Motivating SMEs to Cooperate and Internationalize

Interest in generally expanding the understanding of small and medium-sized enterprises, especially understanding their strategies and operations to enter international markets, is growing rapidly among researchers and academics globally. Government officials, regional and economic specialists, and international trade advisers are directly involved in assisting small and medium-sized enterprises in developing their international marketing expertise.

Motivating SMEs to Cooperate and Internationalize consists of research studies, cases, and experiences obtained by researchers and academics from managers of small and medium-sized enterprises in Northern Europe as they worked closely with managers on issues and problems leading to internationalization of enterprises. This book will not only map the attempts of small and medium-sized enterprises in Northern Europe to enter foreign markets, but also seek to understand how researchers and academics can help small and medium-sized Northern European enterprisers achieve their objectives. This compilation of approaches, perspectives, and experiences will serve as a resource tool for researchers and academics active in international management training programs worldwide and help illustrate how to close the gap between publishing results of their findings and efforts to disseminate their findings among managers of small and medium-sized enterprises in their domains.

This book is the first attempt to integrate results of research studies and practices as an illustration of how knowledge of small and medium-sized enterprises has evolved since the 1980s with the contributions of individual researchers and academics in Northern Europe. It will be of relevance to academics and researchers interested in working closely with small and medium-sized enterprises to meet their goals in entering international markets.

George Tesar is Professor Emeritus of Marketing and International Business at Umeå University in Umeå, Sweden and Professor Emeritus at the University of Wisconsin-Whitewater, USA. He is an Adjunct Professor at Aalborg University, Denmark.

Zsuzsanna Vincze is Associate Professor at Umeå School of Business and Economics (USBE), Head of the Entrepreneurship, and holds a position of Docent of International Business at the University of Turku, Finland.

Routledge Studies in Small Business

Edited by Robert Blackburn, Director of The Small Business
Research Centre, Kingston University, UK

For a full list of titles in this series, please visit www.routledge.com

Motivating SMEs to Cooperate and Internationalize

A Dynamic Perspective

Edited by George Tesar
and Zsuzsanna Vincze

Routledge
Taylor & Francis Group

LONDON AND NEW YORK

First published 2017
by Routledge

2 Park Square, Milton Park, Abingdon, Oxfordshire OX14 4RN
52 Vanderbilt Avenue, New York, NY 10017

*Routledge is an imprint of the Taylor & Francis Group, an informa
business*

First issued in paperback 2019

Library of Congress Cataloging-in-Publication Data
Names: Tesar, George, editor. | Vincze, Zsuzsanna, editor.
Title: Motivating SMEs to cooperate and internationalize : a dynamic
    perspective / edited by George Tesar and Zsuzsanna Vincze.
Description: New York : Routledge, 2017. | Includes bibliographical
    references and index.
Identifiers: LCCN 2017025838 | ISBN 9781138220577 (hardback) |
    ISBN 9781315412610 (ebook)
Subjects: LCSH: Small business—Management. | a International
    business enterprises. | Export marketing.
Classification: LCC HD62.7 .M678 2017 | DDC 658.02/2—dc23
LC record available at https://lccn.loc.gov/2017025838

ISBN: 978-1-138-22057-7 (hbk)
ISBN: 978-0-367-88488-8 (pbk)

Typeset in Sabon
by Apex CoVantage, LLC

Contents

Figures and Tables

Figures

Tables

Preface

Motivating cooperation among and internationalization of small and medium-sized enterprises (SMEs) in Northern Europe is a challenging task. SMEs in Northern Europe are typically located in small remote towns or villages, over large geographic areas, with limited resources. Although in theory they create employment opportunities, stabilize local socio-economic conditions, and contribute to tax revenue, they often require significant managerial know-how and assistance. Their typical local orientation often prevents them looking beyond their perceived boundaries. In order to extend their inherent capabilities, they need to be entrepreneurial, innovative, and international in their managerial abilities.

Most Northern European countries offer assistance to SMEs in numerous forms on local, regional, and national levels. Government assistance is generally directed to the overall operations of SMEs and is seldom directed to improving management of their skills and know-how. Entrepreneurial, innovative, and even international initiatives are personal. Individual managers are sources of ideas, products, programs, and cross border ventures. Northern European SMEs depend on strong managers—managers who understand local strategic dynamics and seize their advantages.

Northern European SMEs do not operate in a vacuum. They frequently cooperate strategically and operationally with other SMEs in their regions. They form industrial clusters with integrated supply chains, internal research and engineering services to develop competitive products and services, and share marketing and sales organizations among other activities. Their futures often depend on exports and on international ventures in some cases.

One of the unique characteristics of SMEs in Northern Europe is their willingness to cooperate with regional universities and other educational institutions. SMEs managers help academics learn about their managerial styles, they respond to academic research, and they open their operations to case research studies. Academics learn from direct contact with SMEs managers. And this is not a one-way street. Managers also learn from the academics.

Academics help managers be entrepreneurial, make better decisions, and think strategically. Transfer of knowledge from academics to SMEs managers represents an important way of growing SMEs. This publication is dedicated to Professor Håkan Boter of Umeå School of Business and Economics at Umeå University. He is one academic who has been extensively involved with the transfer of knowledge from academia to SMEs in Northern Europe.

During his career, Professor Boter initiated and participated in projects designed to foster cooperation and internationalization among SMEs in Northern Europe and facilitate their growth. These projects include the establishment of the Center of Inter-Organizational Innovation Research (CiiR) and the Center for Entrepreneurship, Innovation and Business Development (CEIB) among other initiatives. Professor Boter reached across the borders of academia to SMEs and often served as an advisor, coordinator, facilitator, mediator, and information source. His commitment to developing management expertise in eastern Africa under the auspices of the Swedish International Development Agency has been extraordinary as is his participation in a coalition of major European and North American international universities to promote management education among African universities. Professor Boter has authored and coauthored many widely recognized papers and monographs on managerial aspects of SMEs, their cooperation, and internationalization. His contributions provided an impetus for this project. We thank you, Håkan!

George Tesar, Madison, Wisconsin
Zsuzsanna Vincze, Umeå, Sweden

About the Contributors

Jan Abrahamsson completed his doctoral thesis in the areas of business model innovation and international entrepreneurship at Umeå School of Business and Economics in 2016, with Professor Håkan Boter as a valued co-supervisor. Lately, Jan has been teaching disruptive entrepreneurship and business model design at Toulouse Business School in France along with his position as MBA lecturer at Stamford International University, Bangkok, which is one of the fastest growing business schools in South East Asia. In Bangkok, Jan is also active in export consultancy for Swedish companies as well as with business development of high-tech start-ups. Jan's research interest centers on the nexus of business models, business development and internationalization.

Petri Ahokangas is currently senior research fellow and research group leader at Martti Ahtisaari Institute of Oulu Business School at the University of Oulu, Finland. He is also an adjunct professor of international software entrepreneurship at the University of Oulu. His research interests are in how innovation and technological change affect international business creation, transformation, and strategies and business models in highly technology-intensive or software-intensive business domains. He has over 100 publications in scientific journals, books, conference proceedings, and other reports. He is actively working in several ICT-focused research consortia leading the business-related research streams. Prior to his academic career he worked in the telecoms/software industry.

Irina Atkova is a doctoral candidate at the department of Management and International Business, Oulu Business School, University of Oulu. Her research focuses on entrepreneurship and business models, in particular, how business models are created in the start-up context.

Karl Johan Bonnedahl is an associate professor at Umeå School of Business and Economics. His focus in research as well as in community relations is on sustainability and on the related needs to change business theory and practice. Research has also been conducted within strategy and internationalization. His dissertation was on European integration.

Gert-Olof Boström is an associate professor at Umeå School of Business and Economics. In his research, he has been studying adoption in various contexts. Usually these studies have been undertaken in a service environment. These different adoption situations range from studying the start of use of IT as a process interfering tool to the adoption of sustainability in Swedish. Another paramount topic in his research has been SME firms. Both these referred adoption studies have been conducted in SME firms.

Thommie Burström is an assistant professor at Hanken School of Economics, Helsinki, Finland. His academic interests are in projects, entrepreneurship, business ecosystems, and platform research. Thommie has previously published papers in, for example, the, *International Journal of Management Research Review* and *Journal of Engineering and Technology Management*. For more information see www.hanken.fi/sv/person/thommie-burstrom

Arnim Decker is an assistant professor at Aalborg University in Denmark. He holds a Master degree in Business Administration (Dipl-Kaufmann) from Cologne University and a Doctorate degree in Finance from Complutense University of Madrid, Spain. With a history of having run his own business, his research interests include digitalization processes in the context of internationalization of firms.

Giulia Giunti is an assistant professor at Umeå School of Business and Economics. Her research areas are in the fields of comparative financial accounting and auditing and her dissertation has been awarded the 2015 Outstanding International Accounting Dissertation Award by the AAA.

Jussi Harri studied in the entrepreneurship program at Hanken School of Economics. His research interests can be found in the areas of entrepreneurship. He is currently testing his entrepreneurial capabilities in working in a startup and he is planning to launch his own venture. Jussi is also interested in pursuing a career as a researcher.

Pia Hurmelinna-Laukkanen is Professor of Marketing (International Business) at the Oulu Business School, University of Oulu, and an adjunct professor at the Lappeenranta University of Technology, School of Business and Management. She has published 60 refereed articles in journals such as *Journal of Product Innovation Management, Industrial and Corporate Change, R&D Management, Technovation, and Journal of Service Management*. She has also contributed to book chapters, over 100 conference papers, and other scientific and managerial publications. Most of her research has involved innovation management and appropriability issues in varying contexts like internationalization and interorganizational collaboration.

Leila Hurmerinta is a university lecturer in marketing at the Turku School of Economics, University of Turku, Finland. Her areas of expertise include

innovations and marketing, research methods and the internationalization of small businesses. She has published in various journals, such as
the *International Business Review, Management International Review,*
the *Journal of Marketing Management* and the *International Small Business Journal,* among others. She has also contributed to internationally
published books (Routledge, Edward Elgar Publishing).

Minnie Kontkanen is a university lecturer at the Department of Marketing,
University of Vaasa, Finland. She is a program manager of the Master's
Degree in International Business at the University of Vaasa. Her areas of
interest include international operation mode choices, internationalization of SMEs and international marketing strategies. Her studies have
been published in edited books and in journals like the *Journal of Transnational Management* and the *Journal of Strategic Marketing.*

John Kuada is Professor of International Management at Aalborg University, Department of Business and Management, Denmark. He holds
two doctorate degrees—a PhD from Copenhagen Business School, and
Dr. Merc. from Aalborg University. He has extensive experience as a
business consultant and training advisor in areas of management, marketing and cross-border inter-firm relations in Europe and Africa. He
is author and/or editor of some 18 books on management and internationalization of firms and has written over 100 articles in refereed scholarly and professional journals on a wide range of international business
issues including entrepreneurship, international marketing, intercultural
management, leadership and strategy. He serves on the editorial review
boards of a number of marketing/management journals focusing on business and management in Africa and Asia. He is the founder and editor
of the *African Journal of Economic and Management Studies* (published
by Emerald).

Jorma Larimo is a Professor of International Marketing at the University
of Vaasa, Finland. He is currently the Dean of the Faculty of Business
Studies and Head of the Doctoral program of Business Studies at the
University of Vaasa. His areas of interest include SME internationaliza-
tion and foreign entry strategies of MNEs, especially FDI, M&A, and
IJV strategies and performance. He has edited six books related to various aspects of International Business. His studies have been published in
several journals, including *International Business Review,* the *Journal of
International Business Studies,* the *Journal of International Marketing,*
Management International Review, the *Journal of World Business,* the
Journal of Global Marketing, the *Journal of East-West Business,* and
the *Journal for East European Management Studies,* as well as in several
edited books.

Rolf A. Lundin is Professor Emeritus of Business Administration at
Jönköping International Business School (JIBS), Sweden and Courtesy

Professor-in-Residence at Umeå School of Business and Economics (USBE), Sweden. Professor Lundin received his doctorate from the University of Chicago in 1973 in Management Science. He was the founding dean of USBE and he also served as dean of JIBS. He also was the founding editor of the *Scandinavian Journal of Management*. He has published most recently on projects and temporary organizations. He was the lead author of the Cambridge University Press book *Managing and Working in Project Society*. Professor Lundin can be reached at Rolf.A.Lundin@ju.se.

Liliyana Makarova Jørsfeldt is a teaching assistant at the Department of Business and Administration, Aalborg University, Denmark. She holds a PhD in Sustainable Supply Chain Management, Center for Industrial Production, Aalborg University, a Master's degree (MSc) in Management of Organizations, Odessa State Polytechnic University, Ukraine, and a Master's degree (MSc) in International Business Economics, Aalborg University. Her current research focuses on utilization of Big Data and IoT for development of sustainable business processes.

Hamid Moini is Emeritus Professor of Finance at the University of Wisconsin-Whitewater. Professor Moini received his PhD in Financial Economics and Master of Arts in Finance from the University of Alabama. Over the past 30 years, he has focused on development of global market entry strategies for smaller firms, international mergers and acquisitions, and management education in the contemporary global context. He has published two books and numerous refereed articles in the leading journals in finance and international business. Because of his extensive interest in internationalization of small and medium-sized enterprises, he has been invited to several international networks, study groups, and a number of European universities to give lectures and seminars. In his consulting practice, Professor Moini offers a range of services including planning for foreign direct investments, capital budgeting, and financial structure along with cross-cultural training for managers. He works closely with top management through workshops, seminars, and on-going internal assessment programs.

Niina Nummela is professor of international business at the Turku School of Economics, University of Turku, Finland, and visiting professor at the University of Tartu, Estonia. Her areas of expertise include international entrepreneurship, cross-border acquisitions and research methods. She has published widely in academic journals, including the *International Business Review*, the *Journal of World Business*, *Management International Review*, *Industrial Marketing Management*, the *European Journal of Marketing* and the *International Small Business Journal*, among others. She has also contributed to internationally published books and edited several books for international publishers, such as Edward Elgar Publishing, Palgrave-Macmillan and Routledge.

Eriikka Paavilainen-Mäntymäki is a university research fellow in International Business at the Turku School of Economics, University of Turku, Finland, and an adjunct professor at the University of Vaasa, Finland. Her areas of expertise include research methods, the internationalization processes of firms and the philosophy of science. She has published articles in the *Journal of International Business Studies*, *Management International Review*, the *International Journal of Management Reviews* and *Organizational Research Methods*. She has also contributed to internationally published books (Routledge, Edward Elgar Publishing) and co-edited a book on longitudinal and process research methods for Edward Elgar Publishing.

Erik S. Rasmussen is an associate professor at the University of Southern Denmark, Department of Marketing & Management, and member of the research group of International Business and Entrepreneurship. His publications are in the *International Journal of Innovation Management*, the *International Small Business Journal*, the *Journal of Management & Governance* and the *Journal of Small Business and Enterprise Development*.

Per Servais is an associate professor at the University of Southern Denmark, Department of Marketing & Management, and a member of the research group of International Business and Entrepreneurship. His recent publications are in the *European Journal of International Management*, the *Journal of International Entrepreneurship*, the *Journal of Management and Governance* and *International Business Review*.

Lars Silver is a professor of Retail and Demand Change Management at Umeå School of Business and Economics. He has done previous research in banking as well as small business management. Among his research interests are the financial relationships of small and medium-sized enterprises. Lars has also worked on numerous governmental inquiries on small firm financing.

Tobias Svanström is an associate professor at Umeå School of Business and Economics. He is also an adjunct associate professor at BI Norwegian Business School. His research area is auditing and his work has been published in well-known accounting journals such as *Contemporary Accounting Research*, *European Accounting Review*, *Accounting and Business Research* and the *International Journal of Auditing*. He has also contributed to *The Routledge Companion to Auditing*.

George Tesar is Professor Emeritus of Marketing and International Business at Umeå University in Umeå, Sweden and Professor Emeritus at the University of Wisconsin-Whitewater. Professor Tesar received his doctorate from the University of Wisconsin-Madison and an MBA from Michigan State University. He is a mechanical engineer with several years of industrial experience. He is a founding member of the Product Development and Management Association, a professional association focusing on technology transfer and new product development. He served on two export promotion and stimulation committees to which he was appointed by four Governors of Wisconsin. As a management advisor, he has assisted smaller manufacturing enterprises to export and internationalize. He is a member of the Fulbright Association and assists with international student and faculty exchanges. Professor Tesar can be reached at tesarg@uww.edu.

Vladimir Vanyushyn is an associate professor at Umeå School of Business and Economics. He earned his doctorate in 2011 with a specialization in innovation in SMEs under the supervision of Professor Boter. Vladimir's research lies at the intersection of innovation and entrepreneurship and focuses primarily on inter-organizational collaboration for innovation development and internationalization. His small business papers have appeared in journals such as *Industrial Marketing Management*, the *Journal of Small Business Management, Environment and Planning C* and the *International Small Business Journal.*

Timothy L. Wilson is Adjunct Professor of Marketing and Management at the Umeå School of Business and Economics (USBE), Umeå University, SE-901 87 Umeå, Sweden—previously retired as Professor of Marketing, Clarion University, Clarion, PA, USA. His research interests are in the general areas of business services, project organizations and management, international business, and regional development. On a periodic basis, he offers a PhD seminar in academic writing and works with faculty and staff at USBE with their writing and publication efforts. For more information see http://usbe.se/tiwi0002.

Zsuzsanna Vincze, is an associate professor at the Umeå School of Business and Economic, and Docent of International Business at the University of Turku (TSE). Her areas of expertise include internationalization processes, clusters' transformation, and ecosystems of innovation. She has published a number of single- and co-authored articles in scientific journals; e.g., the *Journal of East-West Business*, the *Journal of Product and Brand Management, Competitiveness Review* and *Thunderbird International Business Review, Industrial Marketing Management* and chapters in books on industrial clusters, grounded theory and longitudinal research. Since 2014, she has been Head of the Entrepreneurship Section at Umeå School of Business and Economics.

Peter Zettinig is University Research Fellow and Adjunct Professor in International Business at the University of Turku, in Finland. Central to his work is a fascination with phenomena in international business related to change on various levels of analysis. His work is published in scholarly journals such as *Thunderbird International Business Review*, the *European Management Journal, Foresight, Critical Perspectives in International Business*, the *International Journal of Cross-Cultural Management, Organizational Dynamics, European Business Review* and *Competitiveness Review*, among others.

1   Motivating SMEs to Cooperate and Internationalize

A Dynamic Perspective—Introduction

George Tesar

1. Introduction

Small and medium-sized enterprises (SMEs) are considered the foundation of economic and social development and provide a platform for industrial growth. Motivating SMEs to cooperate and internationalize is a complex task. They are managed by managers with diverse personalities, ambitions, and managerial skills. SMEs range from low-technology locally oriented, craftsmen-operated shops to sophisticated high-technology manufacturing entities managed by rational managers with extensive decision-making skills.

Successful SMEs, especially high-technology innovative entities, quickly expand and enter markets beyond their initially perceived boundaries. In order to better utilize their resources, because of their own initiatives, or due to external motivations, they realize that they need to cooperate with other SMEs. Their search for markets also leads to their internationalization in addition to cooperation with other SMEs. However, neither cooperation or internationalization is a simple progression of strategic and operations initiatives for most SMEs. These are complicated and time-consuming managerial decisions (Kuada 2016).

From a socio-economic perspective, SMEs are sought after and embraced by communities, municipalities, and localities because they create social and economic value—they create employment, increase tax revenues, and stabilize economic and social conditions. Local, regional, and national governments offer incentives to entrepreneurs, startups, and existing SMEs to expand beyond their current markets and create additional jobs. Some governments provide direct assistance to SMEs to start export operations or obtain additional information to increase them.

SMEs frequently disturb markets because of their entrepreneurial tendencies and through their propensity to innovate. Depending on the environment in which SMEs operate and the nature of their innovation, they dramatically alter traditional markets. Examples in computer technology, telecommunication, or medicine illustrate how SMEs startups disturbed existing markets, developed new industries, and changed consumers' lifestyles. Similarly, the entire service industry was founded by SMEs. Motivations for entrepreneurs such as craftsmen, promoters, or rational managers may differ, but collectively they provide value for customers, consumers, and users.

Northern European SMEs

SMEs in Northern Europe are similar to their contemporaries in other parts of the world in terms of their initiatives, but differ in some ways. The rural environments in which they operate do not provide the same resources as do urban environments endowed with a variety of rich resources. Many Northern European SMEs are in geographically remote areas. They started in remote places because there were opportunities to develop special products or services to established industries such as agriculture, forestry, mining, or ship building. This was the case in the Nordic countries. Similar conditions existed in Northern Germany, Poland, and even the Baltic countries. Over time the technological sophistication of these industries changed. Some SMEs were responsible for innovative initiatives that dramatically changed the industries through automation improvements in production and manufacturing. Some industries ceased operations in those regions and the SMEs that coexisted with them closed their operations or were forced to redefine their missions.

SMEs in Northern Europe need to be flexible, resourceful, and innovative to prosper. Their managements need to understand how to succeed in rapidly changing environments when industries shift their operational emphasis or simply move elsewhere. SMEs cooperate with other SMEs to offset disruptive challenges by forging alliances, developing industrial clusters, or sharing research and development initiatives among other forms of cooperation. However, not all managers of SMEs behave proactively in entering cooperative arrangements; some need to be externally motivated (Tesar and Bodin 2013).

Furthermore, SMEs form cooperatives closely resembling supply chains or even complete value chains in some regions. There are several cooperatives in Northern Sweden, for example, whose range includes maintaining forests, saw mills, carpenter shops, design and production facilities, and marketing and sales organizations. One of the cooperatives specializes in producing staircases, stages for theaters and concert halls, and other custom built wooden indoor structures. In Denmark, agricultural cooperatives produce lines of dairy products for local consumption. In Norway, SMEs join cooperative ventures to maintain and service ships and other marine equipment. Most SMEs that cooperate in various local ventures are concerned about their future and seek opportunities in order to remain profitable and survive (Asheim et al. 2003).

Other SMEs are not as proactive and wait until opportunities develop or until they are approached by other SMEs or some initiators sometimes called vision catchers. They are reluctant to participate in any cooperative ventures until presented with complete plans and strategies they understand. Local governments represented by economic development agencies, universities' business development and innovation centers, and commercial entities such as Chambers of Commerce try to motivate managers of reluctant SMEs to participate in cooperative ventures. Such SMEs need to be assured and have sufficient information to decide if they will join.

SMEs operating in geographically remote regions also require assistance in their attempts to venture beyond their perceived markets. They identify and relate to markets that are close by and familiar to them geographically and culturally. Expansion into regional or national markets is not generally a major challenge; crossing national boundaries is. To cross national boundaries into unknown territory can, in fact, be a major challenge. Crossing national boundaries represents substantial investments for some managers of SMEs in remote regions of Northern Europe.

In addition, SMEs need to restructure strategically and operationally to internationalize. At a minimum, they need to reexamine their products and services to determine if they are suitable and competitive for international markets and if they have the managerial knowledge and skills to enter international markets directly or indirectly. This challenge is difficult for SMEs that operate in remote industrial environments and specialize in products and services tied closely to a single industry. Most SMEs faced with such challenges not only need additional information, but they need additional managerial and marketing skills (Hultman 1999).

It is also important to consider that for SMEs operating in Northern Europe, to be international means to export. Very few SMEs have the resources or knowledge to enter foreign markets as partners in joint ventures, license their products or services, directly invest in an ongoing venture or open a subsidiary. Internationalization occasionally takes on a completely reverse aspect. An SME located in a geographically remote region may be approached and eventually purchased by a foreign entity. In such a case the SME will see internationalization from a different perspective in this situation. This type of internationalization has a completely different impact on the SME and the region in which it operates. An influx of managers, exchanges of information, and even exchanges of technicians and other personnel have a direct impact on internationalization of the region.

The common theme of both cooperation and internationalization among SMEs in Northern Europe is the need for information combined with development of managerial knowledge and skills. The information and knowledge sought by managers of SMEs is relatively specialized, not necessarily because of isolationism, but because of limited mobility of managers, scientists, and other needed specialists. There may be another reason why these SMEs are different: because there is a stigma between the North and the South. Managers and other personnel that have been trained "up north" frequently migrate south. Few of their counterparts trained "down south" seek employment "up north" (Laukkanen 2000).

Consequently, much of the information and managerial knowledge needed by SMEs in geographically remote areas of Northern Europe is generated locally by academics, university researchers, management consultants, or other economic or social development specialists. Regional universities and institutions of learning provide services to SMEs and train their managers. SMEs in these regions are dependent on managerial assistance and technical advice from regional universities. Local and national administrative agencies concerned with economic and regional development encourage close cooperation between the two entities.

The objective of this publication is to highlight how SMEs are motivated to cooperate and internationalize in remote regions of Northern Europe. The efforts to motivate SMEs in remote regions of Northern Europe require special approaches to research, frequently multidisciplinary in nature, and using nonconventional methodologies. Most of all, there is a need for trust and cooperation from managers who manage these entities. In addition, not all academics and researchers are able to conduct research among such SMEs. Conducting research among such SMEs requires an open two-way communication channel—every research project must include exchange of useful information between managers and the researchers.

Universities and SMEs in Northern Europe

Universities in Northern Europe, especially in the Nordic countries, traditionally have had a purpose: to assist with economic and social development of the region in which they were established. Universities and special faculties were founded just for that purpose. Academics and university researchers were expected to work closely with SMEs in their region and help them meet strategic and operational challenges. In return university staff had an open communication channel with SMEs' managers to learn more about them by conducting research studies, writing research cases about their strategies and operations, and occasionally writing masters or doctoral theses. The university staff generate a necessary knowledge to help SMEs in the region to be established and grow.

Some universities cover vast geographic areas with scattered small towns, communities, and an occasional administrative center. Universities are expected to stimulate knowledge and foster innovation and entrepreneurship. Local and regional administrators seek employment opportunities for residents, strive to economically and socially stabilize localities, and generate additional tax revenues. They seek real partnerships with academics and university researchers, management specialists, and academic entrepreneurs to accomplish their objectives. Cooperation among administrators, university staff, and managers is expected to stimulate growth of more SMEs, support SMEs to develop effective and efficient management systems, and expand beyond their regions, both domestically and internationally (Nilsson 2006).

Universities and faculties were founded with different specializations depending on resources in the region such as agriculture, forestry, mines, or fisheries. Sometimes technical universities were founded to develop supporting industries such as manufacturing of agricultural or forestry equipment. In Northern Sweden, for example, technical, agricultural, and comprehensive universities were founded—in Umeå a comprehensive university was founded with an emphasis on medicine and social sciences followed by a separate agricultural university. The social science faculty had a strong focus on economics and business administration. Similar situations can be found across the Bay of Bothnia in Northern Finland—comprehensive universities in Oulu and Vaasa. Norway also located some universities in Northern rural areas such as the Norwegian Technical University in Ålesund and Trondheim. Denmark and Iceland also founded universities in socially and economically important regions. The Northern regions are also serviced by smaller academic institutions, sometimes referred to as colleges, specializing in local educational needs.

The long tradition of symbiotic relationships between academics and SME managers is a two-way street. Managers learn from academics and academics learn from managers. Most of the challenges managers face are resolved with the help of information that is often supplied by academics. Managers of SMEs operating in remote regions of the north outside of major population centers need specialized information that is relevant to their strategies and day to day operations. Because they face complexities related to their communication needs, transportation challenges, and even service of their equipment, they frequently feel that information generated among larger population centers and industrial regions seems superfluous or irrelevant. They perceive the rural environment in which they operate as unique.

When major disturbances occur, such as foreign competitors entering their remote geographic area and beginning to buy up local competitors, suppliers, or enterprises next door, the SMEs become concerned. Introduction of the Internet created substantial changes in strategic and operational strategies that SMEs in many parts of Northern Europe did not expect. Academics who served as management consultants, management advisors, or mentors to top management explained such developments and helped SMEs managers internalize them. Academics at regional universities perform an important role in transferring knowledge gained from their research to local SMEs. SMEs would find it difficult to function without this knowledge.

Management Research in Northern Europe

Much management research conducted among SMEs in Northern Europe is qualitative. Management researchers focus on a small number of subjects, gather data through in-depth interviews, listen to anecdotes, stories, or explanations and later systematically analyze their content. Some researchers rely on observation research: they shadow managers, spend time in their offices, or simply observe their activities. These research approaches are very much based in the social sciences and generate information useful for providing guidance to SMEs' managers. These study results are published in monographs, journal articles, and doctoral dissertations and contribute to an understanding of how SMEs are managed and operate.

Both point in time and longitudinal research studies are conducted. Some longitudinal studies are conducted as participatory research. Researchers sometimes serve in managerial positions with SMEs and observe how decisions are made. Over time, these observations are collected and analyzed, resulting in a variety of management publications. Such publications are useful in generating knowledge of how SMEs perform over time and what the major challenges are, and occasionally question management approaches and techniques.

The migration from managerial positions among SMEs and from managerial positions to academia are important. This approach stimulates the exchange of information and knowledge between academics and managers. Migration between academia and SMEs is not exclusive. Academics exchange positions with banking personnel, insurance companies, engineering firms, and other commercial entities and vice versa. These exchanges serve very important roles in generating localized knowledge.

Lately, mostly due to diversified internationally based studies of SMEs, research approaches among management researchers in Northern Europe are gravitating to quantitative studies that provide information comparable and replicable among SME research in other parts of the world. Much of this research is exploratory and descriptive; some research studies are comparative and support results of studies published from other countries in areas of SME management, entrepreneurship, and innovation.

Recently, greater emphasis has been placed on academic research, qualitative and quantitative, focused on cooperation among SMEs in geographically remote areas of Northern Europe and efforts and approaches to internationalization among SMEs. This research is combined with issues leading to industrial cluster formation among SMEs and their expanded efforts to participate in industrial networks, supply chains, and complete value chains across national boundaries.

The following research among SMEs in Northern Europe is presented along with the conceptual framework that characterizes much of the research, mainly in the Nordic countries. Managers of SMEs must change their local orientation, values, and strategies. They need to cooperate with their equals, but remain competitive in their own core markets. Internationalization of their strategies and operation is frequently an extension of cooperative behavior. Cooperation and internationalization among SMEs in Northern Europe requires a great deal of entrepreneurship—managerial and academic.

2. Framework

The socio-economic environment in which Northern European SMEs operate is distinct due to their geographic conditions and extensive support from administrative units and local universities. Regional administrative efforts motivate them to be more competitive in their domestic and international markets. Although Northern European SMEs tend to be more entrepreneurial, innovative, and conscious of their resources, they are smaller in comparison to their counterparts in the rest of Europe and especially in North America. Some are willing to cooperate with other SMEs in their vicinity and respond to international initiatives individually or collectively. Motivating Northern European SMEs to cooperate and internationalize is a notable challenge for administrators, economic and regional development specialists, and academics.

Northern European SMEs are started by individuals with entrepreneurial tendencies just as SMEs in other parts of the world. They have an idea for a product or service and look for markets. Many startups have a short life span; those that find markets often grow and expand. As they become successful and are managed with better knowledge of market opportunities, they become strategic in their marketing abilities. Successful SMEs usually need assistance from other SMEs in geographically remote areas such as Northern Europe. The needed assistance may be cooperating on marketing and sales of products, combining transportation and distribution options, or sharing manufacturing or production capabilities. More advanced cooperative arrangements can lead to combined research and development and engineering. Cooperation is a necessity to survival for some emerging SMEs in geographically remote regions. The one dominant characteristic among Northern European SMEs is their willingness to communicate with each other and share their experiences.

The internationalization process among Northern European SMEs is complex, but important for their growth and expansion. Some SMEs internationalize in the early stages of operation, especially if they offer high technology products or services and establish a strong market presence via the Internet and a dedicated webpage. These SMEs are generally labeled as born global. However, the first attempt for most SMEs to internationalize is through export activities. Some enter the realm of exports on their own initiative while others are asked to offer export options by others—customers, distributors, or wholesalers among other domestic or foreign institutions. Later, SMEs face options to enter other arrangements to expand their international portfolios. A unique feature of Northern European SMEs is their willingness to cooperate and combine their international activities. Cooperation represents a stronger presence in cross-border markets and a better chance to succeed for most SMEs. They form cooperatives, supply chains, and even entire value chains through which they have a better chance to service domestic or international markets.

In order to fully understand how notions of cooperation and internationalization function among Northern European SMEs, it is important to identify the critical relationships among them. What differentiates those willing to enter cooperative relationships and those that do not from one another? What motivates them and creates motivating forces or do ambient events trigger cooperation and/or internationalization? A framework is needed in order to examine the reasons for cooperation and internationalization. It is important to note that the socio-economic environment in which Northern European SMEs operate is dynamic and temporary, which also makes the framework temporary, and it needs to be constantly monitored.

Cooperation and internationalization are recurrent themes among Northern European researchers, especially in the context of entrepreneurial behavior. Studies describe entrepreneurship, entrepreneurial startups, management of ventures, decision-making propensities by SMEs managers, and managers' responses to external and internal forces formulated to motivate them to cooperate with other entities and internationalize their marketing initiatives. The entire research process among Northern European researchers is focused on entrepreneurial and managerial activities of SMEs and closely linked to innovation research. The overall objective appears to be an attempt to relate entrepreneurial and managerial activities of SMEs to innovation and growth. However, intermediate research objectives include perspectives on entrepreneurship, management, innovation, and growth. In this context research focusing on entrepreneurship and SMEs appears to be synonymous. Entrepreneurs not only start and build SMEs but also manage and grow them.

Although entrepreneurial behavior varies dramatically and not all SMEs are managed by entrepreneurs, many researchers suggest that in some ways, because of these anomalies, a general approach to entrepreneurial research is closely related to SMEs' management. Entrepreneurs are perceived as dynamic, forward-looking individuals who take initiatives and aggressively approach markets. There is also evidence that SMEs are started and managed by individuals who do not fit the current popular conception of entrepreneurs and entrepreneurship. They have the marketable skills needed to craft products or provide specialized services. As long as their SMEs are profitable they are not interested in facing risk or managing operations.

Some SMEs are managed by individuals who do not have apparent entrepreneurial ambitions, are more interested in crafting a product or offering a rudimentary service, and wait until customers come to them. Other SMEs are managed by individuals who strive to sell products or services and increase their net worth in the process. There are also managers who strive to increase their net worth who have entrepreneurial tendencies and manage their SMEs more aggressively. They balance human, financial, and physical resources to meet marketing opportunities and optimize marketing strategies.

Consequently, motivating SMEs to cooperate and internationalize is a highly personal process. Not all entrepreneurs or SMEs managers can be motivated. Decisions to cooperate with other entities and internationalize marketing initiatives are made by individuals who have the propensity to look beyond the current reach of their own SME's singular capabilities. Not all SME managers perceive strength in collective initiatives, just as some do not anticipate rewards from internationalization. Private or public initiatives to motivate Northern European SMEs to cooperate and internationalize have inherent socio-economic or public ambitions. Every external or internal motivating effort has an objective, goal, or common purpose. Individual entrepreneurs willing to respond to external or internal motivations to cooperate and/or internationalize indicate they are willing to build or join industrial networks, form alliances, enter industrial clusters, or participate in other cooperative arrangements.

External efforts typically come from public sources such as local or regional governments, agencies, or influential administrators. Many service providers want to expand SMEs' productivity—including banks, consulting companies, transportations companies, or other facilitators of economic activities. Their purpose is to motivate SMEs to be socio-economically productive because they benefit from such economic activities. Internal efforts come from influential insiders or stakeholders such as an owner-manager, employees who have close contacts with the outside world, or functional specialists such as sales personnel or purchasing agents who frequently communicate with outsiders. It is common to find functional specialists such as engineers who studied abroad, speak a foreign language, and are culturally astute volunteering to service foreign opportunities.

SMEs need to be convinced that they will benefit both in the short and long term before they initiate cooperative ventures or enter foreign markets. Managerial processes inside SMEs suggest that motivation efforts must be coordinated with an SME's mission and core values. Coordination between internal managerial issues and external or internal motivating forces requires intermediary actors who build trust within an SME to consider such actions. Once trust among all potential participants in a decision to cooperate or internationalize has been reached, SMEs may enter mutually beneficial arrangements.

Within such arrangements where a level of trust has been reached, an SME may progress through discovery and learning stages to a stable cooperative state. Building cooperative entities such as industrial networks, joining industrial clusters, or entering a variety of channel agreements dramatically changes managerial styles and strategic perspectives. This can be a long-term learning process for some SMEs operating in geographically remote regions of Northern Europe, depending on how and from what sources an SME obtains its information.

Decisions to cooperate and internationalize are reached because public entities such as economic or regional development specialists target

individual SMEs, offer export assistance, or invite management to participate in a trade mission abroad. These are strategies administratively supported and implemented to improve socio-economic conditions in a region
not only for the benefit of the region but also for national benefit. Additional external motivational efforts may come from customers, suppliers,
members of value chains, and even individual commercial entities abroad.
For example, an SME may be asked to participate in an international supply chain to serve as the local manufacturing licensee for products that are
heavy or difficult to transport.

SME managers suggest that depending on managers' inherent propensity,
overall goals and objectives, the subsequent decision to internationalize may
have two different and distinct approaches. The first approach is personal.
An SME' manager may reach a point where a combination of motivations
produce a level of personal tension which results in the decision to enter
foreign markets directly or indirectly. Such a decision may not be fully con-
vincing and occasionally idiosyncratic. In some cases, an agreement among
key decision makers to explore opportunities to internationalize becomes
the internal motivating force for an SME to make an actual commitment to
internationalize.

3. Integration

The purpose of this publication is to examine the motivating process among
small and medium-sized enterprises (SMEs) in Northern Europe. The motivating process directed to Northern European SMEs requires comprehensive
knowledge of how these enterprises manage their marketing initiatives. There
is sufficient evidence that they manage their marketing initiatives with greater
reliance on local resources and initially expand and grow in the region. The
uniqueness in management styles is attributed to geographic remoteness and
economic isolationism. Yet, SMEs in Northern Europe serve many important economic and regional development roles. SMEs provide a platform for
local economic and social stability by creating employment opportunities and
generating tax revenue, according to economic and development specialists.
Economic development specialists point out that more SMEs need to be fos-
tered and motivated to expand and grow. Based on long-term research and
advising experiences, SMEs managers in the region need to be motivated to
cooperate and internationalize. Cooperation and eventual internationalization among them is an important step in market expansion and growth.

The topic of motivating Northern European SMEs to cooperate and internationalize is a cutting edge of academic researchers in that part of the world.
Many academic researchers also serve directly or indirectly as advisors to
motivate more SMEs to form cooperative entities in the area and expand
into markets across national borders. Some academics with their own
entrepreneurial skills and initiatives advise managers of SMEs in the region
directly while others with less applied experiences work with public and

private organizations to implement research finding. Many research findings published by academic researchers help economic and regional development specialists better understand how managers manage their SMEs and what additional knowledge they need to respond to their recommendations.

A conceptual framework was developed in order to better understand how SMEs in Northern Europe respond to motivating efforts to cooperate and internationalize. The framework is based on contemporary understanding of the regional economic and social dynamics by academics in universities and educational institutions in the Northern European region. The framework also offers a perspective on how SME managers in the region form viable entrepreneurial initiatives, market products and services, and, in general, manage initiatives. The two most important perspectives of the framework are the formation of cooperative initiatives such as industrial networks, including clusters and joint ventures, and internationalization. The framework is presented in Figure 1.1 on page 12.

The process of motivating Northern European SMEs to cooperate and internationalize is complex and requires rapidly evolving specialized knowledge. For this purpose, the resulting conceptual framework consists of four distinct components. The first component examines external and internal forces intended to motivate SMEs to cooperate and internationalize. External and internal motivating forces require entrepreneurial responses leading to willingness to facilitate cooperative and international initiatives. SME managers with entrepreneurial skills must be open to motivating forces, consider their significance, and be willing to respond. Not every SME manager has entrepreneurial propensities to act collectively and be open to cross-border initiatives.

If entrepreneurs respond to motivating forces to cooperate and internationalize, some underlying managerial issues, outlined in the second component of the conceptual framework, need to be explored. Entrepreneurs with a great deal of vision are able to identify opportunities, the advantages of cooperating with others, and share collective goals and objectives. Other entrepreneurs do not have the necessary vision but have the skills to mediate with others to reach goals and objectives beneficial to the proposed initiative. Such entrepreneurs are able to combine resources, communicate among potential participants, and organize activities that go beyond the traditional skills of a manager. Additional entrepreneurial skills are needed to construct the entire cooperative initiative—entrepreneurs who are able to design the initiative, organize the participants into an integrated entity, and make it dynamic.

It may be difficult to find an entrepreneur with all three sets of skills willing to cooperate and internationalize. It is more likely that various entrepreneurs have different managerial skills. Motivating SMEs to cooperate and internationalize is a sequential process consisting of three different entities: (1) vision catcher, (2) mediator, and (3) constructor. The main factor in the process is building trust among the participants. The participants must trust

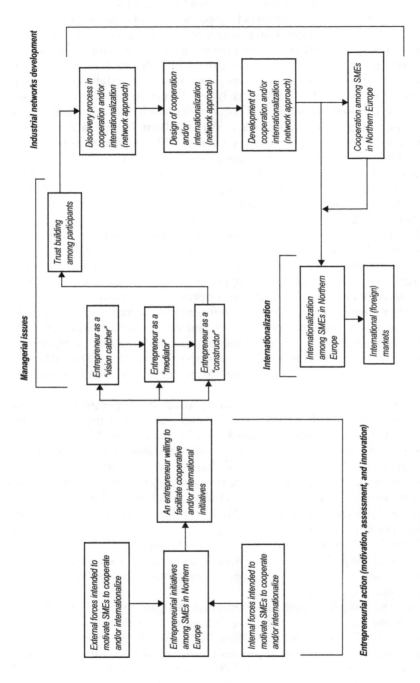

Figure 1.1 Integration of Functions Leading to Motivation of Northern European SMEs to Cooperate and Internationalize

each other and generate consensus. They may not agree all the time on all issues, but they must trust each other to reach consensus.

Once trust building among participants of an initiative to cooperate and/ or internationalize has been accomplished, the developing of a cooperative initiative follows. This process is presented in the third component of the conceptual framework. Development of an industrial network of any type has three distinct steps: (1) discovery, (2) design, and (3) development. The discovery process in cooperation and/or internationalization is an extension of trust. Once the initiative such as an industrial network has been accepted by participants various pressing questions need to be answered and issues resolved. The discovery process examines the fundamental relationships on which any cooperation in the network will be based. The design of the entity depends on the individual strengths and weaknesses among the participants: the strengths each participating SME brings to the network and the weaknesses to be overcome for an optimal network. Development of any cooperation is initially difficult from both entrepreneurial and managerial perspectives. Entrepreneurs may want to develop an entity that looks for innovative and perhaps somewhat uncertain opportunities, while managers may want to protect their interests, carefully manage their resources, and enter less precarious initiatives.

The establishment of a cooperative agreement such as an industrial network does not assure that the initiative will automatically be internationalized. Not all initiatives are developed for the ultimate purpose of entering cross-border markets to expand and grow collectively—some are not. Cooperative agreements, especially those vertically organized such as industrial clusters, are often developed to integrate local SMEs in order to strengthen economic and social conditions without exploring cross-border markets. For example, agricultural clusters developed based on a local industrial base such as aqua-farming require assistance from fabrication shops, welding establishments, plumbing contractors, and other trades. They need to be vertically structured to develop equipment and facilities to grow fresh vegetables or other agricultural crops locally. The cooperation that leads to internationalization must be established early in the development of a network and needs to be mutually accepted.

The final component of the conceptual framework focuses on internationalization of SMEs in remote regions of Northern Europe. A great deal of academic research has covered this topic with mixed results. There appears to be a difference between SMEs that internationalized as single entities and those that internationalized as participants in collective action. The major difference is that the former SMEs typically experienced a longer learning cycle in their efforts to internationalize as compared to the latter. Regardless of how much cross-border experience and knowledge the participants of a cooperative initiative have had, they share experiences and knowledge with other participants—the result is a greater ability to enter international markets.

Researchers and managers view internationalization differently. Researchers tend to consider internationalization as an occurrence that impacts the entire SME, its mission, resources, organization, and marketing activities. The factors that drive an SME to internationalize are concealed in all aspects of managerial responsibilities. Researchers tend to look at the enterprise without dissecting it. This approach can lead to wrong conclusions. Managers point out that motivation to enter international markets is frequently unsolicited, opportunistic, and even unwelcome. Managers may be asked by customers, clients, suppliers, and even competitors to consider an order or opportunity to market products or services to known entities in cross-border markets. In such cases, the decision to export may be a simple manufacturing or production decision and frequently contingent on payment. Managers of SMEs motivated to look for international markets, regardless of how the motivation originated, are aware of the impact the decision to internationalize may have on the entire organization.

Knowledge among academics and managers concerning the motivation of SMEs in Northern Europe to cooperate and internationalize is mounting. Some research is relatively general while some is sharply focused on narrow tangential issues. This publication provides examples of the issues, challenges, and developments presumably important to researchers. Some of the examples clearly support the issues, challenges, and developments faced by SMEs managers, and some do not. It is important to realize that managers are subject to a variety of motivating forces to cooperate with their equals and collectively enter international markets; many SME managers do respond to motivation. The knowledge they need is this: which motivating forces are credible and realistic? How should cooperative entities be managed? What are the best entry modes for them to enter cross-border markets?

This knowledge is available in publications summarizing research studies. However, there is a substantial need for academic consultants to transfer that knowledge to managers managing SMEs and help managers make the difficult decisions about cooperation and internationalization. Only a few academics have the prerequisites to transfer knowledge effectively.

Historical evidence for the founding of regional universities and educational institutions in geographically remote regions of Northern Europe clearly indicates that it was mainly for socio-economic reasons. The responsibilities placed on these institutions include close relationships between them and local startup initiatives, stimulating entrepreneurial actions, assisting managers of local SMEs, and contributing to economic and social development. From an historical perspective, this is an ongoing effort. The only changes that have taken place represent a shifting focus based on local economic or social needs and what information needs to be exchanged between local academics and managers. Consequently, motivating SMEs to cooperate and internationalize is the current cutting edge research focus. The seminal research focused on this topic is promising.

4. Contributions

The research that follows illustrates some of the latest developments and approaches within this framework. Some research approaches illustrate specific advancements in how Northern European SMEs can be motivated to cooperate and internationalize. Other research is formulated as point-in-time research designed to explore narrower issues. The collected examples illustrate the progression from simple case studies generally conducted at the beginning of relationships between academic researchers and enterprises and more advanced qualitative and quantitative approaches to research commonly used today. In all cases, the examples of research that follow are at the forefront of research concerning Northern European SMEs and their cooperative and internationalization efforts.

Part I: Entrepreneurial Action

Rolf A. Lundin (Jönköping International Business School and Umeå University) applied a historical perspective on how Small Business Administration in the early days of Umeå University has played a role in the developments of small business towards internationalized entrepreneurial ventures within the context of Norrland (the northern part of Sweden). He shares with us the view that the small business field started as education for "Bare-feet Business Masters" especially equipped to go out in the "Jungle of Norrland." Rather than specializing in Accounting, Marketing or any other specialty of Business Administration, the students studying Small Business Education were expected to be broad enough to be useful for the entire range of business areas in order to serve the needs of small businesses. His question now is how and where the academia is taken since then.

In the third chapter in Part One, Petri Ahokangas (Martti Ahtisaari Institute at the University of Oulu) and his co-authors Irina Atkova and Pia Hurmelinna-Laukkanen (Oulu Business School, University of Oulu) bring together three streams of discussion that are wide and deep on their own, but are connected to varying extents: innovation, internationalization, and business model literature form an interesting combination. By utilizing a business model as a unit of analysis, their study aims to understand the intertwined nature of innovation, internationalization, and business models. In particular, it explores the process of business model transformation. The research findings indicate that, at the level of entrepreneurial action, business model transformation is an intricate combination of conceptualization and contextualization processes. Conceptualization is an innovation process of the business model anchoring elements, whereas contextualization reflects the interplay between innovation and internationalization processes. From the managerial perspective, their findings imply that going international supports the innovation process in companies.

In the fourth chapter in Part One, George Tesar (University of Wisconsin and Umeå University) argue that smaller manufacturing enterprises (SME) need more information, which helps them solve problems associated with cross-border challenges as they become more active in cross-border marketing activities. SMEs' managers traditionally relied on academic sources for information. With changing research emphases among academics, SMEs' managers look for other sources of information. However, due to the differences in research objectives among alternate information providers, they perceive a conflict in the types of international marketing information that is available. His presentation examines the conflicting issues in information gathering, as viewed by SMEs' managers, and calls for a new research agenda among academics.

Part II: Managerial Aspects of SMEs

The fifth chapter by Vladimir Vanyushyn and Jan Abrahamsson (Umeå University) also applies the business model lens and retrospectively examines the pattern of online channel adoption by Swedish SMEs that occurred between the years 2002 and 2008. Their purpose is to further enhance understanding of the antecedents of substantial business model innovation (BMI). Online channels adoption represents a fitting setting for studying BMI because adoption of such channels may reshuffle the network of external partnerships of an SME as well as allow a firm to bypass the traditional internationalization sequence and effectively become a born-global firm. They identify a firm's willingness to forgo the value of earlier investments in value delivery networks and organizational routines as a precursor of substantial BMI at the early stage of enabling technology development. They further show that market responsiveness becomes the main driver of BMI as enabling technology matures. The study contributes to the business model literature by demonstrating the transient and time-conditioned nature of substantial BMI antecedents.

In the next chapter, Arnim Decker and Liliyana Makarova Jorsfeldt (Aalborg University) investigate how four large multinational corporations with a background in industrial engineering, telecommunication and information technology differ in creating digital platforms and in their collaboration with SMEs and small start-up firms in Northern Europe. Large firms become platform providers to facilitate new processes of digitalization, which results in optimization of existing operations and creation of new products and services, new business processes and new business models. As a result, new entrepreneurial ventures are established as an outcome of joint collaborative activities and initiatives of large companies, SMEs and startups. It is argued that both large companies that create digital platform, and SMEs have their own potential opportunities, which motivates them to collaborate on these platforms. Moreover, Nordic innovative systems, which have cultural and political specificities compared to the rest of Europe, play a significant role in providing SMEs with an innovative business environment. Ultimately, this leads to better innovation and entrepreneurial opportunities and, as a result, economic growth of Northern Europe.

The final chapter in this part is written by Tobias Svanström and Giulia Giunti (Umeå University). They provide a review of the literature on the value of auditor assurance in the process of loan assessment and credit granting of SMEs. Based on the review, they suggest future venues for research in this area. The chapter starts with reviewing the literature on SME and the loan process and the need of SMEs for support services. The authors continue with focus on assurance of financial statements and how audited financial statements impact access to credit and cost of debt according to empirical studies in the area. The role of auditing in this process is to provide assurance to external parties, such as investors and creditors, and thereby facilitate national and international funding which would lead to the internationalization of the SME in question. The evidence is somewhat mixed but suggests that auditing can have a positive impact on access to credit and reduce the cost of debt for SMEs. However, the positive impact should not be overstated and is likely to vary depending on firm characteristics. The conclusion is that further research is warranted, especially from the perspective of creditors, to understand more about how financial statements in general and auditor assurance in particular are used and valued in credit granting to SMEs.

Part III: Industrial Networks Development

In Part Three, Chapter 8 is written by Thommie Burström and Jussi Harri (Hanken School of Economics) and Timoty L. Wilson (Umeå University). The study is based on the following research question: How do networks evolve in the early phases of venture creation? Seven ventures were studied through interviews and visualization techniques. It was found that during the process of managing within networks the content provided by various network contacts changed significantly. A three-phase process was suggested— Conceptualization, Early Foundation and Early Establishment. This chapter contributes to existing literature by defining a conceptual model in which networking in the early phases of venture development can be understood as an ongoing modification through three subprocesses: network mobilization, network utilization and network saturation.

Chapter 9 in Part Three, by Zsuzsanna Vincze (Umeå University) and Peter Zettinig (University of Turku), sets out to explain how and why industrial clusters evolve to new economically viable development paths. Their focus is on the interplay between MNE global strategies and the local SMEs, creating important dynamics leading to cluster change. The authors define the boundary conditions to put the balance of exploitation and exploration into a more applicable framework. Such a framework allows them to present propositions of mindset and behavior in regard to (a) the perceptions and preferences for environmental uncertainty; (b) the focus on exploration and exploitation processes; and (c) the means to balance these processes. Drawing on longitudinal data from a Swedish biorefinery cluster (Örnsköldsvik), archetypical firms are identified and their interactions between the lead MNE and local/regional entrepreneurial SMEs are documented so as to explain the dynamic changes that drive local firms' success in the cluster.

Chapter 10, by Niina Nummela, Leila Hurmerinta and Eriikka Paavilainen-Mäntymäki (University of Turku) focuses on the entrepreneurial decision-making of internationalizing firms and is aimed at answering two research questions: (1) how does decision-making change during internationalization, and (2) what is the role of networks in the entrepreneurial decision-making of internationalizing firms? The findings are based on an empirical survey completed by 160 Finnish food companies divided into three categories: domestic firms (72), potential exporters (44) and exporters (44). The findings indicate that companies' decision-making logic seems to differ by category; that is, it changes over the course of internationalization. While effectual decision-making is often considered to be a characteristic of entrepreneurial behavior, this study finds that internationalizing firms' decision-making becomes less entrepreneurial. This claim is supported by the expansion and increasing sophistication and specialization of the company network over the course of internationalization. The relative importance of personal ties (family and friends) in the network decreases as the role of business ties (suppliers, distributors) becomes more important, and the role of professional ties (experts external to the firm) remains fairly constant or expands only marginally. The number of network-based benefits rises with the growing business ties; the network is increasingly integrated into internationalizing companies' daily business that helps them access international markets.

Part IV: Internationalization

Chapter 11 in Part Four by Gert-Olof Boström, Karl Johan Bonnedahl and Lars Silver (Umeå University) focus on newly started firms. They argue that among SMEs it is possible to find firms whose main intention is to secure a livelihood for the owner/manager, but there will also be firms that are newly started who have not yet proven what development direction they will take. Among newly started firms there will be examples of firms that will challenge the prevailing way of doing business. In order to better understand the potential of small firms, entrepreneurship research, and more specifically the seminal model developed by Gnyawali and Fogel (1994), was used. The three concepts of opportunity, ability to enterprise and propensity to enterprise are central in this model. The newly started firms in the study show a relatively high willingness to grow. About one third of them has the ambition to grow rapidly. In order to achieve this growth, the firms need to be in a market allowing growth (opportunity) and have a chance to obtain resources for this growth (ability). One way to access a larger market is to go international. The results from this study indicate that the newly started firms had a significantly lower degree of internationalization. This result might be understood by the need for the firm to acquire specific skills and time to focus on internationalization. Moreover, the firms need to overcome obstacles such as rules and regulations, as well as financial constraints.

In Chapter 12, Hamid Moini (University of Wisconsin-Whitewater) and John Kuada (Aalborg University) investigate the similarities and differences in the internationalization process of smaller family- and nonfamily-owned firms in Denmark in order to throw additional light on how ownership impacts the internationalization processes of small businesses. Their central finding is that ownership, management decision-making styles, location of firms as well as institutional policies are among the key variables in understanding the resource leveraging processes that shape the internationalization paths of small businesses. They also found that firms with aggressive strategies are more able to expand their markets and to successfully internationalize their operations. Furthermore, both family-owned and nonfamily-owned firms have contributed significantly to their local and regional economies and, to some degree, to the national and global economy.

Jorma Larimo and Minnie Kontkanen (University of Vaasa) explore the similarities and differences between traditionally internationalizing firms (TRs) and the born internationals (BIs) in terms of the adaptation level of marketing strategies and their effect on the export performance, in Chapter 13. Discussion of marketing strategies focuses on product, price, distribution, and communication strategies. The paper highlights the role of contingency factors and their moderating effects on the relationship between adaptation level of marketing strategies and export performance. The empirical part of the study focuses on the strategies used by 221 Finnish firms. The findings indicate surprising similarities between TRs and BIs in the adaptation levels of marketing strategies in general and in the direct performance implications of the marketing strategy elements. However, great differences between TRs and BIs were found in the moderating effects of contingency factors.

In the final chapter of Part Four, Per Servais and Erik S. Rasmussen (University of Southern Denmark) argue that the inward activities of the SME ought to be at least as important as the outward, and there should be a focus on international sourcing as this typically leads to new relations and to exports. Sourcing from abroad can be a way of motivating SMEs to cooperate more internationally and to develop their internationalization further. International purchasing can thus have a relatively large influence on the competitiveness of the firm. In the case of born global sourcers these firms have developed relations with foreign suppliers carefully and this has caused offerings that have enabled the firms to create competitive advantages in the domestic market. Born global sourcers can, as sub-suppliers to firms in their vicinity, serve as an important element in these firms' internationalization. Regional development and internationalization (or globalization) are thus often seen as two opposite poles, but local networks play an important role in the development of the internationalization of especially newly established firms. In the chapter a revised model of born global sourcers is presented, and it is the hope that this could be a stepping stone in the excavation of outward-inward connection in other types of international new ventures, too.

References

Asheim, Bjørn T., Lars Coenen, and Martin Svensson-Henning. 2003. "Nordic SMEs and Regional Innovation Systems." Final report, Nordic Industrial Fund, Center for Innovation and Commercial Development, Department of Social and Economic Geography, Lund University, Sweden.

Gnyawali, Devi R., and Fogel, Daniel S. 1994. "Environment for Entrepreneurship Development: Key Dimensions and Research Implications." *Entrepreneurship: Theory and Practice* 18(4): 43–62.

Hultman, Cleas M. 1999. "Nordic Perspectives on Marketing and Research in the Marketing/Entrepreneurship Interface." *Journal of Research in Marketing & Entrepreneurship* 1(1): 54–71.

Kuada, John. 2016. *Global Mindsets: Exploration and Perspectives.* New York: Routledge.

Laukkanen, Maurila. 2000. "Exploring Alternative Approaches in High-Level Entrepreneurship Education: Creating Micro Mechanism for Endogenous Regional Growth." *Entrepreneurship & Regional Development* 12(1): 25–47.

Nilsson, Jan-Evert. 2006. *The Role of Universities in Reginal Innovation Systems: A Nordic Perspective.* Copenhagen: Copenhagen Business School Press.

Tesar, George, and Jan Bodin. 2013. *Marketing Management in Geographically Remote Industrial Clusters: Implications for Business-to-Consumer Marketing.* Singapore: World Scientific Publishing Co. Pte Ltd.

Part I
Entrepreneurial Action

2 From Small Businesses to Internationalized Entrepreneurial Ventures—Some Personal Notes

Rolf A. Lundin

1. Introduction

In this chapter the effort is made to apply a historical perspective to how Small Business Administration as a tentative field in the early days of the University of Umeå has played a role in the developments. Intertwined, as a parallel, the context in Norrland, the northern part of Sweden, is also attended to. Essentially, the small business field started as a new theme for research and as an education for "Bare-feet Business Masters" especially equipped to go out in the "Jungle of Norrland" (according to the lingo developed) and well prepared for the small businesses situation.

Rather than specializing in Accounting, Marketing or any other specialty of Business Administration the students studying small business education were expected to be broad enough to be useful for the entire range of business areas in order to serve the needs of small businesses. Some questions now are where this has taken academia in Umeå as well as the rest of Sweden, and how it has served business life.

2. The Start

The University of Umeå was founded in 1964 as an initially very small university in Northern Sweden, the first one ever north of Uppsala. It was from the very beginning a university, the fifth one in Sweden (after Uppsala, Stockholm, Lund and Gothenburg), with a full university library including copies of all theses from the entire country. The start was initially regarded as a development investment, partly based on the felt need for dentists and physicians in the remote and sparsely populated areas in the north of the country. Eventually, the university grew into other areas in accordance with a plan, notably also Social Sciences, eventually including also Business Administration. Erik Johnsen from the Copenhagen Business School in Denmark was acting professor in Business Administration when the department was formed, but in 1968 Dick Ramström became the first full professor on the chair in Business Administration. He had been awarded his PhD in 1967 at the University of Uppsala—the early full professors recruited to Umeå mostly came from the prestigious and well established universities in Lund and Uppsala—and the story is that even though his thesis had the title "The Efficiency of Control Strategies," he did not pursue that theme but in practice tried new things to be useful for the business life up north. His thesis can be described as very theoretical and abstract, but his adaptation to the business life up north contributed to a more practically oriented stance in his work. Also, since he was the first full professor in Business Administration in Umeå, he soon became well known in Norrland as well as in the rest of the country, making contacts with business people and with the local chambers of commerce as well as other organizations assisting small businesses.

At the time there were a few huge companies in Norrland, not to say giants (in forestry and mining). Small companies dominated overall in terms of numbers, even though there were some middle-sized companies as well (many of them were in various ways related to the big companies). However, the innovative decision at the department was made to attend to small businesses, both educationally and through research. Courses taught at the very small department covered the traditional specialties, and regarding research, there was no "monoculture"; but the area known as "Small Business Administration" involved several among the personnel and received national attention. So rather than applying the traditional Business Administration specialties (like Marketing, Accounting or Management), the size of the businesses in the Norrland context were attended to. In this way, the relatively young and initially small department made a difference in comparison with the dominating areas and styles of Business Administration in the old universities. Dick Ramström contributed heavily to that direction by appearing at business organizations regularly and by debating and publishing about the small business situation. In an edited book (in Swedish) published in 1971 with the title "Small Companies—Problems and Conditions" (Ramström 1971), some of the early studies at the department with a small business focus were presented. In 1975 another edited book on "Small Businesses—Big Problems" (Ramström 1975) followed up the themes from the previous book, contributing to the national attention to the small business area. Many small businesses in the northern part of Sweden concentrated on physical production as their main line of business, and this fact was alluded to in publications from that time.

A parallel path, which thrived during the early days and also later on, concentrated on regional studies. That path was promoted and supported by arguments that the future of the northern region was very much dependent on the development of small businesses, so there was a strong connection. However, the regional studies were macro-oriented, had less direct impact on the teaching of undergraduate students and did not earn a general reputation to the same degree as the "bare-feet business masters" did. However, a number of prominent theses were published related to the regional perspective. Among them was the thesis by Göran Carstedt and Birgitta Isaksson-Perez (1974) treating business and structural change in industries.

Another thesis was the Carl Fredriksson and Leif Lindmark (1976) study on national and local production systems in Sweden. Jan-Evert Nilsson (1979) wrote a thesis on how the Nordic part of the country would change in the future. However, there were also lots of minor academic publications related to the regional theme.

The focus on small businesses had been confirmed through research activities, resulting in research reports of a minor type but also more traditional academic publications, among the early ones a licentiate thesis by Bengt Johannisson (1971) on how minor companies adapted to changes. Several of the PhD students recruited during the heydays of small business teaching and research eventually produced theses. Among them are Elisabeth Sundin (1980), analyzing changes in subcontracting by minor companies in Norrland. Håkan Bohman and Håkan Boter (1984) scrutinized strategic planning in minor companies; Christer Strandberg (1984) studied convenience stores in the Norrrland region; Christer Peterson (1985) wrote his thesis on family business and mergers; Kerstin Nilsson and Per Nilsson (1992) treated networking and cooperation between minor companies.

The parallel to the small business orientation, regional studies, was then introduced, as well as a relatively new line of research in Business Administration, and also contributed to a broadening of the business administration field in the rest of the country.

Dick Ramström left the department and the group of researchers in the middle of the 70s for a position in Uppsala. Through his personality he had left an imprint not only on the business life in Norrland, but more importantly on the department forming it for several years to come. He is said to have been very much idea-driven and also open-minded in terms of research and teaching efforts. During his years, several female teachers and doctoral students were recruited—which at the time was quite unusual in comparison with the Business Administration departments in the rest of the country. One conspicuous fact is also that many not to say most researchers recruited wrote their theses in Swedish, making their findings less well observed internationally.

In 1978 when I became the successor to Dick Ramström to the full professor position, I came to a department with several doctoral students in the pipeline with partial theses manuscripts to be completed. Also, the educational apparatus was in full swing, with established routines. My personal background was that I had a PhD from what is now the Booth Business School at the University of Chicago in Management Science. During my five postdoctoral years at the business school in Gothenburg, I had been acting full professor for about two years, taking on supervision of many PhD students in the absence of the full professor (Walter Goldberg) there. Concerning research, before the move to Umeå, I had concentrated on studies related to the public sector and organization theory. But rather than pursuing those themes, I felt it to be a duty to assist people at the Umeå department to fulfill their own research ambitions and to adhere to the traditions developed during the previous era. I also made it clear that I would not add to those who stayed in Umeå for a brief stint, but that I was determined to stay. At the same time, and in parallel with my supervisory work in Umeå, I finalized the main supervision task for seven or so PhD students in the Gothenburg business school, thereby adding to my track record as main supervisor (in total, 55 PhD students who finalized their degrees).

3. Norrland and Its Transformation

Most small businesses in Norrland at the time when the university was founded had a line of business mostly limited to fairly uncomplicated physical production (many related to the availability of timber and the use of wood). Wooden furniture and prefabrication of one-family houses are examples. Traditionally, the companies had grown out of local initiatives in order to serve the local or regional market and to make use of the raw materials available. This meant essentially two things: the companies were well integrated with the local population in the vicinity of the company locations at the same time as they often dominated the villages and small towns where they were located. Many locations for the companies can be characterized as limited industrial communities where the villages and small towns were dependent upon the stability of those companies.

As mentioned, most areas up north were extremely sparsely populated. Some towns along the coast had grown to be concentrations of the population. In the inland, the river valleys also had some minor concentrations, but the pattern was generally very low densities of population. There had also been a migration of people from Norrland to southern Sweden. The net migration worried authorities—the lack of population made the Norrland area vulnerable and difficult to defend (as illustrated by the Russian invasion effort in the nineteenth century—a long time ago but still vivid in the minds of many). So, it was high on the political task list to support the Norrland development in various ways.

Much of societal activity in Norrland prior to the foundation of the university in Umeå was directed towards transforming Norrland from being a neglected and underdeveloped part of Sweden to being more in line with the rest of Sweden. It was and still is sparsely populated and considered in need of societal support in various ways. For some people in southern Sweden, Norrland was, however, even described as a burden, but it seems that such an attitude was not shared by many of the politicians. On the contrary, they in general provided serious efforts to support development through the state budget.

The establishment of the new university occurred after a long period of political bickering. The story is that the coastal towns were fighting each other a lot in order to be the town picked as the location for the new university. Umeå won in that competition. Gösta Skoglund, who at the time was a minister in the Swedish government, is described as the main actor in bringing the victory to Umeå. The debate about where the new university should be had been fierce between the towns along the coast of Norrland and caused wounds and antagonism, taking a long time to heal.

As to the earlier transformation, Norrland had become more integrated with southern Sweden through the mining and the forestry industries, since most products were delivered not only to the south but also exported. Later, the development of hydropower stations in the big rivers up north contributed to the integration. Eventually, company activities on other levels became better connected. The study by Sundin (1980) showed that companies working with one-family wooden houses often recruited new CEOs from southern Sweden. The result turned out to be that the new CEOs tended to favor subcontractors (for parts) to their company from southern Sweden in line with their previous purchasing patterns and experiences (from the south). Suppliers from Norrland were often neglected or disregarded, which was a disadvantage to that part of the country, but one effect was also that the business life in Norrland became more integrated with the rest of the country.

This is essentially an example on the company level, but it also made a connection to regional studies where the structure of the business life in the Norrland region connected to other regions and to the national level. As already mentioned there was one dissertation presented in the middle of the 70s (Fredriksson and Lindmark 1976) in which small businesses were studied from a regional, national and even international macro perspective. This also meant that the traditional, academic boundaries between disciplines were broken down and resulted in more or less joint efforts, or at least efforts that were well integrated between business administration, geography, economic history, etc.

The development of the academic environment in Norrland—notably this university but also elsewhere (the technical university in Luleå, for example, became a university in 1997 but had been initiated in 1971 as a college)—made an impact on the structure of the entire business life in Norrland. What is now Mid-Sweden University—the third university in Norrland—was also initiated much later, but the colleges in various locations also started relatively early.

The expansion of university teaching and research made qualified personnel available on various levels, and since several students were recruited from the south, there was an influx of youngsters. Even though students graduating tended to emigrate to the south of Sweden—mostly to Stockholm where business opportunities were regarded as favorable, many of the graduates stayed in Norrland. Those migrating to southern Sweden also tended to come back after a few years in the south (popularly called the Stockholm detour). Fairly quickly the educational institutions developed a strong national recruitment, with students coming from the entire country, and some of those students remained in Norrland after graduation. Together with those returning from their detour to southern Sweden, they contributed in a variety of ways to a stronger connection between Norrland and the rest of the country. The educational investments made in Norrland paid off. In fact, the University of Umeå has retrospectively been described as one of the very best regional investments of all time in Sweden.

4. The Business School of Norrland

Towards the middle of the 80s initiatives were taken to start a business school, initially by me, a few colleagues at the department and the chambers of commerce. The initial idea was that the cities and the educational institutions of Norrland should join forces and form a business school (to be the third one in the country—after Stockholm and Gothenburg). The idea was greeted with enthusiasm by the leadership of Umeå University at the time, with the president, Lars Beckman, on the frontline and also by neighboring cities, but in Luleå and in other places the notion was met with resistance and only approved if the unit was to be placed elsewhere and not in Umeå. The Norrland plan had to be abandoned due to lack of support from other parts of the region and changed to be the Umeå Business School, consisting initially of departments traditionally belonging to a business school.

The business school initiative was not entirely accepted within the entire university. One reason for that is that many of the employees at the university contributed to the outside view of the university as the "red university" by opposing the main components and ambitions of a business school. However, with the strong support of the university leadership and through the fundraising work by the governor at the time of Västerbotten, Sven Johansson, the business school became a fact in 1989 when it was formed as a special unit of the social science faculty. I had worked in various ways together with a group of people on establishing the business school. Among them were Christer Peterson and Nils Wåhlin, and they were part of the liaison between the effort and the regional business life. I was also appointed to be the first dean of the business school.

The business school effort became one part of the expansion of business education and also of the total university. At the inauguration of the business school, happenings were organized, with for instance a public debate on banking in which all CEOs of the major Swedish banks participated. The inauguration contributed heavily to the national attention the effort received. Owe R. Hedström, who is an experienced organizer of events of this type, together with the administrative secretary of the business school at the time, Katarina Pousette, contributed heavily to the inauguration success.

The fundraising efforts had contributed to an internal fund, in particular used for adding business administration full professorships in the traditional areas. The fund had also some room for seed money for research efforts. The new school provided a strong impetus for developing student exchange with educational institutions abroad. Soon the Umeå business school was leading in the university in international student recruitment and exchange.

It still holds that position. Some personnel were also recruited from abroad in the internationalization efforts. George Tesar—one of the two editors of this volume—was one of the professors who spent extended time teaching at the business school. In a similar way, Tim Wilson was recruited and has served for a long time at the business school. The habit of inviting international guests was also initiated strongly during the first years of the business school. Many of the teachers and also the PhD students today have an international origin.

5. Attending to Entrepreneurship and Internationalization

As alluded to, the small business concentration received a lot of attention not only from the regional business environment but also from the academic environment nationally. "Bare-feet Business Masters" caught on as a label in regional businesses and among the "friends" of small businesses devoted to promoting business development in the northern areas of Sweden, with a threatening net out-flux of habitants in relation to southern Sweden. With a basis in studies on small businesses, and with the thesis of Bohman and Boter (1984) on conditions for that part of business life, the small business field developed to also focus on entrepreneurship. Academically, the focus on entrepreneurship might partly be conceived as an extension of the small business area; in addition, my predecessor, Dick Ramström, has been regarded as one of the forefront personalities of entrepreneurship research. Whereas the small business area focused on making small businesses work and survive in a less than benevolent environment, though, entrepreneurship put attention on creating and growing businesses (without the notion of smallness).

Most of the early studies made on small businesses used a case methodology. The case orientation in a sense was natural since the main thrusts in cases could be used in direct communication between the researchers involved and company representatives. An entrepreneurship researcher, Per Davidsson, was recruited from the Stockholm School of Economics directly upon being awarded his PhD in 1989. His preferences for quantitative research opened up another type of research efforts on macro related matters and growth rather than on individual business leaders and their actions. This was one factor influencing governments' opinions of the usefulness of entrepreneurship research. Not too long ago there were very few efforts particularly devoted to the entrepreneurship specialty. Nowadays, governments all over the world have emphasized the idea that entrepreneurship might be a means of achieving good economic developments and improved figures of employment, and almost all universities allude to their interests in and focus on entrepreneurship. Interest in entrepreneurship has spread throughout the world practically and academically, with a focus on not only how entrepreneurs become entrepreneurs but also entrepreneurship on a macro level. Put differently, the world has been opened up to internationalization of entrepreneurship.

With the expansion of the university, the areas treated in research and teaching were transformed in various ways, attracting an increasing number of students from southern Sweden. With the ambitions of a young university, Umeå eventually favored start-ups in new industries and a concentration on knowledge related companies. Modernizing appeared on the scene, with less concentration or direct connections to the traditional small companies working with physical production. Rather than focusing on the fact that small companies are small, the faculty with support from the university transformed the direction of the research (and the teaching) into other areas than those which had been traditional. Entrepreneurship with an international focus is one example of such a new direction.

Håkan Boter has developed his interests from the early doctoral thesis and in different ways alluded to entrepreneurship at the same time as he has kept a keen interest in small businesses in the region from a practical perspective. However, he has also contributed to the idea that small businesses need to complement internal expertise with capabilities from the outside (Boter and Lundström 2005). He has demonstrated his interests in open innovation (Wincent *et al.* 2009) and its connection to small firms. His idea on the role of the internet and marketing (Bengtsson et al. 2007) in achieving this aim is an example of his wide interests.

Another line of his research has been internationalization. One well cited article already published in 1996 by Boter and Holmquist (1996) focuses on internationalization processes in small firms, adding to the stream of internationalization research in business administration. Eventually, internationalization issues have been given even more importance in business research. One reason is that research in this area has been in line with how the environments of companies have developed over time. Early studies mostly described internationalization as a step-by-step process in which real bold steps were avoided or absent. Incremental learning and starting internationalization work in neighboring countries dominated practice and also the main advice based on research activities. However, more recent studies have also analyzed a growing number of cases of instant globalization, where entrepreneurs seem to adhere to notions like "fortune favors the brave." Currently, research focuses very much on what happens and what is done after the brave initiation. Boter has been touching indirectly also on that area by being a supervisor for a PhD thesis recently defended at USBE with the catchy title "Beyond Going Global," on how international new ventures develop past early internationalization (Abrahamsson 2016).

Entrepreneurship is being supported not only from local and regional sources but also from national and international bodies. On the regional level, the developments are supported by start-up facilities related to universities, often called "science parks." Some foundations are now devoted to support entrepreneurial ventures of a completely different character than the traditional small businesses. One way to describe such a turn is to use the term "knowledge-intensive" firms, where physical production is relatively unimportant and where the market is fast moving. Examples can be found in the gaming industry, tapping the market created by the younger generation. Those industries are extremely project oriented and with a much shorter time horizon than traditional industrial companies with large investments in heavy machinery.

However, entrepreneurship is not only about inventing advanced ways to satisfy needs in the market but also about making things happen. Academically and practically, we will see a merger combining entrepreneurial activities and inventiveness with efficient project handling. In practice, entrepreneurship has links with project management. But not until lately has that connection been made in the academic literature. In a study published by Kuura and coauthors (2014) the conspicuous finding is that essentially only one (American) researcher has published well in both entrepreneurship and in project-related themes.

This example serves to show how entrepreneurship is on its way to diversification. The major theme of entrepreneurship has developed into a set of related specialties, but the proponents of those specialties also tend to become a bit isolated in relation to the main theme of which they are an offspring. I think that there is a danger in this development. Social sciences are in need of an ability to relate special and detailed studies to other related areas and to be inspired by putting their specialties in relevant contexts.

Thus, I do find it promising that connections have been made between entrepreneurship and gender research. Holmquist and Sundin have alluded to that joint theme in a publication from 1988 and also continued publishing in related areas since that time, thus being role models for how research should develop.

6. Migration of Academics

During the early years of the University of Umeå, the dominant pattern was that senior academics tended to come from the more prestigious universities in southern Sweden. Many of those early recruitments of senior academics tended to move back south at the first opportunity to do so. Initially, most of the teaching personnel were recruited locally, though. In 1978 when you walked the corridors at the department of business administration, almost all names indicated a Swedish heritage. The department had three teachers from Finland, however. The reason was that academic business education in northern Finland had yet to develop, and it was relatively easy for people from Finland to settle in Umeå. Nowadays, when you walk the corridors of Umeå School of Business and Economics, there are lots of names indicating foreign descent. This goes for PhD students as well as for senior professors. As mentioned previously, USBE was early in developing international contacts with other universities and business schools in the world. It is still leading in that development at the University of Umeå.

However, there has also been a migration of senior academics from the University of Umeå to prominent and important positions elsewhere in Sweden. Bengt Johannisson moved to Växjo, and eventually he became a full professor at that university (now Linneus University). A group of researchers—among them small business researchers like Christer Strandberg—went to assist in the development of the academic context in Sundsvall. Leif Lindmark was asked to be the dean of Jönköping International Business School (where he was my predecessor before I was invited to accept the same position at that school), and eventually he became the rector of Stockholm School of Economics (SSE). Elisabeth Sundin eventually became full professor at Linköping University. And Carin Holmquist became full professor in entrepreneurship at SSE. Anders Söderholm, who served as dean of USBE for a couple of years, was recruited to be the rector (or Vice Chancellor) of Mid-Sweden University and has now been appointed Chancellor over all Swedish universities. Håkan Boter became a full professor of the Mid-Sweden University at the Östersund campus and had a stint there for a few years. Another prominent position has been held by Sigbrit Franke (coming from education) when she became the Chancellor of all Swedish universities and held that position for a couple of periods. So, all in all, this once-tiny university has grown and become an important influence in the country.

The examples provided only cover academically relevant careers. Many also went to prominent managerial positions in businesses and in public administration organizations.

To summarize the history thus far one might say that the University of Umeå and the present business school has moved a long way from being a nascent idea to the present situation without losing sight of initial concerns for teaching and research. The context of the university and the business school has changed. At that, the development of the university has been very strong. In 1978 it had close to 7,500 students, and thus far it has peaked at 36,000 students, not to mention research and its other impacts.

References

Abrahamsson, Jan T. 2016. "Beyond Going Global—Essays on Business Development of International New Ventures Past Early Internationalization." PhD diss., Umeå University.

Bengtsson, Maria, Håkan Boter, and Vladimir Vanyushyn. 2007. "Integrating the Internet and Marketing Operations a Study of Antecedents in Firms of Different Size. "International *Small Business Journal* 25(1): 27–48.

Bohman, Håkan, and Håkan Boter. 1984. "Planering i mindre och medelstora företag: den strategiska planeringens utmaningar och faktiska villkor (Planning in Small and Medium-sized Companies—Challenges and Real Conditions for Strategic Planning)." PhD diss., Umeå University.

Boter, Håkan, and Anders Lundström. 2005. "SME Perspectives on Business Support Services: The Role of Company Size, Industry and Location." *Journal of Small Business and Enterprise Development* 12(2): 244–258.

Boter, Håkan and Carin Holmquist. 1996. "Industry Characteristics and Internationalization Processes in Small Firms." *Journal of Business Venturing* 11(6): 471–487.

Carstedt, Göran, and Birgitta Isaksson-Perez. 1974. "Företag i strukturomvandlingen (Businesses in Structural Development)." PhD diss., Umeå University.

Davidsson, Per. 1989. "Continued Entrepreneurship and Small Firm Growth." PhD diss., Stockholm School of Economics.

Fredriksson, Carl, and Leif Lindmark. 1976. "Nationella och lokala produktionssystem: en strukturstudie av svenskt näringsliv (National and Local Production Systems: A Study of the Structure of Businesses in Sweden)." PhD diss., Umeå University.

Holmquist, Carin, and Elisabeth Sundin, E. 1988. "Women as Entrepreneurs in Sweden: Conclusions from a Survey." In *Frontiers of Entrepreneurship Research*, edited by Bruce A. Kirchhoff, Wayne A. Long, W. Ed McMullan, Karl H. Vesper, and William E. Wetzel Jr. Center for Entrepreneurial Studies Wellesley, MA: Babson College.

Johannisson, Bengt. 1971. "Företagens anpassningsprocesser: En systemanalys med tillämpning på mindre företag. (Adaptation Processes in Companies: A System Analysis of Small Companies), Studier i företagsekonomi (Studies in Business Administration)." Umeå University.

Kuura, Arvi, Robert A. Blackburn, and Rolf A. Lundin. 2014. "Entrepreneurship and Projects—Linking Segregated Communities." *Scandinavian Journal of Management* 30(2): 214–230.

Nilsson, Jan Evert. 1979. "Norrland År 2001: Drivkrafter Bakom Ett Regionalt Skeende Från Historia Till Framtid. (Industrial Development and Regional Interaction-the Case of Northern Sweden)." PhD diss., Umeå University.

Nilsson, Kerstin, and Per Nilsson. 1992. "Småföretag i flerpartssamverkan: En studie av aktörer, byggstenar och fogmassa vid nätverksbyggande (Small Business in Cooperation: A Study of Actors, Building Blocks and Glue for Networking)." PhD diss., Umeå University.

Peterson, Christer. 1985. "Familjeföretag i omvandling: en studie av fusionsförlopp och utvecklingsmönster (Family Businesses in Change: Studies of Merger Developments)." PhD diss., Umeå University.

Ramström, Dick. 1967. "The Efficiency of Control Strategies." PhD diss., Uppsala University.

Ramström, Dick, ed. 1971. "Mindre företag-problem och villkor: företagsekonomer vid Umeå universitet diskuterar de mindre och medelstora företagens problem och möjligheter." Prisma i samarbete med Svenska civilekonomföreningen. (Small Companies—Problems and Conditions), Prisma and Association of Swedish Civil-Economy, Stockholm.

Ramström, Dick. 1975. "Små företag-stora problem. (Small Companies—Big Problems)." Norstedt and Association of Swedish Civil-Economs, Stockholm.

Strandberg, Christer. 1984. "Glesbygdsbutiker: en studie av tillkomst, köptrohet och socialt samspel. (Convenience Stores in Sparsely Populated Regions)." PhD diss., Umeå University.

Sundin, Elisabeth. 1980. "Företag i perifera regioner: fallstudier av företagartra-dition, företagsmiljö och företags framväxt i Norrbottens inland (Industries in Peripheral Regions: Case Studies of Industrial Tradition, Industrial Environment and Growing Firms in the Interior of Norrbotten)." PhD diss., Umeå University.
Wincent, Joakim, Sergey Anokhin, and Håkan Boter. 2009. "Network Board Conti-nuity and Effectiveness of Open Innovation in Swedish Strategic Small-Firm Net-works." *R&D Management* 39(1): 55–67.

3 Come to the Northern Side— We Have a Business Model

*Petri Ahokangas, Irina Atkova,
and Pia Hurmelinna-Laukkanen*

Dream a dream: Late 1960s, Rovaniemi, Lapland, Finland. Antero Ikäheimo has a dream to build a Santa Claus Land in his hometown. Some fifty years later, Johanna Ikäheimo, Antero's daughter, is the chairman of the board of Lappset group, a family business that focuses on story-based activity attractions, generates over MEUR 50 turnover with MEUR 20 from abroad, employs over 350 staff in seven countries, and has distributors in 46 countries globally . . .

1. Introduction

The nature of the relationship between innovation and internationalization represents a long-standing debate in the extant research. Originally, internationalization was understood as a process of learning in adopting innovation (Bilkey and Tesar 1977; Czinkota 1982). Later, the two concepts were studied separately, and it was only recently that the interrelated nature of innovation and internationalization has become a target of wider interest.

Innovation and internationalization have been linked to other concepts as well. Within the business model literature, business model innovation has become an established research stream wherein a business model is approached as one of the innovative key elements in analyzing, designing, and implementing strategic activities in companies. Less is known about the internationalization aspect. However, entrepreneurship and strategic management literature provides us with research examples that combine business models with an international business context, especially in the ICT sector and among start-up companies. However, the internationalization process itself remains unaddressed. In addition, traditional industries, established companies, and family firms represent those areas of research that still call for attention regarding the utilization of a business model in exploring and understanding the internationalization of companies.

Utilizing a business model as the boundary-spanning unit of analysis, this chapter explores the intertwined nature of internationalization and innovation with a more specific aim to understand the process of business model transformation. We start by reviewing the current literature on business models, innovation, and internationalization in order to reveal and understand the interconnections between these phenomena. We continue by describing the longitudinal research approach. Next, we proceed to the case description wherein we explore and depict the innovative, business model-based internationalization of the family-owned manufacturing firm Lappset Oy (Rovaniemi, Lapland, Finland) over a period of more than 40 years. Finally, we present a model of the business model transformation process that reflects the interrelatedness of business models, innovation, and internationalization concepts. We conclude by describing the limitations of this study and sketch avenues for future research. From a theoretical perspective, the chapter adopts an integrative approach with the purpose of contributing to the existing body of knowledge through a longitudinal case study.

2. Business Model and Innovation

Like a kaleidoscope, the business model concept changes meaning depending on the perspective or purpose of the knowledge creation (Jensen 2013). The business model phenomenon has been understood as "an architecture for the product, service and information flows" (Timmers 1998; 4), logic for value creation and capture (Chesbrough 2007; Johnson *et al.* 2008; Linder and Cantrell 2000; Shafer *et al.* 2005; Zott and Amit 2007), "stories that explain how enterprises work" (Magretta 2002, 87), a set of activities (Afuah 2004), a scale model (Doganova and Eyquem-Renault 2009), and cognitive structures (Doz and Kosonen 2010), just to name a few examples. This diversity reveals different ways of thinking about the business model concept, yet value creation and value capture seem to be the common denominators in the majority of the definitions (Ahokangas and Myllykoski 2014; Boons and Ludeke-Freund 2013; Nenonen and Storbacka 2010). Whatever definition is adopted, at the practical level, entrepreneurial decisions and subsequent actions reveal the specifics of a business model (Klein 2008; Mason and Spring 2011). From the entrepreneurial action perspective, a business model helps to answer the questions regarding what companies offer to their customers in terms of products/services and value proposition, how and where they plan to do that in practice, and why they think they can do it profitably (Ahokangas *et al.* 2013, 2014).

Similarly to the business model concept, there are several interpretations of what business model innovation is (cf. Magretta 2002; McGrath 2010; Morris *et al.* 2005; Sosna *et al.* 2010). Previously, innovation was generally understood as a new idea, product or service, and was largely confined to the realm of technology and R&D (Chesbrough 2007). However, there is growing consensus that, in order to stay ahead of the product innovation game (Amit and Zott 2012), companies need to integrate their innovation processes with their business models (Chesbrough 2007). This implies approaching business models simultaneously as a vehicle and an object of innovation (Zott *et al.* 2011). In other words, magic happens when a product or service innovation is matched with business model innovation as "the same idea or technology taken to market through two different business models will yield two different economic outcomes" (Chesbrough 2010, 354). It is noteworthy that companies are increasingly making business model innovation a strategic priority—even above product or service innovation (Martins *et al.* 2015).

Reflecting the variety in approaches, in the extant literature, business model innovation refers to processes that are different in scale and scope. For instance, for Wirtz *et al.* (2010) business model innovation is largely about reaction and adaptation to the external environment. On the other hand, Morris *et al.* (2005) see adaptation only as a part of the business model innovation process. For them, business model innovation is a cyclical process involving specification, refinement, adaptation, revision, and reformulation. In a similar vein, Sosna *et al.* (2010) describe business model innovation as the process of experimentation, revision, adaptation, and fine-tuning based on trial-and-error learning. Contrary to Wirtz *et al.* (2010), Demil and Lecocq (2010) understand business model innovation as a proactive process of anticipating and responding to the changes in the external circumstances. For Zott and Amit (2010), business model innovation is a design process of an activity system (content, structure, governance), and a source of value creation (novelty, lock-in, complementarities, efficiency). Adopting action learning perspective, Ahokangas and Myllykoski (2014) understand business model innovation as consisting of four parallel practices—visioning, strategizing, practicing, and assessing.

Martins *et al.* (2015) differentiate between three major perspectives within the business model innovation literature. According to the rational positioning view, business model innovation is a process of optimization and adaptation in response to the external changes, whether that is technological or regulatory. From the evolutionary perspective, business model innovation is a process of incremental modification under the circumstances of external uncertainty. Finally, the cognitive view explains business model innovation in terms of schema change, through analogical reasoning or conceptual combination. Analogical reasoning implies the transfer of knowledge from a familiar to a novel domain, whereas conceptual combination entails identifying the differences between a modifier concept and the existing business model schema (Martins *et al.* 2015) In other words, according to the revolutionary and evolutionary perspectives, change in the external environment (including shifts in the international landscape) is a primary driver of the business mode innovation process, whereas a cognitive approach allows for explaining business model innovation in the absence of exogenous change.

If business model innovation implies unique changes in the business model (e.g. Voelpel *et al.* 2004), the transformation process can refer to the life cycle of a business model (Cavalcante *et al.* 2011) or to the less radical business model changes (Wirtz *et al.* 2015). Cavalcante *et al.* (2011) differentiate between four stages in the business model transformation process, i.e. creation, extension, revision, and termination. In turn, van Putten and Schief (2012) distinguish nine levels where a business model change can occur: value proposition, target customer, distribution channel, relationship, value configuration, core competency, partner network, cost structure, and revenue model. These transformations connect business models to innovation and internationalization-related aspects.

Transformation does not come easily, however. Although companies increasingly understand the importance of business model innovation as a source of competitive advantage and industry change (Johnson *et al.* 2008), such revolutionary stories as iTunes or Uber are quite rare. Johnson *et al.* (2008) differentiate between two factors that make business model innovation difficult to pull through. The first is a lack of research into dynamics and the business model development process. The second one is a poor understanding of business models—most companies do not comprehend their existing business models well enough for timely change. Christensen (1997) interprets disruptive innovation as a potential barrier for business model innovation where an existing business model conflicts with the emerging one. Zott and Amit (2010) view novelty, lock-in, complementarities, and efficiency concurrently as the key aspects of business model innovation and as sources of conflict when it comes to the change of the traditional business model configurations. By adopting a cognitive perspective, Chesbrough (2010) talks about "dominant logic" as hindering business model innovation.

In sum, business model innovation, though difficult to achieve, is crucial for companies. It is the source of sustainability, competitive advantage, and a key to company performance in the long run. This is particularly true in relation to innovation and internationalization as well as their intertwined nature.

3. Internationalization and Innovation

During the past few years, new players from emerging countries, recession, and weakening entrepreneurial activity have created a novel competitive environment wherein an ability to recognize new opportunities, innovate, and operate on the global scale have become a key to the firm survival and growth (Boter 1996; Hagen *et al.* 2014). Accordingly, in the extant research, entrepreneurship, innovation, and internationalization are increasingly seen as interrelated phenomena with entrepreneurship tying the other two together (Hagen *et al.* 2014; Onetti *et al.* 2012; Zucchella and Siano 2014). However, the relationship between innovation and internationalization remains complex and difficult to determine unambiguously.

First, the causality between innovation and internationalization is controversial (D'Angelo 2010; Hurmelinna-Laukkanen 2014; Sterlacchini 1999). Some authors argue that innovation activity and the related unique knowledge assets enable and drive internationalization (Boter 2003; Caves 1982;

Kogut and Zander 1992; Pla-Barber and Alegre 2007; Zucchello and Siano 2014). Hitt *et al.* (1997) suggest that innovating companies are incentivized to expand globally in search of higher returns on investment. Others emphasize that innovation enables the creation of firm-specific assets thereby achieving a competitive advantage and ensuring survival on the international markets (Giovannetti, Ricchiuti and Velucchi 2009; Porter 1990; Zucchello and Siano 2014).

On the contrary, relying on the resource-based view and organizational learning theory, Bettis and Hitt (1995) identify internationalization as an innovation trigger. According to Hitt *et al.* (1997) internationalization enables the exploitation of the local market advantages, whereas innovation allows overcoming the disadvantages. Furthermore, involvement in the international activities influences the firm's innovation capacity by generating R&D resources and reducing the costs of R&D inputs (Kobrin 1991; Kotabe *et al.* 2002), providing access to the globally available resources (Kotabe 1990), networking with the local actors (Santos *et al.* 2004), accessing the larger pool of knowledge, and improving the process of knowledge accumulation thereby increasing organizational learning (Hitt *et al.* 1997; Kafouros *et al.* 2008). Yet, together with positive effects, internationalization also brings along versatile challenges, such as knowledge leakage, tacit knowledge transfer, and management of a complex global network (Fisch 2003; Hurmelinna-Laukkanen 2014; von Zedtwitz and Gassmann 2002).

Similarly to Bettis and Hitt (1995), Kafouros *et al.* (2008) argue that a company can reap innovation benefits, provided that a certain degree of internationalization exists. In other words, the degree of internationalization preconditions the possibilities for innovation monetization. If international operations are below a threshold level, companies are unable to enjoy the innovation benefits (Kafouros *et al.* 2008). In turn, Hitt *et al.* (1997) suggest that the relationship between the two may be two-directional. Likewise, Hagen *et al.* (2014, 111) emphasize the reciprocal nature by stating that "internationalization and innovation are two major options to achieve firm growth" and "most important strategies determining business success in today's competitive markets" (Zucchela and Siano 2014, 35).

The second (somewhat related) challenge relates to the fact that the effects of innovative activity and internationalization remain unclear. Some authors find that innovation and internationalization positively influence firm performance (Kafouros *et al.* 2008; Pla-Barber and Alegre 2007), whereas others claim that firms with limited international presence might not be able to cover the costs associated with innovation (Hitt *et al.* 1997).

In sum, the concepts of a business model, internationalization, and innovation have been mostly addressed separately, thereby causing a lack of research focusing on the nexus of these phenomena (Onetti *et al.* 2012). Furthermore, even though business model innovation is a widely researched topic, the links between the concepts of a business model and internationalization remain virtually unexplored. Therefore, by approaching a business model as a unit of analysis (Zott *et al.* 2011), this research aims to explore how a business model accommodates the global presence and fast-paced innovation, especially in the non-high-tech context.

4. Methodology

The aim of this study is to provide an analysis of the context and processes that illuminate business model transformation. Therefore, a longitudinal single case study was chosen as the methodological approach. This research strategy is particularly suited for understanding social and organizational processes, especially when "the boundaries between the phenomenon and context are not clearly evident" (Hartley 2004; Yin 1994, 13). A case study allows for inductive theory building by systematically patching together the detailed evidence (Hartley 2004). This broad strategy allows for multiple methods to be used. Therefore, Stake (2000, 435) does not consider case studies as a methodological choice but rather as "a choice of what is to be studied . . . by whatever methods, we choose to study the case".

For the purposes of this study, the analysis of the documents over the last 45 years was combined with semi-structured interviews with the CEO and chairman of the board of the case company. Lappset has nearly 50 years of experience in the production of playground equipment and is one of the benchmark companies in the industry in the international arena. Therefore, the case company provides an exclusive opportunity to trace the business model transformation process. In the following, the story of Lappset is laid out and blended with analytical observations.

5. Unfolding of the Lappset Story

The Modern Playground is Born and Spreads Internationally . . .

The dream of the "Santa Claus land" conceived in the late 1960s started to become reality in 1970 when Lappset was established as Pohjoiskalotti Oy by Antero Ikäheimo. The starting idea for Lappset was to develop and manufacture innovative and unique playground equipment made of Lappish wood. Antero Ikäheimo began to develop an innovative idea of furnishing living environments with warmer and softer-looking play equipment. The hope was to replace metallic carousels and climbing frames that were fashionable at the time. In the new environment, children could have fun by climbing and playing independently. The very first playground equipment was produced under a Swedish license and subcontracted by a carpentry workshop in the nearby town of Pello, which is close to the Swedish border. Before long, the two northern play experts, Antero and his brother Risto, were known throughout Finland and even beyond: by the 1970s, the brothers were already making sales calls in Scandinavia, the Benelux countries, and even Japan. Long delivery distances and the demands for efficient production presented challenges for the young company. In response, Lappset began to develop new innovative solutions, such as modular construction, and invested heavily in product and business development with a keen eye on market trends. In fact, already the original vision of Antero Ikäheimo was to develop all-round environmentally sustainable play equipment and playgrounds.

During the 1970s and early 1980s, the innovation of Lappset was in the idea of producing Nordic wooden playgrounds and street furniture. In the beginning, all of the production was outsourced locally, but when the subcontractor started to copy the products, the company was forced to establish its own production. That was also the point when modular design and a special type of grooving were first introduced to the products. This special type of grooving increased the quality of the products, and modular design provided children with the opportunity for playful learning. At that time, the public sector was seen as the main paying customer. As a visionary, Antero Ikäheimo had the insight that the Finnish market alone would be too small for the company and would not provide enough opportunities for growth. The export logic applied by the company was also innovative: where most companies would start exporting to the familiar, close markets, Lappset chose to enter the most difficult and demanding countries first, as success in those markets would mean faster growth in the other, easier markets. The planning for specific export products was started in 1975, at a time when the company trademark was registered and product designs were legally protected. The company succeeded in starting their own exports to Belgium, Germany, Switzerland, Denmark and Japan, although Japan did not turn out to be a success. Moreover, the US market was studied with the idea of licensed production in Mexico, but due to high customs and excise costs in Latin America, the company decided to look elsewhere. In the early 1980s, France, Hong Kong, Great Britain, Singapore, and Arab countries were added to the list of export countries. This was also the time when Antero Ikäheimo laid the foundations for a company culture with strong Lappish identity thereby understanding the value of the brand with a focus on sustainability and social responsibility.

In order to secure further growth in the mid-1980s, the owners of the company decided to sell the majority of the ownership to a private equity investor that brought professional management into the company. The innovative thinking of the company was channeled into seeking efficiency that made Lappset, among other things, the first company in the industry to adopt computer aided design (CAD) tools. The public sector was still the main customer group of the company. Foreign acquisition options were examined, and the first subsidiaries were established in Germany and then in Great Britain. In 1988, all of the shares were sold to the equity investor. However, the financial crisis in 1990 forced the equity investor to divest from certain industries and, in 1994, Lappset became family owned again.

The 1990s marked a strong international expansion for Lappset. China, Greece, Italy, Taiwan, Thailand, and South Korea were included as new export countries, and a subsidiary was started in Sweden. By the end of the 1990s, Lappset had grown into one of the biggest players in the industry. The increasing range of countries served by Lappset brought about the need to develop the skills needed for international business. Not everything went smoothly, though, as there were several occasions of agreement problems as well as financial losses in export markets. But the company remained profitable every year.

Already at this stage, the Lappset business model, innovation, and internationalization show a close connection mutually influencing each other. Lappset initially targeted mostly public customers by offering modular play equipment made of Lappish wood—a relatively straightforward, well-defined approach. The innovation process of the company was focused on eco-friendly sustainable materials and modular design, which provided it with a unique character and competitive advantage. The innovation activities influenced the formation of corporate brand and identity: brand and strong technical capabilities were utilized to strengthen each other. At the heart of the organization identity, Lappset saw itself as a company that furnishes a pleasant living environment with sustainability. The limitedness of the local market motivated the company to explore international markets, and the distinctive and emotive brand message helped to get started with the first export operations. In other words, product innovation called for changes in the core or anchoring elements of the business model—product, corporate brand, and identity, thereby leading to the business model reconceptualization and its subsequent transformation. At the same time, serving as the environmental factors innovation and internationalization provided contextual cues for the business model development. Thus, innovation and internationalization surrounded the process of business model transformation helping to illuminate the phenomenon.

Playgrounds Get Digitalized . . .

The new millennium brought about digitalization and a generation change to company management. Antero Ikäheimo started handing over the reins of the company to his daughter Johanna Ikäheimo. Having several stages, the transition took six years, and was completed by 2006. Before retirement, Antero initiated a new stage of innovation. He saw that the company needed to grow bigger even though a financial crisis in Europe had brought about fierce price competition and an expansion to new countries had started to slow down. Being just different and effective was not enough anymore: he suggested that the new management "include a microchip in the wood." In 2002, a nonfamily CEO with a strong strategy orientation and focus on corporate governance, as well as external board members, joined the company. In 2003, Lappset started a smart playground project called SmartUs.

The SmartUs project was a huge investment for the company; the total budget exceeded MEUR 2. It aimed to bring together the traditional playground, new technology, and innovative and interactive applications for different age groups. In the core was the idea of supporting learning, physical, and motor development as well as creativity. In addition, the project brought together design thinking, architecture, and digital technologies in the playground context. The results of the project took Lappset further than they expected. A series of new tailored, modular product lines was introduced that helped Lappset to expand to serve new end users, adults, and seniors as well as enter new customer groups in the private sector, such as wellness centers, shopping malls, and holiday resorts. The idea was not to sell sets of individual playground products, but rather to provide customers with an opportunity to build fully equipped and versatile playgrounds anywhere. Play and sport equipment, park and street furniture, digitalized playgrounds, and service (installation and maintenance), were examples of the Lappset product lines. With the new offering, Lappset became the benchmark for the industry, the first one to introduce digital content, concept thinking, and new materials to the markets. In parallel, a new brand strategy started taking its shape: playful learning and growth through play became the brand focus.

At the time, the company had about 50 distributors all over the world. Sales in many countries were, however, quite small, but altogether company turnover exceeded MEUR 30. Regarding the internationalization strategy, Lappset took its first steps with acquisitions with the aim to grow in big countries and to achieve stronger control of operations. By 2012, Lappset had made acquisitions in Sweden, Germany, Finland, the Netherlands and France. As the customer segmentation expanded in the private sector, customer intimacy became even more important for the company. By 2005, Lappset had representatives in 26 countries and subsidiaries in Finland, Spain, Germany, the UK, and Sweden. In 2006, a new marketing and sales oriented CEO joined Lappset. Toward 2010, the scale of operations started to call for a revision in the management logic. The company refocused to accelerate organic growth, improve cost efficiency and optimize the value chain, rationalize the product portfolio, and enhance brand awareness.

The digitalization of playgrounds marked changes in the dynamics of internationalization, innovation, and the business model. Disruptive product innovation required reconceptualization of the existing business model and its anchoring elements. At this second "development stage," the company customer base expanded from within to include not only public but also private customers, as Lappset started offering them digitalized product lines for different end-user groups. This suggests that a proactive approach was taken to change the market for Lappset, and it implies that product innovation triggered business model transformation that in turn further affected the innovative and internationalization aspects. The change in the product and customer segments gave a new boost to international markets, forming a new context for the company. Lappset moved from producing individual products to creating a range of innovative product lines that gave a customer a unique opportunity to assemble his or her own playground that matched specific requirements. Together with the new product lines, the end-user groups extended to account not only for children, but also adults and seniors. By incorporating the digital element into the product lines, the company was able to accommodate an emerging trend in the education technologies of lifelong playful learning. At this stage, "growth through play" was at the core of the company brand. The company's organizational identity had developed to cover not only sustainability, but also life -long playful learning. At the same time, Lappset attracted an external investor that allowed benefiting from the company learning curve and accelerating its internationalization process by acquiring companies and establishing regional subsidiaries. With the help of the business model transformation, the benefits of innovation and internationalization could be realized, and the interconnection of the two could be utilized to the fullest extent.

Playgrounds Start Telling Stories . . .

In 2010, Rovio's Angry Birds landed in Lappset's backyard and started to build a nest. Rovio needed a partner to build "Angry birds' parks" internationally. Suddenly, Lappset had to start re-conceptualizing their offering in terms of stories, characters, and themes that placed increased demands also for the design, manufacturing, marketing, and selling capabilities of the company. The standard existing elements, the playground equipment with a modular digitalized design, formed the core of the new product concept— the activity theme parks. In turn, brand thinking became even more pronounced for Lappset. The company saw its mission in inviting mankind outdoors, i.e. creating environments that would persuade people to spend more time outside.

Rovio's visit to the company backyard led Lappset to think about brand owners as potential partners. Maybe Thomas and Friends, Bob the Builder, Peter Rabbit, Barbie, and Angelina Ballerina could have their own activity theme parks? This revelation accidentally opened up a blue ocean opportunity for Lappset. None of the global competitors were in this business.

Parallel to the reconceptualization of the offering, the internationalization strategy of the company turned from seeking new entries to increasing sales and penetration in the existing markets. Customer segmentation was renewed and prioritized to cover public and private projects, resorts and shopping malls, and designers and amusement parks. The activity park business became the first spin-off from Lappset with an idea not to sell products but to create business cases. Johan Granholm, head of Lappset Creative, puts it as follows: "I am not here to sell a product—I would like to sell you a lucrative business case and an investment that generates a quick return." The pillars of the scalable new concept included market, space, business, and experience models. At the heart of each theme park was a brand with an internationally known set of characters and story, such as Thomas and

Friends. Thus, the new customers were the companies owning the IP of the characters and stories, and theme park operators. In a couple of years, Lappset built a team that was capable of designing, producing, delivering, and realizing an activity park based on any story or character, meaning that the size of one business case could grow from the traditional few tens of thousands to millions, with a possibility to offer extensions and updates on an annual basis.

At this third stage, as a result of an external trigger, Lappset started to offer story-based activity theme parks for public and private customers that implied a shift from product towards conceptual thinking. Its connectedness with contextual and conceptual aspects allowed it to react to an opportunity emerging from the outside, and turn it into a company-specific springboard for further development. The company focused not just on offering products, but also started to highlight concepts covering design and play. Being a benchmark in the international market, the company brand started reflecting its global mindset and the desire to promote outdoor activity among people who easily get stuck inside. The societal impact became a new element in the core of the organizational identity that was already characterized by sustainability and playful learning. Although the pace of the international expansion slowed down, the company established itself as an influential global player in the industry. With the help of business model transformation, the innovative ideas were transferable to the wide market, and yet another round was given a start for international opportunities.

What about the future? To stay as the innovation benchmark, Lappset is already running the SmartUs 2.0 project and is thinking about the digital revolution of play. And, finally, Antero Ikäheimo's original dream of Santa Claus land has become real: the true feeling of Lapland can soon be found not only in Rovaniemi, but also in China. ☺

6. Discussion and Contribution

The Lappset case initiates numerous "take-aways." The above presented storyline allows for distinguishing among three phases in the development of the company that are characterized by opportunity and business model transformation. At the very beginning of the company history, Lappset saw an opportunity in transforming unattractive metal play equipment into a pleasant living environment by utilizing local sustainable materials. When the new digital and educational technologies emerged, the company focused on incorporating a digital element into its product lines, thereby accounting for the requirements of playful learning. At a later stage, by bringing a story to the playground, Lappset created a whole new concept of story-based activity theme parks. In turn, the changing opportunities influenced the innovation and internationalization processes of the company and brought about business model transformation. The offering developed from play equipment to theme parks to accommodate new opportunities that, in turn, led to the extension of the customer base and end-user groups.

Lappset moved from building individual products and product lines to offering a holistic play concept that was accompanied by the extension of the customer base and end-user groups. Product innovation progressed from modular play equipment to digital playgrounds and to story-based activity theme parks. The internationalization process of the company grew in scope and scale, whereas the company brand and identity developed to reflect its values and global mindset. In other words, similarly to the observations of Hitt *et al.* (1997) and Hagen *et al.* (2014), the relationship between business model transformation and innovation and internationalization processes was reciprocal. Business model transformation was driven by the innovation and internationalization processes. And, at the same time, changes in the business model structure influenced the way the company expanded to the international markets and developed its product.

The extant literature is copiously supplied with a variety of business model conceptualizations (cf. Doz and Kosonen 2010; Magretta 2002; Timmers 1998; Zott and Amit 2007) that lack unanimity and breed confusion. This situation can be partially explained by the kaleidoscopic nature of the business model concept: at the level of entrepreneurial actions, each business model is unique in one way or another and is distinguished by a distinctive set of anchoring elements. By anchoring elements, we mean those business model components that allow a company to create value and exploit its competitive advantage. For example, in the case of Lappset, an offering can be considered as an anchoring element in the business model structure. Viewing a business model as a unit of analysis (Zott *et al.* 2011) allows for identifying unique anchoring elements of a business model and reduces the need for a single business model definition.

If the current research aims at establishing causal links between innovation and internationalization (Giovannetti *et al.* 2009; Hitt *et al.* 1997; Zucchello and Siano 2014), the case of Lappset clearly indicates that the relationship between the two is rather intricate. Innovation and internationalization seem to be closely intertwined and frequently inseparable supporting and complementing each other. Taken together, they define the operational context of the company that changes as the business opportunity evolves and calls for business model transformation. In turn, the innovation of the anchoring elements of a business model brings about new business model conceptualization requiring adjustments and transformations in the business model. Thus, business model transformation can be viewed as framed by conceptualization and contextualization processes that highlight the intertwined nature of the internationalization, innovation and business model concepts. Figure 3.1 on page 47 illustrates the business model transformation process, where the colored lines indicate the transition between the different stages.

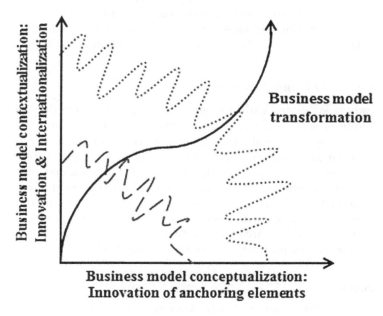

Figure 3.1 Business Model Transformation Process

Martins *et al.* (2015) suggest analogical reasoning and conceptual combination as two main cognitive mechanisms of business model innovation process. The internationalization process of Lappset followed the pattern of analogical reasoning where the knowledge and experience acquired in one foreign market was utilized to enter the new ones—although not in the traditional fashion starting from more familiar markets, but risk was incorporated in this process as well. Conceptual combination is revealed in the company product innovation where first the digital element and then a narrative served as modifier concepts. Thus, where the current literature on business model innovation stipulates that the innovation process can follow either an evolutionary, revolutionary, or cognitive path (Martins *et al.* 2015), the case of Lappset clearly illustrates that the nature of the business model innovation changes at different stages of the business model transformation process. It implies that business model innovation is of an eclectic nature that does not follow just one path.

Taking a step further at the company level, if for the creative or digital industries internationalization from inception appears almost as a standard, for the traditional sectors the industry traditions may not support international aspirations. However, the Lappset case shows that internationalization can be a source of innovation and competitive advantage both in international and domestic markets. From the managerial perspective, our findings thus imply that going international supports the innovation process in companies. Moreover, business models can be innovated by going international—something that we would like to encourage all companies to do.

Limitations and Future Research

This study is associated with the single case research design that limits the opportunities for generalization across different contexts. Thus, the exploration of the business model transformation as a combination of the conceptualization and contextualization processes in other geographical and industrial contexts and using multiple-case and/or longitudinal approaches is one avenue for future research. In addition, a deeper understanding of the business model anchoring elements is required. Comprehending the nature and diversity of the anchoring elements would provide insight into the business model concept. Research into brand and identity as anchoring business model elements is of particular interest for future studies.

References

Afuah, Allan. 2004. *Business Models: A Strategic Management Approach*. New York: McGraw-Hill.

Ahokangas, Petri, Marko Juntunen, and Jenni Myllykoski. 2014. "Cloud Computing and Transformation of International E-business Models." *Research in Competence-Based Management* 7: 3–28.

Ahokangas, Petri, Marja Matinmikko, Seppo Yrjola, Hanna Okkonen, and Thomas Casey. 2013. " 'Simple Rules' for Mobile Network Operators' Strategic Choices in Future Cognitive Spectrum Sharing Networks." *Wireless Communications, IEEE* 20(2): 20–26.

Ahokangas, Petri, and Jenni Myllykoski. 2014. "The Practice of Creating and Transforming a Business Model." *Journal of Business Models* 2(1): 6–18.

Amit, Raphael, and Christoph Zott. 2001. "Value Creation in E-Business." *Strategic Management Journal* 22(6): 493–520.

Amit, Raphael, and Christoph Zott. 2012. "Creating Value through Business Model Innovation." *Sloan Management Review* 53(3): 41–49.

Bettis, Richard A., and Michael A. Hitt. 1995. "The New Competitive Landscape." *Strategic Management Journal* 16: 7–19.

Bilkey, Warren J., and George Tesar. 1977. "The Export Behavior of Smaller Sized Wisconsin Manufacturing Firms." *Journal of international Business Studies* 8(1): 93–98.

Boons, Frank, and Florian Ludeke-Freund. 2013. "Business Models for Sustainable Innovation: State-of-Art and Steps Towards a Research Agenda." *Journal of Cleaner Production* 45: 9–19.

Boter, Håkan. 1996. "Industry Characteristics and Internationalization Processes in Small Firms." *Journal of Business Venturing* 11(6): 471–487.

Boter, Håkan. 2003. "Management Perspectives as Catalysts for Exporting: A Study of Nordic SMEs." *Journal of Global Marketing* 16(3): 31–52.

Cavalcante, Sérgio André, Peter Kesting, and John P. Ulhøi. 2011. "Business Model Dynamics and Innovation: (Re)establishing the Missing Linkages." *Management Decision* 49(8): 1327–1342.

Caves, Richard E. 1982. *Multinational Enterprise and Economic Analysis*. Cambridge: Cambridge University Press.

Chesbrough, Henry. 2007. "Business Model Innovation: It Is Not Just About Technology Anymore." *Strategy and Leadership* 35(6): 12–17.

Chesbrough, Henry. 2010. "Business Model Innovation, Opportunities and Barriers." *Long Range Planning* 43(2): 354–363.

Christensen, Clayton M. 1997. *The Innovator's Dilemma: When New Technologies Cause Great Firms to Fail*. Boston, MA: Harvard Business School Press.

Czinkota, Michael R. 1982. *Export Development Strategies: US Promotion Policies*. New York: Praeger Publishers.

D'Angelo, Alfredo. 2010. "Innovation and Export Performance: A Study of Italian High-Tech SMEs." *Journal of Management and Governance* 16(3): 39–58.

Demil, Benoit, and Xavier Lecocq. 2010. "Business Model Evolution: In search of Dynamic Consistency." *Long Range Planning* 43(2): 227–246.

Doganova, Liliana, and Marie Eyquem-Renault. 2009. "What Do Business Models Do? Innovation Devices in Technology Entrepreneurship." *Research Policy* 38(10): 1559–1570.

Doz, Yves L., and Mikko Kosonen. 2010. "Embedding Strategic Agility: A Leadership Agenda for Accelerating Business Model Renewal." *Long Range Planning* 43(2): 370–382.

Fisch, Jan Hendrik. 2003. "Optimal Dispersion of R&D Activities in Multinational Corporations with a Genetic Algorithm." *Research Policy* 32(8): 1381–1396.

Giovannetti, Giorgia, Giorgio Ricchiuti, and Margherita Velucchi. 2009. "Size, Innovation and Internationalization: A Survival Analysis of Italian Firms." *Applied Economics* 43(12): 1511–1520.

Hagen, Birgit, Stefano Denicolai, and Antonella Zucchella. 2014. "International Entrepreneurship at the Crossroads Between Innovation and Internationalization." *Journal of International Entrepreneurship* 12(2): 11–114.

Hartley, Jean. 2004. "Case Study Research." In *Essential Guide to Qualitative Methods in Organizational Research*, edited by Catherine Cassel and Gillian Symon, 323–333. Thousand Oaks, CA: Sage.

Hitt, Michael A., Robert E. Hoskisson, and Hicheon Kim. 1997. "International Diversification: Effects on Innovation and Firm Performance in Product-Diversified Firms." *Academy of Management Journal* 40(4): 767–798.

Hurmelinna-Laukkanen, Pia. 2014. "Appropriability Regimes in the International Playground for Innovation." *European Journal of International Management* 8(6): 621–643.

Jensen, Anders Bille. 2013. "Do We Need One Business Model Definition?" *Journal of Business Models* 1(1): 61–84.

Johnson, Mark W., Clayton Christensen, and Henning Kagermann. 2008. "Reinventing Your Business Model." *Harvard Business Review* 86(12): 58–68.

Kafouros, Mario I., Peter J. Buckley, John A. Sharp, and Chengqi Wang. 2008. "The Role of Internationalization in Explaining Innovation Performance." *Technovation* 28(1): 63–74.

Klein, Peter G. 2008. "Opportunity Discovery, Entrepreneurial Action, and Economic Organization." *Strategic Entrepreneurship Journal* 2(3): 175–190.

Kobrin, Stephen J. 1991. "An Empirical Analysis of the Determinants of Global Integration." *Strategic Management Journal* 12: 17–31.

Kogut, Bruce, and Zander, Udo. 1992. "Knowledge of the Firm, Combinative Capabilities and the Replication of Technology." *Organization Science* 3(3): 383–397.

Kotabe, Masaaki. 1990. "The Relationship Between Offshore Sourcing and Innovativeness of US Multinational Firms: An Empirical Investigation." *Journal of International Business Studies* 21(4): 623–638.

Kotabe, Masaaki, Srini S. Srinivasan, and Preet S. Aulakh. 2002. "Multinationality and Firm Performance: The Moderating Role of R&D and Marketing Capabilities." *Journal of International Business Studies* 33(1): 79–97.

Linder, Jane, and Susan Cantrell. 2000. *Changing Business Models*. Chicago: Institute for Strategic Change, Accenture.

Magretta, Joan. 2002. "Why Business Models Matter." *Harvard Business Review* 80(5): 86–92.

Martins, Luis L., Violina P. Rindova, and Bruce E. Greenbaum. 2015. "Unlocking the Hidden Value of Concepts: A Cognitive Approach to Business Model Innovation." *Strategic Entrepreneurship Journal* 9: 99–117.

Mason, Katy, and Martin Spring. 2011. "The Sites and Practices of Business Models." *Industrial Marketing Management* 40(6): 1032–1041.

McGrath, Rita Gunther. 2010. "Business Models: A Discovery Driven Approach." *Long Range Planning* 43(2–3): 247–261.

Morris, Michael H., Minet Schindehutte, and Jeffrey Allen. 2005. "The Entrepreneur's Business Model, Toward a Unified Perspective." *Journal of Business Research* 58(6): 726–735.

Nenonen, Suvi, and Kaj Storbacka. 2010. "Business Model Design: Conceptualizing Networked Value Co-creation." *International Journal of Quality and Service Sciences* 2(1): 43–59.

Onetti, Alberto, Antonella Zucchella, Marian V. Jones, and Patricia P. McDougall-Covin. 2012. "Internationalization, Innovation and Entrepreneurship: Business Models for New Technology-Based Firms." *Journal of Management and Governance* 16(3): 337–368.

Pla-Barber, José, and Joaquín Alegre. 2007. "Analyzing the Link Between Export Intensity, Innovation and Firm Size in a Science-Based Industry." *International Business Review* 16(3): 275–293.

Porter, Michael E. 1990. *The Competitive Advantage of Nations*. New York: Free Press.

Santos, Jose, Yves Doz, and Peter Williamson. 2004. "Is Your Innovation Process Global?" *Sloan Management Review* 45(4): 31–37.

Shafer Scott M., Jeff H. Smith, and Jane C. Linder. 2005. "The Power of Business Models." *Business Horizons* 48(3): 199–207.

Sosna, Marc, Rosa Nelly Trevinyo-Rodrigez, and Ramakrishna S. Velamuri. 2010. "Business Model Innovation Through Trial-and-Error Learning." *Long Range Planning* 43(2–3): 383–407.

Stake Robert E. 2000. "Case Studies." In *Handbook of Qualitative Research*, edited by Norman K Denzin and Yvonna S. Lincoln, 435–455. Thousand Oaks, CA: Sage.

Sterlacchini, Alessandro. 1999. "Do Innovative Activities Matter to Small Firms in Non-R&D Intensive Industries? An Application to Export Performance." *Research Policy* 28(8): 819–832.

Timmers, Paul. 1998. "Business Models for Electronic Markets." *Electronic Markets* 8(2): 3–8.

van Putten, Bart-Jan, and Markus Schief. 2012. "The Relation Between Dynamic Business Models and Business Cases." *The Electronic Journal Information Systems Evaluation* 15(1): 138–148.

Voelpel, Sven, C., Marius Leibold, and Tekie B. Eden. 2004. "The Wheel of Business Model Reinvention: How to Reshape Your Business Model to Leapfrog Competitors." *Journal of Change Management* 4(3): 259–276.

von Zedtwitz, Maximilian, and Oliver Gassmann. 2002. "Market Versus Technology Drive in R&D Internationalization: Four Different Patterns of Managing Research and Development." *Research Policy* 31(2): 569–588.

Wirtz, Bernd W., Adriano Pistoia, Sebastian Ullrich, and Vincent Göttel. 2015. "Business Models: Origin, Development and Future Research Perspectives." *Long Range Planning* 49(1): 36–54.

Wirtz, Bernd W., Oliver Schilke, and Sebastian Ullrich. 2010. "Strategic Development of Business Models: Implications of the Web 2.0 for Creating Value on the Internet." *Long Range Planning* 43(2–3): 272–290.

Yin, Robert K. 1994. *Case Study Research: Design and Methods* (2nd ed.). Newbury Park, CA: Sage.

Zott, Christoph, and Raphael Amit. 2007. "Business Model Design and the Performance of Entrepreneurial Firms." *Organization Science* 18(2): 181–199.

Zott, Christoph, and Raphael Amit. 2010. "Designing Your Future Business Model: An Activity System Perspective." *Long Range Planning* 43(2–3): 216–226.

Zott, Christoph, Raphael Amit, and Lorenco Massa. 2011. "The Business Model: Recent Developments and Future Research." *Journal of Management* 37(4): 1019–1042.

Zucchella, Antonella, and Alfonso Siano. 2014. "Internationalization and Innovation as Resources for SME Growth in Foreign Markets: A Focus on Textile and Clothing Firms in the Campania Region." *Journal of International Studies of Management and Organization* 44: 21–41.

4 Managerial Initiatives, Internationalization and Smaller Manufacturing Enterprises

Perspectives and Approaches

George Tesar

1. Introduction

Driven by marketing and technological capabilities, many smaller manu-facturing enterprises (SMEs) are evolving into complex multidimensional organizations and in various configurations are operating in diverse inter-national markets. Managers of SMEs have traditionally been confronted with a range of cross-border challenges, most of which can be classified as structural, strategic, or operational. These challenges are particularly appar-ent from the perspective of international marketing. SMEs are challenged to introduce new organizational structures to effectively and efficiently enter international markets, which require such structures by market behavior or legal requirements. These challenges present decision-making complexities to SME managers, who need substantial and reliable information concern-ing rapidly changing international markets.

Information about international markets is available from a variety of public and private sources. Governmental agencies, university faculty, or local economic development organizations may be able to assist managers of SMEs in facing their challenges by suggesting how information could be used. Private sources of information such as consulting agencies, banks, or freight forwarders may help SMEs managers solve specific problems in entering international markets. However, managers often need to exchange suitable ideas related to entering specific markets or how to modify products for international markets. In other words, information is essential to under-standing the dynamics of international markets, but cooperation in the form of exchanging ideas is also important, especially in rural areas. The funda-mental need to discuss ideas in rural and geographically remote areas is the primary motivating reason for industrial cluster development found in sev-eral regions of Northern Europe, North America, Australia and elsewhere.

Organizational types and managerial styles vary a great deal among SMEs. It is important to understand that some SMEs involved in cross-border activities are very much proactive regardless of their managerial types and marketing capabilities, while others are fundamentally reactive. Proactive SMEs need more information and frequently cooperate on the interpretation or meaning of the information in crossing borders. Managers of reactive SMEs wait until they need information and typically anticipate that they will find appropriate public sources for it.

Managers of SMEs differ substantially and consequently structure and manage their enterprises accordingly. The traditional craftsman-owner-entrepreneur who typically started an SME either evolved into a rational manager capable of managing a multifunctional technologically complex international organization or was consequently replaced by a professional manager with the appropriate managerial skills needed as the SME grew and expanded across borders and acquired new markets. Most cross-border growth among SMEs is relatively slow and complex under natural evolutionary circumstances. Managers of SMEs face many internal and external challenges such as securing venture capital, identifying technological capabilities suitable for entering specific markets, defining optimal markets, or facing unique technology-based cross-border marketing opportunities. To solve these challenges, managers need substantial information from reliable sources. In geographically remote regions, often the necessary information may be obtained locally from management specialists in regional universities.

SMEs face even greater challenges as they assume complex organizational structures and increase their cross-border initiatives. Each market requires its own unique definition, competitively viable strategic and operational approaches, and most of all, appropriate levels of marketing and technological sophistication. Identifying the technological capabilities of an SME and positioning it accurately in any market requires specific information on which international marketing perspectives can be formulated by managers (Tesar and Moini 1999).

SME managers repeatedly signal that accurate and reliable information concerning international markets is increasingly more difficult to acquire due to a variety of conflicting information sources. Managers of dynamic and cross-border active SMEs suggest that the fundamental formulation and modeling of information needs do not correspond to the information they need to make decisions. Research based on conceptual and theoretical foundations which is predominantly academic does not respond to their current needs Van der Arend 2014). At the same time, information generated from other sources, such as management consultants, think tanks, government agencies, or international agencies which may be useful in addressing some of SMEs' cross-border challenges is frequently misdirected and often formulated to answer much broader questions. The conflicts in research, research perspectives, and approaches to research in international marketing present a major dilemma for managers of SMEs (Tesar *et al.* 2010).

Most critical concerns among SME managers today is the need for substantial and reliable information regarding structural, strategic, and operational challenges. The concern is that traditional sources of information, especially conventional academia sources, are refocusing their research efforts on other aspects of management in general, including social phenomena, that do not help managers confront their growing challenges—particularly as they relate to international marketing and more specifically to cross-border marketing (Bartlett and Ghoshal 1989). This presentation explores these concerns from the perspectives and approaches of SME managers and considers their needs for a new research agenda.

2. Border Crossing Marketing Challenges

Management of SMEs, because of their natural character, is a complex process of internal and external activities, initially combined with managerial reluctance, followed by frequently misdirected entrepreneurial exuberance, that can later lead to levels of rational management (Tesar *et al.* 2010, 15–17). SMEs are typically started by craftsmen-type individuals who are most interested in their technical resources, personal capabilities, and unique knowledge. The products they can create are their inherent objectives. Craftsmen-type managers are not necessarily interested in markets or eventually how their products are used. They tend to respond passively to market demand and often become reluctant actors in international markets.

If, despite a craftsmen-type manager, an SME is successful and demand for its products increases, it begins to grow. This transition requires a new type of manager—one who can stimulate growth and respond to market demand. The craftsman-type manager often evolves into a promoter-type manager who is interested in promoting the SME and its products in any accessible markets, even with limited knowledge and information. Promoter-type managers seek information opportunistically, and only when information is needed, because acquisition of information is an expense.

Successful promoter-type managers may eventually evolve into rational-type managers. In the process, some promoter-type managers acquire the necessary professional experience and education and can rationally manage their SMEs. They systematically allocate their resources and successfully manage across markets. Rational-type managers make decisions based on their ability to recognize problems and realize the timely necessity to solve them. When they need information, it is to solve a problem. Rational-type managers consider information as an investment.

All three types of SMEs managers tend, at various times, to operate in cross-border markets. Craftsman-type managers tend to be reluctant exporters, promoter-type managers tend to seek export opportunities along with other forms of cross-border market entry activities, and rational-type managers consider international marketing opportunities as part of their portfolio of markets. Thus, SMEs managed by any of the three types of managers are at some point confronted with structural, strategic, or operational challenges (Tesar *et al.* 2010, 19–22).

Cross-border marketing represents a present-day dimension in the overall management of SMEs. Every SME entering cross-border activities makes decisions about how to enter each market, selects optimal strategies for entering markets, and identifies the necessary operations to be successful and competitive (De Bodinat 1984). The selection of cross-border entry may be complicated, due to the nature of an SME, primarily its marketing abilities and technological sophistication, and its target markets and consumers.

Traditionally, cross-border market entry was less complicated from SMEs' perspectives. SMEs were assumed to enter foreign markets as exporters, partners of convenience, or investors (Root 1994). The situation is different today. SMEs expand their direct export activities into complex industrial networks, supply chains, and entire value chains. They also became importers of necessary and economically competitive supplies. SMEs are becoming partners of convenience. They establish an array of exclusively owned divisions, subsidiaries, or operating units such as sales agencies and warehousing facilities among competitively viable operations. As a result of such broadening activities, SMEs managers develop cross-border alternatives differently and with much more emphasis on information needs and modeling procedures. Even the smallest SMEs attempt to manage a variety of alternative strategies and operations in order to enter optimal international markets, be competitive, and survive (Berger 2013, 97–100).

Structural Challenges

Decisions to enter cross-border markets today take place on much higher managerial levels in SMEs. Such decisions require resource allocation on an enterprise level consistent with its mission and technologically competitive posture. SMEs today need to approach cross-border markets from the perspective of top management and structure their market approaches appropriately using a variety of enterprise actions, such as: (1) focusing of the entire enterprise as a direct exporting entity, (2) forming a division— an autonomous entity designated to act internationally, (3) establishing a subsidiary—an entity wholly controlled by the enterprise for purposes of exploiting its technological and marketing capability in designated markets, (4) introducing managerial functions—a group of related managerial actions contributing to a large enterprise action such as international marketing research, (5) designating units—a single managerial group such as a legal arm of an enterprise facilitating cross-border transactions, and (6) entering into affiliated ventures—a risky or speculative undertaking from a managerial perspective (see Appendix 1 for corresponding short scenarios).

The individually distinct structural alternatives listed above offer a portfolio of potential strategies for SMEs to enter international markets and maximize their presence and market position. Various structural alternatives are differently suited for diverse technological and market levels of cross-border sophistication and managerial abilities. An SME whose marketing and technological abilities vary greatly in sophistication, ranging from low technological applications to very high technological applications, depending on the sophistication of its markets, may opt to export products into markets with low technological demands. At the same time, the SME may open a subsidiary in markets with high technical demands. The level of managerial aptitudes and ratios between marketing and technological abilities provide the foundation for an SME's alternative structural approaches to cross-border opportunities.

In order to overcome structural challenges, SME managers need an understanding of marketing and technological capabilities, and need substantial and consistent information to make decisions. SME managers making structural decisions need detailed information about potential markets as well as a deep understanding of how their technology can be integrated into such markets. Information gathering tools and models are typically SME specific, and each SME needs information specific to solving its own discrete problems.

Most SMEs have resolved the structural challenges directly connected with functional and unit specific decisions. For example, they have formed management functions and designated organizational units to solve cross-border challenges and design and manage marketing strategies and operations. However, few SMEs have addressed the structural issues of setting up a division or forming a subsidiary to exclusively manage international activities. And an even smaller number of SMEs have entered affiliated ventures to attempt riskier international undertakings. Those SMEs that successfully entered international markets using structural alternatives often suggest that the strategic and operational challenges tend to be greater than the structural ones (Berger 2013, 119–120, Tesar *et al.* 2010, 79–80).

Strategic Challenges

Strategic challenges among SMEs can be divided into two categories, sometimes referred to as the dimensions of an enterprise—internal and external. Internal strategic dimensions involve: (1) the resource base and (2) the mission. The resource base determines the level of enterprise action and the level of managerial activities. It consists of the financial, physical, and human resources owned or mobilized by an SME and, in its broader context, it includes both tangible and intangible resources. A given SME may own all its resources, while another may use its financial strength to purchase needed resources for cross-border initiatives. For example, instead of maintaining its own manufacturing facilities, an SME may subcontract its manufacturing; or, it may subcontract with a human resource provider—such as an engineering or design contractor—to provide the necessary specialists it needs.

An SME's resource base is the fundamental element of managerial action that determines the parameters, limits, and scope of enterprise action in terms of how the SME approaches cross-border activities—through the enterprise itself, organizing a division, establishing a subsidiary, specifying a management function, forming a unit, or undertaking an affiliated venture. Depending on the selection of its particular structural approach to cross-border activities, an SME may choose to use external sources to supplement its activities—it may source for venture capital needed to establish its foreign operations or it may seek foreign partnership to establish a subsidiary. One of many managerial challenges related to optimally utilizing an SME's resource base depends on its managerial abilities to be entrepreneurial, creative, and willing to face risk.

An SME's mission is the second internal strategic factor; its mission statement is not only a road map for the entire SME, but also a statement of technological and marketing abilities and actions. Conversely, a mission statement anticipates what an optimal combination of resources, formulated by its managers, may accomplish depending on the SMEs level and nature of technological and marketing activities. Managers, in the early stages of SME development, do not necessarily formulate mission statements. Craftsman-type managers generally operate in a perfunctory manner, while scientifically inclined craftsman-type managers may have clearly defined enterprise missions because a mission statement was required in the "business plan" when the SMEs sought external funding. As SMEs grow and assume complex structures, well formulated mission statements with sufficient time dimensions become essential.

When a rational-type manager assumes a top position in an SME, one of the first steps, if the SME does not have a mission statement, is to formulate one. There is also a point in the life of an SME managed by a promoter-type manager when it becomes important to define its mission so it has direction to expand, grow, and be competitive.

Additional dimensions internally managed by an enterprise include: (1) markets, (2) target markets, (3) market segments, (4) consumers, (5) consumption, and (6) post consumption. These dimensions are defined as controllable variables in marketing management. In general terms of contemporary marketing practice, products and accompanying services are the results of a combination of technological know-how and managerial skills. Conversely, given an SME's technological capabilities and managerial skills, markets determine the nature of suitable products and accompanying services.

Strategic challenges determine how managers can combine their marketing skills and technological capabilities to introduce optimal products in markets they identify. Both academic and consulting approaches suggest that a marketing strategy needs to include a combination of marketing factors that facilitate placement of specific products into market segments to satisfy consumers' consumption and meet societal requirements—that is social responsibilities. This approach suggests that the marketing strategy for a given market segment, where a specifically designed product needs to be introduced, is a function of the product's market segment internal adjustability, its communication needs, distribution channel requirements, and price flexibility. Furthermore, the marketing strategy is constrained by its budget and the market's external environmental variability. This is the classic traditional approach to marketing.

From an information gathering perspective this assumes that market conditions change constantly and are influenced not only by competitive pressures but also by such external factors as changing lifestyles, economic conditions, and social and political forces among other unexpected developments and regulations. SMEs with relatively homogeneous products, indirectly operating in foreign markets, can be faced with major difficulties, often due to broad environmental changes that come unexpectedly. The more advanced an SME is the more likely it will gather information to prevent unexpected developments. Some SMEs constantly scan the external environment for information and tend to conduct periodic market assessments to adjust their marketing strategies and operations.

Operational Challenges

SMEs that implement cross-border operations are frequently confronted with two types of operational challenges—indirect and direct. Some SMEs, especially in the early stages of cross-border operations, contract for whatever operations they need with local contractors. In such attempts to indirectly manage their operations, they seldom gather the necessary information to understand their operations and eventually lose control. Local contractors need training; they must know how to market the product, inform consumers, and service the product. The indirect approach is very much symptomatic in the early stages of exporting, licensing, or using exclusive agents. As SMEs expand cross-border operations they begin to directly control foreign market operations and establish marketing centers, sales organizations, warehousing and retailing functions, and product service centers.

Managing cross-border operations directly requires a great deal of information. Depending on the marketing activities an SME introduces in given markets, it has a variety of information gathering options. It can collect and monitor information internally or externally. International divisions, subsidiaries, and even affiliated ventures typically collect and monitor their own information internally in cross-border markets. Enterprise functions and units responsible for cross-border operations tend to collect and monitor information externally by conducting surveys, processing checkout data, addressing consumer panels or using market informants. Managers of SMEs actively involved in cross-border marketing activities suggest that they gather more information in their domestic markets than in cross-border markets.

In summary, managers of SMEs point out that although the structural challenges they face are enterprise-level challenges faced by top managers and decision makers, they are viewed in the context of marketing management. This is because many SMEs, especially high-technology SMEs, consider marketing the overall philosophy of management. International marketing is considered an extension of domestic marketing and has not changed dramatically over the past twenty-five years or so (Terpstra 1972; Czinkota 1998).

Consequently, some SME managers are convinced that structural challenges are essential to accommodate optimal cross-border strategies and operations. These convictions also imply that there is a major shift when entering cross-border markets from relying on strategic and operational variations to higher levels of enterprise action. This shift and the resulting decisions require new organizational structures and additional information to reinforce them.

3. Marketing Management in SMES

Marketing management among SMEs drives cross-border expansions. Within the framework of a mission statement, the traditional marketing management functions include: (1) identification of marketing opportunities, (2) assessment and selection of marketing opportunities, (3) fostering of managerial skills leading to decision-making potential, (4) building enterprise structures capable of implementing achievable marketing opportunities, and (5) qualitative and quantitative control of implemented marketing opportunities. Marketing management in SMEs depends on an uninterrupted vertical and horizontal flow of information with unbiased feedback.

When examined in the context of cross-border marketing activities, there are two approaches to how marketing management is implemented in SMEs. Some SMEs clearly differentiate between domestic and international marketing such that top management tends to value its domestic marketing activities differently than its international marketing activities (Tesar *et al.* 2010, 57–61). These SMEs allocate necessary resources per sets of priorities that reflect marketing opportunities in their domestic market. International opportunities are perceived as secondary that carry marginally more financial risk. Other SMEs do not differentiate between domestic and international activities; they have a more holistic view of markets. Functional differentiation of marketing management activities between domestic and international reflects the fundamental mission and market preferences of top managers.

Depending on the preferences of marketing management, SMEs managers also have different informational needs. Some managers make decisions based on minimal information and rely on their own instincts and intuitions—typically craftsman-type or early promoter-type managers. Rational-type managers tend to rely on qualitative and quantitative information generated internally and/or externally. Some managers gather information from secondary sources before they determine specifications for information to be gathered from primary sources.

SMEs require additional information as they generate more cross-border activities. Information needed to facilitate marketing management decisions ranges from initial identification of marketing opportunities to implementation and control. SME managers need more specific information as the marketing management process intensifies. In the opinion of some SME managers, availability of information from a variety of reliable secondary sources is growing (Moini and Tesar 2005). Among high technology SMEs with greater abilities to gather information, availability of information is not necessarily a managerial concern but rather the concern of marketing research specialists (Hamill 1997). Such SMEs may also look for relevant academic sources for information generated on the bases of theoretical and/ or conceptual research.

Managers of SMEs, especially among highly cross-border active SMEs, indicate that academic research may formulate and test theories and concepts that have little practical value to them. Consultants and other SMEs advisors point out that academic research is not sufficiently problem focused and not intended to be so. Academics are expected to publish, use their experience and research findings to stimulate enterprise formation and growth, and assist with economic development among other productive activities. Dissemination of information to management of SMEs is secondary.

4. Research Landscape

Managers of SMEs routinely face a variety of complex problems and need reliable information to solve them. This is particularly apparent when SMEs face periods of growth, expansion, or diversification. Given the recent emphasis on building supply and value chains, industrial networks, regional clusters, and even local industrial councils, SME managers need quality information to make better decisions. Some SMEs, especially high-technology SMEs, maintain their own marketing research functions, gather their own information and monitor their markets in real time. SMEs also purchase information from outside sources such as consultants, government agencies, think tanks or international agencies. Smaller and less skilled SMEs frequently purchase needed information from sources that may be only marginally capable of collecting information.

SMEs located near universities, or in university-owned incubators or industrial parks, often cooperate with faculty and rely on their information. Faculty members may also serve as consultants. In most cases these relationships are symbiotically favorable and productive. But many are not because they tend to distort the boundaries between academically based theoretical or conceptual research and the applied research needed by SME managers (Shugan 2004).

Managers concerned with cross-border activities indicate that there is significant conflict between the types of research, and related research perspectives and attitudes towards research, among the different types of information suppliers. Information needed to face managerial challenges among SMEs and the resulting problems, particularly when needed to solve cross-border related problems, is predominantly conflicting (Thorelli and Tesar 1994).

Most SME managers suggest that their information needs were satisfied in the past by results from academic research delivered through media such as publications, public faculty seminars, workshops, or training. According to SME managers, sales and marketing in general benefited greatly from interactions with major universities when faculty were directly involved in generating information applicable to problems faced by managers daily. A review of recent publications focusing on international issues suggests that published information resulting from academic studies today tends to be too sophisticated to be considered by SME managers as relevant. Such information focuses on abstract issues only tangentially related to the day-to-day problems of SMEs managers (Kulik 2014).

Contemporary sources of information available to SME managers consist of five distinct sources: (1) conceptual, theoretical, and experimental academic research; (2) consulting research with a problem-solving focus; (3) think tank research with a futuristic focus; (4) government agencies' research with a focus on economic growth; and (5) international agencies' research with a focus on economic development, growth, and stability. The argument that these sources of information tend to be less and less useful as inputs into managerial decision-making is real Moutray 2008).

Each current source of information has different research objectives and generates different information outcomes. When SMEs' decision makers consider the resulting information, it has a relatively low decision value. Academic research, in both the domestic and international context, is decreasing in its ability to assist SME managers in resolving their structural, strategic, or operation problems. According to SME managers, academic research needs to be redefined and its content refocused to address current issues of innovation, entrepreneurship, managerial functions, and organizational development, among other managerial issues that evolve in current cross-border challenges. From an alternative point of view, academic research needs to consider two approaches: (1) theoretical and conceptual and (2) applied. This also suggests that results of academic research studies need to be presented both to academia and industry (Burke and Rau 2010).

The major issue with consulting research is that it generally ignores broad social, economic or even technological issues in environments external to individual SMEs and predominantly focuses on current distinct incremental challenges or problems. Consulting research is contracted research designed to solve specific problems faced by the manager of an SME today—managers may contract for new research tomorrow because they must solve a new problem tomorrow. Consulting agencies also use the same information in offering solutions to problems specified by other individual SME managers who have not commissioned the research. This means that consulting agencies frequently provide managers with a solution to a stated problem, and in the process, generate the type of information they think managers need to solve the problem—a form of rolling research. Both academic and professional researchers consider consulting research as problem conditional.

Research studies conducted by industry think tanks tend to be mainly futuristic. They address and research issues that have a long-term impact on a variety of concerns including the future of SMEs. Typical think tank research objectives include growth of industrial sectors, diffusion of technology, market concerns and regulations, among others. Think tanks operate under defined agendas and frequently with a specific philosophical, political, or social bias. Although some of the information generated by think tanks may be useful to a limited number of SMEs managers, it is not typically considered for direct input in solving day to day problems; its character is mostly informative.

Research conducted by think tanks can be useful in an SME's decision when attempting to open new markets. Since think tanks focus on broad future issues, including environmental issues, the information they generate can be used in assessing political, social, or technological risk factors in various markets. Future market stability is an important factor, especially for SMEs operating cross-border with limited resources. However, since few industrial think tanks provide direct advising services and the results of their research are published by in-house publications, newsletters, or personalized briefings for members, they are considered secondary sources of information.

Government agencies are responsible by law for tracking industries, import-export data, growth of industries, sales of consumer and industrial goods and services, and patent applications among other types of statistics. Some government agencies, mostly in the advanced economies of North America, Europe, Australia and New Zealand, Japan, and more recently in China, try to identify and publish trend data which can be used by SMEs to identify growth of markets or even increases or decreases in product or service consumption (Jaffe and Trajtenberg 2002).

Statistics offered by government agencies present a major dilemma for SME managers. Unless they have a deep understanding of their enterprise, its markets, competitors, and cross-border activities, it is difficult to abstract the relevant information they need to solve their day-to-day problems from government reports. SMEs managers need specific problem formulation and definition of markets and market context before they can use any statistical information generated by government agencies.

Information available from international agencies such as GATT, United Nations, or the European Union is even more abstract from SMEs' point of view. International agencies collect data which they combine into statistical reports and make available to other domestic or international agencies, the academic community, or interest groups with specific agendas. They also conduct a limited number of assessment research studies such as those from the United States Government Accountability Office or the International

Labor Organization which maintains the ILOSTAT—ILO database of labor statistics.

Although the information generated by international agencies is informative and useful for a variety of industrial enterprises, it has limited value for SME managers. Perhaps the only time SME managers are exposed to this type of information is in training sessions, industry briefings, or training courses offered by major universities.

SME managers are faced with challenges and problems specific to their individual enterprises. Their information needs are unique. SMEs seek information for cross-border activities that is specific to their current problems—such as entering a market, modifying a standard product to meet local specifications, or finding an appropriate mode of distribution. Academics refer to this type of research and information as problem solving research. Industrial research specialists, consultants, and even government agencies approach it as main stream research (Berger 2013, 119–120).

The divergence in research activities among the five major sources of information creates conflicts among SME managers. They question what information and from which source is useful for their decision making. This conflict is particularly evident in international marketing initiatives, especially cross-border activities. Managers of SMEs, especially smaller low-technology SMEs, have difficulty understanding the perspectives and approaches that the five major sources of information follow. They perceive the information generated by think tanks, government agencies, and international agencies as not relevant to their information needs—unless the information is filtered or interpreted by a specialist, sometimes an academic or consultant.

The current state of academic research presents conflicts for SME managers. Traditional academic research that supported resolution of challenges and helped solve problems is no longer available; it has been replaced by abstract theories and concepts that have little relevancy to day-to-day challenges and problems faced by SME managers. Thus, readership of results of academic research, or opinions derived from such research, routinely published by in-house university publications, by SME managers is declining. SME managers need new and more relevant information. Academics need to refocus their theories, concepts, and models to address structural, strategic, and operational challenges and help managers solve day-to-day problems. A new research agenda is needed by academics who study the broad range of managerial activities among SMEs (Berger 2013, 119–120; Trajtenberg 2002, 25–49).

SME managers perceive a major conflict among the sources of information available to them. Although their information needs are substantial, they have significant difficulties finding the information they need to help them address challenges and solve problems. Their major information needs in the discipline of international marketing may be divided into two major categories: (1) information formulated to address problems symptomatic of how SMEs as entities structure their organizations and use these structures in cross-border activities, and (2) enterprise activities that address development of strategic alternatives and selection of operations fundamental to selection and management of cross-border markets. The two major categories represent the research agenda that needs to be addressed by academic researchers and cross-border marketing specialists.

5. Conclusion

This presentation explores conflicts faced by managers of SMEs in their attempts to identify and utilize viable information for cross-border activities. The managers are confronted with challenges and problems in their day-to-day activities. They need relevant information. The traditional information sources that SME managers relied on in the past are changing. Academic research is becoming more complex and the information generated by academics is becoming less and less relevant to SME managers. Consultants provide SMEs with information designed to resolve specific problems individually without sufficient continuity for on-going knowledge acquisition by SME managers.

The remaining sources of information, according to SME managers, are too broad and macro oriented to offer any significant input into their decision-making process. Although some information provided by think tanks, government agencies, or international agencies is relevant about trends, growth patterns, or economic development in markets, SME managers find it cumbersome and overwhelming to use.

The research agenda presented above is designed to narrow the gap between academic research and information needs of SME managers. Academics on all levels need to reexamine their research objectives, consider the real focus of their institutions, and focus on research questions relevant to managerial concerns of smaller manufacturing enterprises as they attempt to cross borders in today's internationally dynamic environments.

Appendix 1

Scenarios

The following scenarios illustrate different information needs among SMEs. Although these scenarios are not taken directly out of the Northern European context, they can serve as examples. Academic literature seldom addresses the types of information needs presented in these scenarios.

Scenario 1: Electro-Plating Services

Electro-Plating Services (E-PS) is a small privately held enterprise located in a northern part of a mid-Western state. It employs twelve hourly employees working one shift. E-PS provides electroplating services primarily to ship builders, agricultural machinery manufacturers, and medical equipment fabricators. Its clients are located all over the mid-West and several are across the border in Canada. Parts that require plating are shipped to E-PS by private trucking companies and generally returned the same way.

Recently, the state's economic development specialists called on E-PS to invite Mr. Adam, the owner, to join a state trade mission to Mexico. This is the first-time E-PS had contact with the state, and consequently Mr. Adam was surprised. Why would a small operation such as his participate in an international trade mission? The few occasional clients in Canada are just across the border, and if necessary, the local bank and freight forwarder take care of the necessary documents, if any documents are needed. The economic development specialists pointed out that their agency tracks exporters and that E-PS is considered to be an exporter.

Scenario 2: Furniture Craftsmen

Furniture Craftsmen (FC) is a semi-automated manufacturer of fine home furnishings located on the east coast of the United States. FC has been building furniture for about eighty-five years. Over time, it was transformed by its owners from a carpenter shop to a semi-automated medium-sized furniture builder. Most furniture is fabricated by using computerized machinery from design specifications to final finishing. Some of the finishing and staining on custom built pieces is done by highly skilled craftsmen that have been with FC for a long time. FC is a family-owned enterprise.

To meet the growing demand for their products the management recently decided to expand its operations. To fully understand the increasing demand for their furniture, the CEO reviewed recent deliveries, backlog orders, and the origin of orders, and discovered that many of the orders originated in major international cities, closely correlated with sales of luxury homes and condominiums. Based on this information the CEO presented an interesting and challenging proposal to the board: he proposed to open three sales showrooms in three major cities abroad where most of the orders originated.

Several family members challenged his proposal on the basis that they are furniture builders, customers are coming to them, and that FC is not a marketing operation. FC simply does not have sales experience abroad. The CEO pointed out that the proposed showrooms could be staffed by local sales specialists. One of the senior family members asked the CEO this: would opening the three sales showrooms make FC an international player?

Scenario 3: Leisure Shoes

Leisure Shoes (LS) is a rapidly growing enterprise located in one of the mid-Western states. After several years of growth, it offered a limited number of shares to its managers, employees, and interested friendly investors. LS started out as a family business; after a recent expansion into international markets, it was noticed by one of the leading equity capital firms on the East coast, which decided to purchase LS. The new management added a few new lines of shoes, some leather accessories, and clothing lines for men and women. This strategy proved to be very successful. With on-line sales, mail order sales, and several strategically placed retail outlets, LS's sales revenue grew significantly. Even sales abroad expanded.

The initial foreign demand for LS's shoes came from U.S. executives, managers, and diplomats abroad. Recently more professional foreign customers found value in LS's line of products. LS has considered its foreign retail operations unique international marketing ventures and wanted to be more aggressive in markets abroad.

Top management felt that by expanding their foreign operations they would face major accounting and tax problems. A consulting agency suggested a solution to the problem—open a sales entity abroad to shelter some of the profits from abroad. Owners of LS called for a special stockholders' meeting to discuss this option. The consultants that suggested this option insisted that this is a management decision, not a decision for stockholders.

Scenario 4: Custom Fabricated Parts

Custom Fabricated Parts (CFP) is a large custom fabrication facility located in one of the Northern European industrial centers. CFP was established over one hundred years ago as a small machine shop to service local manufacturers and build custom machinery for them. CFP now has over two hundred employees, mostly skilled machinists and fabricators, engineers, and automation specialists.

Recently CFP was asked by one of its long-time clients in the aircraft industry to support their operations in other European and North American aircraft building facilities. This would be a major step for CFP and especially for its management, who believe that their success is based on closely controlling their operations in one location. The managers feel that CFP would lose its competitive advantage by setting up new locations in foreign markets.

What would it involve? To meet the needs of their clients, CFP would have to replicate its facilities in other parts of Europe and in North America. The management is skeptical; could it maintain its professional reputation and successfully compete in other locations?

Scenario 5: Danish Furniture Builders and International Packing

Danish Furniture Builders (DFB) is an experienced designer and fabricator of furniture known internationally as Danish-style furniture. DFB ships its furniture all over the world. Its major markets are in Europe, North America, Australia, and more recently, Japan. DFB has exceptional skills in shipping its furniture disassembled to reduce weight volume ratios and to reduce the cost of shipping. Increasing costs of shipping forced DFB to open a wholly owned subsidiary in Canada.

Shortly after DFB opened its subsidiary, it was approached by a well-known Canadian packaging company, International Packaging (IP), to cooperate in a joint venture that would focus its research and development efforts on improving how unassembled furniture could be packaged and shipped more efficiently. A key aspect of this joint venture is to also use recycled cardboard stock to make the packaging more preferential to customers and reduce shipping costs at the same time.

This would be a win-win situation—DFB contributes its know-how in designing collapsible furniture and IP would contribute its understanding of packaging technology. DFB's management is reluctant to enter this venture and believes that it would give up too much of its key knowhow that IP could use in favor of other clients.

References

Bartlett, Christopher A., and Sumantra Ghoshal. 1989. *Managing Across Borders: The Transnational Solution.* Boston: Harvard University School of Business.
Berger, Suzanne. 2013. *Making in America: From Innovation to Market.* Cambridge, MA: MIT Press.
Burke, Lisa A., and Barbara Rau. 2010. "The Research-Teaching Gap in Management." *Academy of Management Learning & Education* 9(1): 132–143.
Czinkota, Michael R., and Ilkka A. Ronkainen. 1998. *International Marketing* (5th ed.). Forth Worth: The Dryden Press.

De Bodinat, Henri. 1984. "Influence in the Multinational Enterprise: The Case of Manufacturing." In *Technology Crossing Borders*, edited by Robert Stobaugh and Louis T. Wells, Jr., 265–292. Boston: Harvard Business School Press.

Hamill, Jim. 1997. "The Internet and International Marketing." *International Marketing Review* 14(5): 300–323.

Jaffe, Adam B., and Manuel Trajtenberg, eds. 2002. *Patents, Citations and Innovation: A Window on the Knowledge Economy*. Cambridge, Massachusetts: The MIT Press.

Kulik, Carol T. 2014. "Working Below and Above the Line: The Research-Practice Gap in Diversity Management." *Human Resource Management Journal* 24(2): 129–144.

Moini, Hamid A., and George Tesar. 2005. "The Internet and Internationalization of Smaller Manufacturing Enterprises." *Journal of Global Marketing* 18(3, 4): 79–94.

Moutray, Chad. 2008. "Looking Ahead: Opportunities and Challenges for Entrepreneurship and Small Business Owners." monograph. Office of Advocacy Working Paper number 332. www.sba.gov/content/looking-ahead-opportinities-and-challenges-entrepreneurship-and-small-business-owners.

Root, Franklin R. 1994. *Entry Strategies for International Markets: Revised and Expanded*. New York: Lexington Books.

Shugan, Steven M. 2004. "Editorial: Consulting, Research, and Consulting Research." *Marketing Science* 23(2): 173–179. http://dx.doi.org/10.1287/mksc.1040.0078.

Terpstra, Vern. 1972. *International Marketing*. New York: Holt, Rinehart and Winston, Inc.

Tesar, George, and Hamid A. Moini. 1999. "Long-Term Analysis of Technologically Focused Smaller Manufacturing Enterprises." *Scandinavian Journal of Management* 15(3): 239–248.

Tesar, George, Moini A. Hamid, John Kuada, and Olav J. Sørensen. 2010. *Smaller Manufacturing Enterprises in an International Context: A Longitudinal Exploration*. London: Imperial College Press.

Thorelli, Hans B., and George Tesar. 1994. "Entrepreneurship in International Marketing: A Continuing Research Challenge." In *Marketing and Entrepreneurship: Research Ideas and Opportunities*, edited by Gerald E. Hills, 255–268. Westport, CT: Quorum Books.

Trajtenberg, Manuel. 2002. "A Penny for Your Quotes: Patent Citation and the Value of Innovation." In *Patents, Citations & Innovation: A Window on the Knowledge Economy*, edited by Adam B. Jaffe and Manuel Trajtenberg, 25–49. Cambridge, MA: MIT Press.

Van der Arend, Jenny. 2014. "Bridging the Research/Policy Gap: Policy Officials' Perspectives on the Barrier and Facilitators to Effectively Link Between Academic and Policy Worlds." *Policy Studies* 35(6): 611–630.

Part II
Managerial Aspects of SMEs

5 Triggers of Substantial Business Model Innovation

Lessons Learned from Swedish SMEs

Vladimir Vanyushyn and Jan Abrahamsson

1. Introduction

Business models have been a vital concept for economic activity since the advent of trade, because creation, delivery and appropriation of value has always been tacitly integrated in the economics of doing business (Teece 2010). The lion's share of the initial scholarly interest in the term was in business models geared towards new technology, especially Internet-based technology, becoming commercially viable in the booming "dot.com" economy of the early 2000s, when venture capitalists inquired how start-ups would create value and how that value could be captured as a surplus or profit (Brea-Solís *et al.* 2015). Overall, e-business and online-based companies have been the primary phenomenon triggering (Amit and Zott 2001; Magretta 2002) and driving (Mezger 2014; Michel 2014) academic business model research in general and business model innovation (BMI) research in particular.

Such emerging scholarly interest in business models was a natural response to societal and technological trends. In the late nineties, the Internet was hailed as a new technology that would bring the world closer together and re-write the rulebook of competition. In other words, the Internet was seen as technology that was very close to a radical innovation in the way that it was formulated by Tushman and Anderson (1986). The Internet was perceived as a technological discontinuity in that it had the capability to destroy the competence of firms in an industry. Implicit or explicit commonality between Internet and radical innovation has been discussed both in the small-business context (Bengtsson *et al.* 2003, 2007; O'Toole 2003) and on the level of fundamental marketing theory. For example, Srinivasan *et al.* (2002) explicitly defined e-business as radical technology that disrupted old industries and fundamentally re-shaped business models and practices of organizations, and the Internet-based models of companies such as Amazon, Netflix and AirBnB continue to change the ways we shop, consume media and travel (Abrahamsson 2016; Michel 2014; Ritala *et al.* 2014).

In the context of smaller firms, adoption of the Internet-based, or online, channels represent a fitting setting for studying business models and business model innovation for two reasons. First, adoption of such channels may reshuffle the network of external partnerships of an SME by breaking away from traditional value chain, disintermediation and opening for logistics and delivery modes for innovation (Abrahamsson 2016). Second, such online channels may allow a firm to bypass the conventional internationalization sequence (Johanson and Vahlne 1977) and effectively become a born-global firm (Hennart 2014; Sinkovics *et al.* 2013). However, even though both effects—reaching a more favorable position in a value chain and faster internationalization—are highly desirable, in the early days of the Internet many SMEs found it difficult to innovate their existing offline-focused business models and engage in new online-based ones. Prior work has shown that adoption of online channels required substantial changes in underlying resources and capabilities of the firm (Bengtsson *et al.* 2007; Vanyushyn 2008a) in line with the recent notion of substantial business model innovation (Gerasymenko *et al.* 2015) and of the barriers to business model innovation (Chesbrough 2010; Kim and Min 2015) proposed in the literature.

Organizational antecedents of business model innovation decisions in incumbent firms are still not well understood and more research is explicitly called for (Chesbrough 2010; Mezger 2014). Longitudinal empirical studies on business model innovation would allow further insights from case-study research that dominated business model literature (Clauss 2017) and thus contribute to the debate regarding potential costs and benefits of BMI for incumbent firms (Björkdahl and Holmén 2013). As a response to these calls, we retrospectively apply a business model lens to examine the pattern of online channel adoption by Swedish SMEs and raise two questions. We first ask, what are the antecedents of substantial business model innovation in Swedish SMEs? We further ask, how do these antecedents change as the enabling technology matures?

We answer these questions by using an original firm-ID matched dataset consisting of a two-wave survey of 124 Swedish SMEs initially collected as a part of the research effort at Umeå University under the leadership of Håkan Boter. The first wave of data collection took place in 2002 and the second in 2008. This period represents an excellent setting for examining the antecedents of business model innovation as the proportion of households with access to broadband connection increased from about 5 percent in 2000 to 80 percent in 2009; 82 percent of all companies in Sweden used high speed Internet connections in 2005 compared to 44 in 2001 (SCB 2005). By exploiting the matched-pair nature of our data and the rapid development of enabling technology that occurred during the study period, we identify firms' willingness to forgo the value of earlier investments in value delivery networks and organizational routines as a precursor of substantial BMI at the early stage of the enabling technology development. We further show that market responsiveness becomes the main driver of BMI as enabling technology matures. Combined, our findings contribute to the business model literature by demonstrating the transient and time-conditioned nature of substantial BMI antecedents and by identifying changes in managerial perceptions of BMI magnitude.

2. Background

Business Models

Business models in their most unpretentious conceptualization can be seen as how firms do business (Zott and Amit 2010). However, more detailed definitions have offered some rather divergent perspectives over the years. For instance, Shafer *et al.* (2005) have the view of business model as the core logic of how to create and capture value within a value network of external partners; Doganova and Eyquem-Renault (2009) see business models as a scale model of a new venture, which has the purpose of indicating the venture's feasibility and attracting necessary external partnerships, such as financing, customers or suppliers, to the venture. Perhaps Osterwalder *et al.* (2005) and Teece (2010) provide a more tangible representation of business models, which ties back to the mechanisms of value creation and value capture provided by Shafer *et al.* (2005). They share a generally similar view of business models as the design of how to identify, create and deliver value and how to capture and return parts of this value back to the focal firm.

Moreover, Shafer *et al.* (2005) claims that business models could facilitate testing and validation of strategic choices and their logic, for instance, moving from a brick-and-mortar business to an online equivalent. This is moreover broadly consistent with the more recent lean start-up approach originating from Silicon Valley, which is focusing on an iterative process of business model generation through prototyping, minimum viable products and customer feedback (Blank 2013).

Regarding the concept of value capture in a business model, it is claimed by Teece (2010) that understanding how to capture value from innovation is a key element of business model design and that a "good" business model allows for sufficient value capture by the focal firm. These two logics of creating and capturing value are therefore intertwined, interdependent and difficult to separate, particularly in situations of co-creation of value with other actors especially so when considering cost structure issues, which heavily influence what could be seen as created value and value to be captured (Cortimiglia *et al.* 2016, Jelassi and Enders 2005). Similarly, Spieth *et al.* (2014) take note of the relevance of looking at value capturing when studying business models in the context of business development. Michel (2014) argues that value capture aspects have been receiving less attention than they deserve in business model research, which per his argument has been focusing too heavily on value creation aspects.

One example of such value capture focus is how Internet-based new entrants such as Netflix innovated the value capturing aspect of the industry standard business model (i.e. paying to rent or watch movies individually) towards a subscription service, giving more stable and recurring revenue streams (Michel 2014), and consequently moved elements of their business model to their current fully online-based business model. The Netflix example highlights how firms could innovate in different dimensions of the business model as well as the necessity of BMI as such, to ensure further growth.

Business Model Innovation

A firm's business model can constitute a competitive advantage, but hardly an enduring one, as business model mechanics are rather transparent from the outside view of the firm and thus replicable by new entrants to that market (Teece 2010). Such transparency combined with ever-present environmental dynamism suggests that business models cannot remain static. In the context of the rapid technological developments of the Internet of the early 2000s, Swedish SMEs were obviously facing external pressure from the business environment to innovate their business model towards online-based models.

The argument regarding the business environment driving BMI decisions is further reinforced by Demil and Lecocq (2010), who established that proactive scanning of the external and internal business environments ought to guide business model innovation decisions. This is furthermore much in line with Sosna *et al.* (2010), who observe that business model experiments driven by the top management and trial-and-error learning could fuse business model innovation. Again, this notion also echoes the lean start-up approach of experimental business model innovation in iterations (Blank 2013). Additionally, consistent with McGrath's (2013) thoughts on transient advantages, business model innovation can be seen as a tool for a firm for moving along the waves of emerging transient advantages over time.

Teece (2010) argues further that technological innovations by firms often should be accompanied by business model innovations, for maximizing the value capturing effect of the technological innovation, such as the swift emergence of Internet technology in the early 2000s in the context of this study. Moreover, business model innovation can simply be thought of as changes made by the firm in "how to do business," considering that even a rather small change in a business model could have substantial effects on the business as a whole (Amit and Zott 2012). This argument is largely echoed by Cortimiglia *et al.* (2016), who notes differences between developing an existing business model and designing a completely new business model, while noting that both business model innovation types could have considerable effects. A more specific operationalization of the term *business model innovation* was provided by Björkdahl and Holmén (2013, 214): ". . . to redefine an existing product or service, how it is delivered to customer and/ or how the firm profits from the customer offering."

Obviously, there is an opening for a discussion here in regards to how momentous or large such changes should be to be defined as an actual innovation and not just an incremental change of a business model. Gerasymenko *et al.* (2015, 2) approach this issue by using the term "substantial business model change." By substantial business model change, the authors suggest that the business model change should not only impact how the focal firm generates revenues or manages its costs, but also consider areas such as core resources, competences/capabilities or relationships. The core argument is that changes in resources, capabilities and relationships, along with revenue generation and costs management mechanisms, have a substantial firm-wide effect on how its business is being done.

This reasoning by Gerasymenko *et al.* (2015) can be seen as consistent with Björkdahl and Holmén's (2013) definition of business model innovation. However, Gerasmyenko *et al.* (2015) contributes by acutely highlighting the differences between more incremental or minor changes in the business model and more significant or substantial changes therein.

As the empirical focus of our study is on SME implementation of online channels, it does meet the above definition of substantial business model innovation. By its very nature, moving online from brick-and-mortar operations requires new resources and capabilities for the firm (Teece 2010). Furthermore, the Internet changes the value created and proposed to the customer, the delivery modes and the underlying revenue models and cost structures (Mezger 2014; Michel 2014).

Business Model Innovation Deterrents

As described previously, business model innovation might have different internal and external triggers in a firm. However, several factors also inhibit BMI efforts, especially poignant in incumbent firms, where established business models and ways of doing things already are in existence. These deterrents towards BMI can be exemplified by the new business model conflicting with the firm's traditional asset configuration and thus threatening how the firm generates ongoing value (Amit and Zott 2001; Kim and Min 2015). For instance, human capital tied up in a sales force will be under threat by a business model based on online sales. Similarly, Christensen and Rosenbloom (1995) and Christensen *et al.* (2016) takes on the lens of disruptive innovation, where Internet technology in the early 2000s can be included, and finds that incumbents fail to innovate their business model to counter threats from new, disruptive, entrants due to perceived lower initial margins with the new business model. Put differently, Christensen and Rosenbloom (1995) recognize that the business model for the established technology might conflict with the business model of new technology, leading to lower margins, at least in the short term.

Furthermore, Chesbrough (2010) takes note of cognitive barriers in an organization which prevents BMI. The knowledge-based resources and capabilities needed for creating and designing new business models simply get lost or filtered out in the organization's inherent logic of how value should be created and captured. Unlike for instance Amit and Zott (2001) and Christensen *et al.* (2016), Chesbrough (2010) thus sees that managers consequently fail to recognize what the "right" business model should be, due to internal organizational obstruction and legacy.

Hypotheses Development

Having reviewed the core elements of business model, business model innovation and its deterrents, we proceed to developing a set of hypotheses that are contextualized in the setting of online channel adoption. The study's conceptualization of an online-based business model follows the first-wave design of the studies of online channel adoption reported in Bengtsson *et al.* (2007) and Vanyushyn (2008a, 2008b, 2011). Following that conceptualization, the online business model included three basic features—using a website for a firm's presentation, displaying information about products, and communicating via e-mail with customers. These three features are complemented by four more advanced forms of online channel—ordering via a firm's website, collecting feedback from customers, integrating a firm's website with the rest of the firm's systems and collecting information about customers' on-line behavior. These features and the degree of their implementation will separately and jointly affect how the focal firm creates, delivers and captures value, as well as its resources and capabilities. Hence, the implementation of an online-based business model can be seen as a substantial business model innovation.

Considering business model innovation, its drivers and deterrents, the implementation of BMI could be further scrutinized in terms of the exploration-exploitation dichotomy (March 1991). The literature on e-business, as well as that on IT, that emerged in the late 90s and early 2000s presents two sets of conflicting views. The first view emphasized the innovative core that IT and the Internet developments would bring to the industries and to the firms and forecast that e-business would redefine the rules of strategy. Seen as a radical technological innovation, understanding of the e-business adoption by firms relied on inputs from the theoretical frameworks on the adoption of innovations (Rogers 1995). The radical innovation focus implied a shift in the existing practices of the organization, and such a shift could lead to an organizational change and abandonment of investments in the earlier routines and practices. A good exemplification of this approach is the work of Srinivasan *et al.* (2002) who used e-business as an empirical setting to develop the construct of 'technological opportunism.' Starting with the assumption that e-business is a radical technological innovation, Srinivasan *et al.* (2002) linked e-business adoption to a sense-and-respond capability of an organization with respect to new technologies.

An alternative view on e-business is encapsulated in the title of Carr's (2003) article "IT doesn't matter," voted the best article of 2003 in *Harvard Business Review*. The core of the argument is that as such IT cannot be a source of strategic advantage and eventually transforms into some type of infrastructural technology, or common utility like electricity. Thus, while innovative investments can provide a lead and contribution to organizational performance, the opportunities for gaining IT advantages are dwindling. Carr (2003, 49) concludes that IT should become "boring," and that a firm's focus should shift from an aggressive search for opportunities to careful management of costs and risks. In this view, the innovativeness factor dissipates and the decisions regarding IT are to be taken within the basic cost-benefit framework.

Thus, the processes of investing in an online-based business model from the innovation viewpoint is akin to the process of exploration, and from Carr's (2003) view, they parallel that of exploitation. It is important to point out that these are not mutually exclusive categories, but rather polar ends of a continuum. A general proposition to be examined in this study is that adoption in 2002 was driven by exploration, while in 2008 the adoption is driven by exploitation. Translating these rather abstract categories into a set of measurable antecedents is not a straightforward task. Furthermore, the design of the study is constrained by the original first-wave survey conducted in 2002. As such, an inquiry into the adoption and subsequent use of the Internet requires addressing two key questions: (1) the sequence of steps in the adoption process and (2) identification and evaluation of the relative influence of factors that affect the adoption process. The process of implementing and adopting an online-based business model for an incumbent firm can be hypothesized to follow the general stages of the organizational adoption process (Wolfe 1994) of first becoming aware of a channel feature, evaluating the feature, deciding to adopt, implementing the feature, and then finally using it. Hence:

H1: Firms' online-based business model implementation will follow the linear adoption sequence.

The explorative implementation of online-based business models had an embedded prerequisite of making a choice between keeping and potentially ruining existing routines, practices, and prior investments in technology and distribution channels. It is envisaged that a firm that decided to invest in the e-business in the late nineties was willing to accept that trade-off. Porter (2001) suggested that the Internet is cannibalistic in its nature in that it can replace the existing business models. A firm's existing technologies and employees, such as call centers and sales force, are also not immune (e.g., Eyuboglu and Kabadayi 2005; Johnson and Bharadwaj 2005). Thus, from the exploration perspective, a firm had to be willing to bet on new technology even if its past investments would lose value, and it had to be able to replace one set of abilities with a different set of abilities to adopt, for instance Internet-based sales. The ability of a firm to accomplish that depended on prior investments (Chandy and Tellis 1998).

The potentially competence-destroying and cannibalistic nature of the Internet at the time (Deleersnyder *et al.* 2002; Ghosh 1998) suggests that a firm must have exhibited willingness to invest in a new technology even though in so doing it could possibly cannibalize earlier business model investments. In the examination of radical product innovation, Chandy and Tellis (1998) introduced the construct "willingness to cannibalize"—an attitudinal variable that captured "the extent to which a firm is prepared to reduce the actual or potential value of its past investments" (p. 475). Fundamentally, their study confirmed that to be radically innovative, firms should be prepared to give up the old and embrace the new (Chandy and Tellis 1998), which is a notion largely echoed in more recent studies on business model cannibalization in incumbent firms (e.g. Kim and Min 2015). After some modification, the construct has been used in the online business model context (Bengtsson *et al.* 2007; Host *et al.* 2001; Vanyushyn 2008a) and has been shown to be significant in the datasets collected in the early 2000s. The key insight gained from these studies was that willingness to cannibalize existing business models contributed to the understanding of why firms invested in online-based business models. Thus, we propose:

H2. Willingness to Cannibalize will be positively associated with the implementation of an online-based business model

Given the unit of analysis in this study—a small firm—it is necessary to consider the perceived degree of congruence between the offerings by the firm and the online business model. If a firm finds that an online-based business model lacks relevance for the firm in terms of creating, delivering and capturing value with its products, the usefulness of such a model becomes questionable. Thus, the perceived relevance of the online channel needs to be taken into consideration (Vanyushyn 2008a). To be implemented the cost and the complexity of running an online business model must be evaluated as well. If the IT costs of establishing such as business model are too high, then it is unlikely that a firm will commit resources to such a channel (Vanyushyn 2008a; cf Davis 1989 in the individual case); this approach is akin to conventional cost-benefit analysis (Carr 2003) of implementing a new business model.

Finally, any business operates in an environment where customers and competitors represent two major forces, and a firm must respond to them in order to stay in business. If a firm's customers exhibit the desire to purchase or evaluate products through the Internet and if the market is perceived as ready for electronic activities overall, then a firm is likely to respond by investing in an online-based business model. The need to stay on par with competition may force a firm to do the same as well. Hence, we propose:

H3a. Relevance will be positively associated with online business model adoption

H3b. Ease of Use will be positively associated with online business model adoption

H3c. Market Pressure will be positively associated with online business model adoption

3. Research Method

Sample

The data for this study were collected via two mailed questionnaires: the first sent out in 2002 and the second in 2008 to a sample of SMEs in Sweden. The questionnaires contained three measures of the elementary Internet use and four measures of the advanced use, and a range of items capturing internal and external conditions and managers' attitudes. In 2002, the questionnaire was sent to a random sample of manufacturing SMEs in four different regions of Sweden. The major industries represented include wood, publishing/printing, chemicals, metal, machinery and electrical equipment. Out of the initial mailing of 1,037 questionnaires, 479 were returned, although 100 surveys contained non-systematic missing data. Then, in 2008, these responding firms were traced using unique organizational numbers as search criteria. Out of the original 478 responding firms, 366 were still registered as active at the end of the fiscal year of 2007. A questionnaire, containing identical questions presented a format and layout identical to the original questionnaire, was mailed to the 366 firms that were still registered as active. After two reminders that emphasized the two-wave nature of the study and highlighted the importance of the response for the research project, 124 usable surveys, that is, with no missing values and full responses from 2002, were returned.

Measures of Online Channel Adoption

The questionnaire contained four measures of online business model use: ordering via a firm's website, collecting feedback from customers, integrating a firm's website with the rest of a firm's systems and collecting information about customers' on-line behavior. Items for measuring the basic use of the Internet contained three questions: using a website for the firm's presentation, displaying information about products, and communicating via e-mail with customers. The available response categories for each item were "not considered," "considered," "planned," "under implementation," "implemented," and "successfully implemented." Because of the final sample size of 124 and the requirements of cell count of the general loglinear model (GLA), the categories "planned" and "under implementation" were merged; categories "implemented" and "successfully implemented" were also merged. Table 5.1 (page 82) summarizes the frequency of responses to the channel adoption questions both in 2002 and 2008.

Table 5.1 Levels of Online Channel Feature Adoption, Years 2002 and 2008

	Not considered	Considered	Planned or being implemented	Implemented
Responses in 2002				
Presentation of our firm	9	9	16	66
Providing information about company's offerings	9	10	18	63
Communication with customers via e-mail	9	7	10	73
Receiving orders via the website	41	21	19	19
Getting feedback from customers	38	19	16	27
Our website is integrated with other systems	54	24	18	4
Collect information on how our customers use our website	48	24	18	10
Responses in 2008				
Presentation of our company	7↓	5↓	9↓	78↑
Providing information about company's offerings	7↓	4↓	11↓	78↑
Communication with customers via e-mail	7↓	3↓	10↕	81↑
Receiving orders via the website	40↓	23↑	13↓	24↑
Getting feedback from customers	40↑	20↑	13↓	28↑
Our website is integrated with other systems	53↓	23↓	15↓	9↑
Collect information on how our customers use our website	43↓	20↓	13↓	25↑

Note: The table reports row percentages, rounded to the nearest integer, of responses in each category. N = 124, identical firms in both 2002 and 2008. For convenience, the table indicates the direction of change: ↑—percentage of firms in the category increased compared to 2002; ↓—decreased; ↕—remained unchanged.

Measures of Antecedents

Willingness to cannibalize, market pressure, relevance and ease of use are measured on a multiple-item Likert scale ranging from 1, "strongly disagree" to 5, "strongly agree." The scale for willingness to cannibalize is adapted from Chandy and Tellis (1998). CFA was used to evaluate the discriminant and convergent validities of the measures for the first survey period. The fit of the model turned out acceptable: GFI = .908, AGFI = .871, CFI = .906, SRMR = .0618. The 95% confidence interval for pairwise correlation between constructs was well below 1 (p < .05), and all factors loadings were high and significant at p < .05. Therefore, conditions for convergent and discriminant validity were met for the period 1. The alphas and confidence intervals for the multiple item-constructs (Duhachek *et al.* 2005) are reported in Table 5.2 (page 83). For the purpose of the analysis, equally weighed additive scales were developed.

Table 5.2 Measures in the Study

Measure	Items
Willingness to Cannibalize α_{p1} = .77 ± .035	1. We are ready to support Internet projects even if it will jeopardize our sales through existing channels.
	2. We are willing to sacrifice sales through our existing channels to implement Internet-based sales.
	3. We are willing to bet on new technology even if our past investments will lose value.
	4. We can easily change the organizational scheme to fit the needs of the Internet-based sales.
	5. We can easily replace one set of abilities with a different set of abilities to adopt the Internet-based sales.
	6. We can easily change the manner in which we carry out tasks to fit the needs of Internet-based sales.
Market Pressure α_{p1} = .71 ± .04	1. Our customers want to buy our products through the Internet.
	2. Our market is ready for e-business.
	3. Our closest competitor has started to use the Internet for marketing and sales.
	4. We are forced to use the Internet as our competitors already do so.
Ease of Use α_{p1} = .73 ± .049	1. IT costs of establishing Internet-based marketing are too high.
	2. Internet-based trade is too complex.
Relevance α_{p1} = .76 ± .029	1. Our products are too complex to be sold via the Internet.
	2. Clients often want to have a presentation before purchase.
	3. Our products are customized to individual needs of clients.
	4. We discuss our products before purchase.

Note: wave one estimates (Vanyushyn 2006)

4. Data Analysis and Results

Table 5.1 presents the overall frequencies of the features implementation stages for the years 2002 and 2008. For all seven attributes of the Internet adoption, there appears to be a shift from the lower end of the scale, "not considered," to the higher end of the scale, "implemented." In particular, the percentage of firms that have implemented any of the seven features has increased. These increases, however, are not as large as might be expected, with only nine percent of firms having the website fully integrated with other systems in 2008.

Implementation Sequence

The next step is to investigate whether the firms followed the linear adoption sequence in their implementation of online-based business models. Between the two waves of the study some firms switched between different levels of adoption, for example, moved from "considered" to "being implemented" or vice-versa. For example, out of 23 firms which had the feature "receiving orders via web site" fully implemented in 2002, only 15 remained at the same stage in 2008; 16 firms that were at one of the first three stages in 2002 moved to implemented.

By the virtue of the research design, the adoption levels for each individual firm are known for both periods. Therefore, models for matched pairs, or paired data, can be applied (Agresti 2007). Level of adoption of each individual feature can be represented by a 4 × 4 matrix. To determine whether a statistically significant change in the adoption level between the two periods has occurred, a test of marginal homogeneity can be conducted. Omitting the technicalities in the interest of brevity, we report that the marginal homogeneity does hold (that is $p > .1$) for the attributes 3, 4, 5, and 6. For these attributes there was no change in the general adoption level because the number of firms that moved to a particular stage will be compensated by the firms that left this stage. The marginal homogeneity did not hold for attributes 1, 2 and 7 suggesting that for these features a statistically significant number of firms moved to the implemented stage. Intuitively, this result is reflected in Table 5.2—for these attributes, the implemented stage increased substantially, while the number of firms in the other three stages decreased. Thus, H1 is only partially supported as not all features followed linear adoption sequence.

Determinants of Adoption

The relationship between the advanced use of the Internet and the drivers of the online business model implementation were tested using regression analysis. The dependent variable is an index calculated as a sum of features four through seven, that is, of the advanced use features. Table 5.3 on page 85

Table 5.3 Model of Factors Behind the Advanced Use of the Internet: Regression Results

	2008			2002		
	β	s.e.	p	β	s.e.	p
Constant	2.20	.57	.00	2.23	.48	.00
Willingness to Cannibalize	−.02	.10	.81	.17	.10	.08
Market Pressure	.28	.09	.00	.16	.10	.10
Ease of Use	.04	.08	.60	.08	.07	.24
Relevance	.18	.08	.03	.24	.07	.00
R^2	.179**			.218**		
Adj R^2	.153**			.194**		
$\beta = 0$	7.02**			9.00**		
$\beta_{02} = \beta_{08}$			11.3**			

Note: **—significant at p < .01. Largest VIF = 1.34.

reports the coefficients, their standard errors and significance, R^2, adjusted R^2, and test of the overall model significance for 2002 and 2008. The last row in the table reports the result of the Chow test for structural break. Willingness to Cannibalize, Market Pressure and Relevance were significant at p < .1 in 2002. On the other hand, in 2008 Willingness to Cannibalize is no longer significant, and the explained variance decreased somewhat (from .218 to .179). The significant result for the structural break test indicates that the data from 2008 and 2002 cannot be pooled as the intercept and the slopes are different for 2002 and 2008. Thus, H2 is supported only in the first wave, H3a is supported for both waves, H3b is not supported, and H3c is supported in both waves.

5. Discussion

In this study, we applied a business model perspective and examined the patterns of online channel adoption by SMEs in Sweden that occurred during the first decade of the 21st century. The context of rapid development of the Internet as an enabling technology gave us an opportunity to compare and contrast various drivers that triggered business model innovation manifested in online channels adoption—innovation that had a potential to reshuffle the network of external partnerships as well as to speed up the internationalization process. The underlying theoretical contrast of adoption of innovation (Bengtsson *et al.* 2007, Srinivasan *et al.* 2002) versus conventional cost-benefit analysis (Carr 2003) showed that the composition of drivers behind a BMI decision is dynamic and context-dependent. While a firm's willingness to cannibalize, or to forgo the value of earlier investments, turned out as a significant precursor of substantial BMI at the early stage of the enabling technology development, market responsiveness overtook the main driver of BMI as enabling technology matured.

A comparison of the different features of the online business model use revealed that the proportion of firms that have fully implemented the online business model aspects increased overall. However, some firms that previously had these features implemented stopped using them. Moreover, the results of the GLA procedure suggested that no particular transition between the adoption stages has occurred. A firm that stated in 2002 that it was planning to invest in an online business model is no more likely to have this feature up and running than a firm that had no such intention. Moreover, firms that had a certain aspect fully implemented in 2002 may be at the "not considered" stage in 2008. What these findings suggest is that there is no clear pattern in contrast to what the sequential adoption models suggest. An explanation of the changes observed might be that the decisions made in 2002 were driven by exploration (March 1991) and thus resulted in opportunistic adoption, which failed to deliver and were withdrawn. On the other hand, firms that were unwilling to commit resources in 2002 did so in 2008 after deciding that the benefits of such decisions outweighed the costs. Such an explanation is also consistent with the investigation of the factors that drove the firm's implementation of the more advanced online features, as willingness to cannibalize (Chandy and Tellis 1998), a general proxy for the degree of innovativeness perceived by a firm, did not affect the online business model implementation in the wave two of the study.

Another implication that falls out from this study is that the make-up of factors that explain the decision to adopt, implement, and use the online-based business model changed over time during the time frame of the study. The results of the studies based on the 2002 survey showed that the adoption of the online business models can be likened to the adoption of a radical innovation (Bengtsson *et al.* 2007) and that such adoption is affected by a firm's innovativeness, perception of the information technology, and competitive strategy (Vanyushyn 2008a). The 2008 results, on the other hand, suggest that the degree of implementation of an online business model aspect is more closely linked to the conventional cost-benefit analysis. Factors that had been drawn from the literature on innovation and found significant in early 2000 had lost their explanatory power, albeit not entirely. The most notable change is that a firm's willingness to lose the value of its past investments was significant in 2002, a finding consistent with the views expressed during that time (Deelersnyder *et al.* 2002; Ghosh 1998; Porter 2001). In 2008, however, this factor lost its explanatory power. This finding further reinforces the exploration-exploitation dichotomy of decisions advocated here. While the research focusing on innovation generation and adoption attempts to explain why firms behave outside of the usual cost-benefit approach (Crossan and Apaydin 2010; Wolfe 1994), for example, internal resistance precluding the firm from pursuing beneficial technology, at the later stage a more conventional cost-benefit approach and its derivatives should contribute more to the understanding of the processes involved.

The findings of the study should be treated with a great deal of caution, though. Certain factors may persist over time, such as disintermediation and the threat potential of a channel conflict (Eyuboglu and Kabadayi 2005) and will contribute to the online business models implementation decision. On the other hand, over time the balance of costs and benefits and the perceptions thereof are likely to change. Advances in technology lead to better, cheaper, and easier-to-use systems, and the increases in the numbers of trained professionals lead to the supply of necessary competence. One must not disregard the effects of network externalities (Zott and Amit 2010)—the more Internet users there are, the higher incentive, or utility, there is to implement online business models. At the same time, as decision makers become better and better informed about the Internet and related technologies, their perceptions of its benefits will be altered as well and will mirror the true situation more accurately, thus requiring less risk-taking. Nonetheless, a firm's innovation culture will still influence the way an online business model is used and the performance outcomes of such use (Adam *et al.* 2009).

Overall, the study reinforces the notion that the spread of the Internet as enabling technology follows a predictable path, along which the "innovativeness" component starts to wear off. As time goes by, the reduction of costs, increase in the availability of trained specialists, and improved productivity of digital technology should go hand in hand with the classical S-shaped curve of the saturation. The findings of the study imply that small firms' implementation of online business models, at least to the extent it is conceptualized here, involves less "risk-taking, experimentation, flexibility, discovery, innovation" and more "refinement, production, efficiency, implementation, execution," if one is to use March's (1991) descriptors.

Limitations and Suggestions for Future Research

The design and context of this study have limitations that need to be addressed. First, the design of the study is constrained by the original first-wave survey conducted in 2002. The aspects of online business models studied did not include web 2.0 applications, such as use of social media. Examining how a small firm uses social media to create, deliver and capture value is a promising area for future research. Second, the sample used is a purposive one, as only firms responding to the original survey were included in the study. A longitudinal representative panel of firms would allow for generalization and potentially uncover a more refined pattern of adoption of online business models. Third, the findings of this study can be country specific. An examination of drivers of online business models adoption in a multiple country setting with dissimilar availability of the infrastructure may further advance the understanding of the drivers of online channel use.

Finally, this study does not consider whether the existing offline business models were dismissed or not. It is however likely that offline and online business models often were, and are, used in parallel, thus creating business model portfolios (Abrahamsson 2016) among the SMEs.

6. Conclusions

For more than two decades, the entrepreneurship research track led by Håkan Boter at Umeå University has recognized the importance of cooperation and internationalization for small firms in sparsely populated areas of northern Sweden. The interface among innovation, internationalization and cooperation has been the focal point of interest for scholars from this track, whose work resulted in numerous findings and insights. This study looks back at some of the earlier findings on online channels adoption through a modern lens of business models. Such retrospective application identifies willingness to forgo the value of earlier investments in value delivery networks and organizational routines as a precursor of substantial business model innovation. Yet as enabling technology that underlies business models matures, an SME's decision to transform a business model no longer depends on organizational-level antecedents and is driven by market responsiveness and conventional cost-benefit analysis. Combined, our findings contribute to the business model literature by demonstrating the transient and time-conditioned nature of substantial business model innovation antecedents and by uncovering changes in managerial perceptions of the magnitude of business model innovation.

References

Abrahamsson, Jan. 2016. "Beyond Going Global: Essays on Business Development of International New Ventures Past Early Internationalization." PhD diss., Umeå University.

Adam, Stewart, Andrea Vocino, and David Bednall. 2009. "The World-Wide Web in Modern Marketing's Contribution to Organisational Performance." *Marketing Intelligence & Planning* 27(1): 7–24.

Agresti, Alan. 2007. *An Introduction to Categorical Data Analysis.* Hoboken, NJ: Wiley-Interscience.

Amit, Raphael, and Christoph, Zott. 2001. "Value Creation in e-business." *Strategic Management Journal* 22(6–7): 493–520.

Amit, Raphael, and Christoph, Zott. 2012. "Strategy in Changing Markets: New Business Models—Creating Value Through Business Model Innovation." *MIT Sloan Management Reviews* 53: 41–49.

Bengtsson, Maria, Håkan Boter, and Vladimir Vanyushyn. 2003. "The Challenge of Building Marketing Channels via the Internet." Paper presented at the *International Council for Small Business (ICSB) Conference*, Belfast, Northern Ireland.

Bengtsson, Maria, Håkan Boter, and Vladimir Vanyushyn. 2007. "Integrating the Internet and Marketing Operations: A Study of Antecedents in Firms of Different Size." *International Small Business Journal* 25(1): 27–48.

Björkdahl, Joakim, and Holmén Markus. 2013. "Editorial: Business Model Innovation—The Challenges Ahead." *International Journal of Product Development* 18(3–4): 213–225.

Blank, Steve. 2013. "Why the Lean Start-Up Changes Everything." *Harvard Business Review* 91(5): 63–72.

Brea-Solís, Humberto, Ramon Casadesus-Masanell, and Emili Grifell-Tatjé. 2015. "Business Model Evaluation: Quantifying Walmart's Sources of Advantage." *Strategic Entrepreneurship Journal* 9(1): 12–33.

Carr, Nicholas G. 2003. "IT Doesn't Matter." *Harvard Business Review* 81(5): 41–58.

Chandy, Rajesh K., and Gerard J. Tellis. 1998. "Organizing for Radical Product Innovation: The Overlooked Role of Willingness to Cannibalize." *Journal of Marketing Research* 35(4): 474–487.

Chesbrough, Henry. 2010. "Business Model Innovation: Opportunities and Barriers." *Long Range Planning* 43(2): 354–363.

Christensen, Clayton M., Thomas Bartman, and Derek Van Bever. 2016. "The Hard Truth About Business Model Innovation." *MIT Sloan Management Review* 58.

Christensen, Clayton M., and Richard S. Rosenbloom. 1995. "Explaining the Attacker's Advantage: Technological Paradigms, Organizational Dynamics, and the Value Network." *Research Policy* 24(2): 233–257.

Clauss, Thomas. 2017. "Measuring Business Model Innovation: Conceptualization, Scale Development, and Proof of Performance." *R&D Management*. 47(3): 385–403. doi:10.1111/radm.12186.

Cortimigla, Marcelo Nogueira, Ghezzi Antonio and Germán Frank Alejandro. 2016. "Business Model Innovation and Strategy Making Nexus: Evidence from a Cross-Industry Mixed-Methods Study." *R&D Management* 46(3): 414–432.

Crossan, Mary M., and Marina Apaydin. 2010. "A Multi-Dimensional Framework of Organizational Innovation: A Systematic Review of the Literature." *Journal of Management Studies* 47(6): 1154–1191.

Davis, Fred D. 1989. "Perceived Usefulness, Perceived Ease of Use, and User Acceptance of Information Technology." *MIS Quarterly* 13(3): 319–340.

Deleersnyder, Barbara, Inge Geyskens, Katrijn Gielens, and Marnik G. Dekimpe. 2002. "How Cannibalistic Is the Internet Channel? A Study of the Newspaper Industry in the United Kingdom and the Netherlands." *International Journal of Research in Marketing* 19(4): 337–348.

Demil, Benoît and Lecocq Xavier. 2010. "Business Model Evolution: In Search of Dynamic Consistency." *Long Range Planning* 43(2–3): 227–246.

Doganova, Liliana, and Marie Eyquem-Renault. 2009. "What Do Business Models Do?" *Research Policy* 38(10): 1559–1570.

Duhachek, Adam, Anne T. Coughlan, and Dawn Iacobucci. 2005. "Results on the Standard Error of the Coefficient Alpha Index of Reliability." *Marketing Science* 24(2): 294–301.

Eyuboglu, Nermin, and Sertan Kabadayi. 2005. "Dealer-Manufacturer Alienation in a Multiple Channel System: The Moderating Effect of Structural Variables." *Journal of Marketing Channels* 12(3): 5–26.

Gerasymenko, Violetta, Dirk De Clercq, and Harry J. Sapienza. 2015. "Changing the Business Model: Effects of Venture Capital Firms and Outside CEOs on Portfolio Company Performance." *Strategic Entrepreneurship Journal* 9(1): 79–98.

Ghosh, Shikar. 1998. "Making Business Sense of the Internet." *Harvard Business Review* 76(3): 126–135.

Hennart, Jean François. 2014. "The Accidental Internationalists: A Theory of Born Globals." *Entrepreneurship: Theory and Practice* 38(1): 117–135.

Host, Viggo, Niels P. Mols and Jorn Flohr Nielsen. 2001. "The Adoption of Internet-Based Marketing Channels." *Homo Oeconomicus* 17(4): 463–488.

Jelassi, Tawfik, and Enders Albrecht. 2005. *Strategies for e-business: Creating Value Through Electronic and Mobile Commerce: Concepts and Cases.* Harlow, UK: Pearson Education.

Johanson, Jan, and Jan-Erik Vahlne. 1977. "The Internationalization Process of the Firm—A Model of Knowledge Development and Increasing Foreign Market Commitments." *Journal of International Business Studies* 8(1): 23–32.

Johnson, Devon S., and Sundar Bharadwaj. 2005. "Digitization of Selling Activity and Sales Force Performance: An Empirical Investigation." *Journal of the Academy of Marketing Science* 33(1): 3–18.

Kim, Stephen K., and Sungwook Min. 2015. "Business Model Innovation Performance: When Does Adding a New Business Model Benefit an Incumbent?" *Strategic Entrepreneurship Journal* 9(1): 34–57.

Magretta, Joan. 2002. "Why Business Models Matter." *Harvard Business Review* 80(5): 3–8.

March, James G. 1991. "Exploration and Exploitation in Organizational Learning." *Organization Science* 2(1): 71–87.

McGrath, Rita Gunther. 2013. "Transient Advantage." *Harvard Business Review* 91(6): 62–70.

Mezger, Florian. 2014. "Toward a Capability-Based Conceptualization of Business Model Innovation: Insights from an Explorative Study." *R&D Management* 44(5): 429–449.

Michel, Stefan. 2014. "Capture More Value." *Harvard Business Review* 92(10): 78–85.

O'Toole, Thomas. 2003. "E-Relationships—Emergence and the Small Firm." *Marketing Intelligence & Planning* 21(2): 115–122.

Osterwalder, Alexander, Yves Pigneur, and Christopher L. Tucci. 2005. "Clarifying Business Models: Origins, Present, and Future of the Concept." *Communications of the Association for Information Systems* 16(1): 1–25.

Porter, Michael. 2001. "Strategy and the Internet." *Harvard Business Review* 79(5): 62–79.

Ritala, Paavo, Arash Golnam, and Alain Wegmann. 2014. "Coopetition-Based Business Models: The Case of Amazon.com." *Industrial Marketing Management* 43(2): 236–249.

Rogers, Everett M. 1995. *Diffusion of Innovations* (4th ed.). New York: Free Press.

SCB. 2005. *Företagens användning av datorer och Internet 2005* [Companies' use of computers and Internet 2005]. Stockholm: Statistiska centralbyrån [Stockholm: Statistics Sweden]

Shafer, Scott M., H. Jeff Smith, and Jane C. Linder. 2005. "The Power of Business Models." *Business Horizons* 48(3): 199–207.

Sinkovics, Noemi, Rudolf Sinkovics, and Ruey-Jer Jean. 2013. "The Internet as an Alternative Path to Internationalization?" *International Marketing Review* 30(2): 130–155.

Sosna, Marc, Rosa Nelly Trevinyo-Rodríguez, and S. Ramakrishna Velamuri. 2010. "Business Model Innovation Through Trial-and-Error Learning: The Naturhouse Case." *Long Range Planning* 43(2–3): 383–407.

Spieth, Patrick, Dirk Schneckenberg, and Joan E. Ricart. 2014. "Business Model Innovation – State of the Art and Future Challenges for the Field." *R&D Manage* 44(3): 237–247. doi:10.1111/radm.12071.

Srinivasan, Raji, Gary L. Lilien, and Arvind Rangaswamy. 2002. "Technological Opportunism and Radical Technology Adoption: An Application to e-business." *Journal of Marketing* 66(3): 47–60.

Teece, David J. 2010. "Business Models, Business Strategy and Innovation." *Long Range Planning* 43(2–3): 172–194.

Tushman, Michael L., and Philip Anderson. 1986. "Technological Discontinuities and Organizational Environments." *Administrative Science Quarterly* 31(3): 439–465.

Vanyushyn, Vladimir. 2006. *Antecedents of Innovative Behavior in Smaller Firms: Application to E-business Adoption and Exporting.* FE-publikationer 2006:185. ISSN 0349–2230. Umeå, Sweden: Umeå Universitet.

Vanyushyn, Vladimir. 2008a. "Innovation at the Intersection of Market Strategy and Technology: A Study of Digital Marketing Adoption among SMEs." In *Entrepreneurship, Sustainable Growth and Performance: Frontiers in European Research*, edited by Hans Landström, Hans Crijns, Eddy Laveren and David Smallbone, 299–323. Cheltenham, UK: Edward Elgar.

Vanyushyn, Vladimir. 2008b. "The Dual Effect of Resellers on Electronic Business Adoption by SMEs." *International Journal of Entrepreneurship and Innovation* 9(1): 43–49.

Vanyushyn, Vladimir. 2011. "Innovative Behaviour of Small Firms: Essays on Small Firms' Internationalisation and Use of Online Channels." PhD diss., Umeå University.

Wolfe, Richard A. 1994. "Organizational Innovation: Review, Critique and Suggested Research Directions." *Journal of Management Studies* 31(3): 405–431.

Zott, Christoph, and Raphael Amit. 2010. "Business Model Design: An Activity System Perspective." *Long Range Planning* 43(2–3): 216–226.

6 Digitally Enabled Platforms

Generating Innovation and Entrepreneurial Opportunities for SMEs

Arnim Decker and Liliyana Makarova Jørsfeldt

1. Introduction

The Internet, one of the greatest technological innovations, has brought significant opportunities to create new products, processes and businesses. "Digitalization," "Industry 4.0," and "IoT" are the terms that are used to depict these changes in the business world. Technological developments are attracting both large companies and small businesses as a source for creation of new products and services.

Following the major changes in technology development large companies are creating digital platforms with the aim to enhance and develop their businesses to prosper. Such platforms are developed to facilitate cooperation and collaboration and provide support to new business initiated by SMEs and start-ups.

The evidence of success of companies originated in northern Europe, such as Skype and Spotify amongst others, raises an interest in further investigation of factors which underpin the success of northern European business models in innovation and entrepreneurship. Therefore, the aim of this paper will be twofold. First, we aim to describe how large companies that own digital platforms collaborate with SMEs and start-ups originated in northern Europe. Secondly, we aim to understand what motivates both large companies and SMEs to engage in collaborative effort on the basis of digital platforms and what are the unique characteristics of such cooperation in northern Europe.

The rest of the chapter is structured as follows. Firstly, digital platform competition will be described. Secondly, to shed light on the topic, concepts of IoT and Industry 4.0 will be presented and effects of digitalization and new technologies discussed. The "data collection" subsection will include examples of Siemens AG, Inter Corporation, Huawei Technologies Co., Ltd and Ericsson AB digital platforms. In the "Analysis" subsection we will examine the differences and similarities of the processes that support entrepreneurship in connection with innovation of the digital platforms. Further, we will discuss the nature of collaboration between large companies that provide technological platforms and SMEs. By presenting the Danish incubator "NOVI" we will illustrate the particularities that are specific to innovation models in northern Europe. Finally, the "Conclusion" subsection will be presented.

2. Platform Competition

Large companies create and lead industrial platforms to facilitate innovation and entrepreneurship. However, to be successful and scale out rapidly, they are also dependent on a network of external partners. Large firms support new business start-ups by providing access to capital and technology. When collaborating with SMEs and entrepreneurial start-ups, large firms profit by partnering with multiple firms so they can strengthen their own platform, especially as some of the SMEs and start-ups eventually grow into larger firms themselves. During the earlier stages of collaboration, large firms can expect feedback in the form of information with regards to viability of business models and generation of new technological knowledge. This helps to sustain the technological platform that the large firm is building up.

Even for large firms that act as platform providers, it is scarcely feasible to scale out an industrial platform without external partner firms, since the requirements for resources and capabilities are substantial. Furthermore, opening up to a third party creates room for new ideas which might not have been generated internally. Successful initiators of industrial platforms succeed in attracting a sufficient number of complementary firms who contribute to the overall success of the platforms through providing space for a niche in which complementary technologies can be built on the core technology created by the dominating platform firm. Time is a factor when emerging technologies open new possibilities for new market situations where Metcalfe's law is likely to apply (Hendler and Golbeck 2008). In such markets, the first firm that is able to successfully establish a new platform is likely to become the dominant player. When platform leaders combine efforts with innovative SMEs and entrepreneurial start-ups, the overall value created is likely to increase.

One of the most remarkable results of transformation towards digitalization is that increasingly, not individual firms, but networks compete against each other (Katsamakas 2014). As digitalization accelerates, firms more and more recognize the value of taking leadership by creating networked industrial platforms. Aspiring firms that aim for platform leadership need to establish an underlying technological design that can serve as the foundation on which the technological platform is built. The technological core (or kernel) needs to be stable and should not change—or at least should change as little as possible—in the long run. Based on this fundament, new technologies can continuously be developed building on a stable kernel to create new products and related services.[1] The basic trade-off is related to finding the appropriate balance between functionality and performance (Baldwin and Clark 2000). An essential requirement for a successful platform is the

ability to create sufficient stability to satisfy the needs of networked partners who use the platform to develop products and related services for their
end customers. If the underlying technology becomes too complex, however,
successful adaptation can be obstructed. Complexity can be mitigated by
modularity and well-defined interfaces, shielding the complexity which is
embedded in the individual modules. With reduced complexity, it becomes
more feasible to scale out the technology rapidly so that benefits from networking cannot be achieved.

Industrial platform leadership can be lost when the leading firms make
wrong strategic decisions. For example, IBM lost its grip on the upcoming
personal computer platform to Microsoft by ceding control over the operating system. Then together with Intel, Microsoft took over control of the
platform, which it still maintains. By committing the error of handing the
central part of the industry platform to Microsoft, IBM unwillingly reduced
itself to a complementary provider and in consequence lost the ability to
exercise leadership. A good example of a successfully established industrial
platform is Apple. The firm shifted the boundaries of the music industry
by creating a new ecosystem around its I-pod music player. Later Apple
revolutionized the industry for mobile telecommunications by extending
the ecosystem towards the new I-phone platform. Both platforms are now
forming the base for a variety of business models for competing SMEs to
emulate. As digitalization is about to become ubiquitous, other companies
are entering the race to build new platforms and profit from upcoming
opportunities. New platforms enable SMEs and start-ups to create innovative business models for offering new and competitive products and services.
In this new competitive environment, aspiring platform leaders need to find
the right strategy to attract third parties to their platforms, including SMEs
and entrepreneurial start-up companies.

Internet of Things and Industry 4.0

Internet of things (IoT) or Industry 4.0 (Siemens 2016a) are expected to
lead to revolutionary changes in global economic structures. The term *IoT*
describes a world of ubiquitous computing in which information technology has become omnipresent in practically all aspects of life (Weiser 1993).
Industry 4.0 and IoT depict the same ongoing phenomenon of increasing
digitalization; however, there are some subtle underlying differences in what
these terms actually mean.

In Europe, the term "Industry 4.0" is more commonly used. This term is
frequently used to depict the ongoing digitalization in society. With regards
to the economy, digitalization is perceived predominantly as a process of
complementing or replacing existing parts of a value chain, including production of products and services, with new digital technologies. The term
industry is also used to emphasize manufacturing as the cornerstone of stability and growth of the economy. Generally, such an approach can be seen

as one of a gradual evolutionary nature. Contrary to the above described view, many researchers argue that the predominant understanding is that digitalization opens up new opportunities to create new types of business models with the potential for disruptive innovations (Christensen 1997). Such a view comes closer to the American way of looking at digitalization. Similar to the European perspective, the term *IoT* carries the association of upgrading existing processes by increasing the intensity of digitalization. However, digitalization seems to be understood as upcoming opportunities to create new start-up companies with a potential to drive existing industries by leveraging innovative types of business models.

American start-ups seem particularly able to create business models by leveraging opportunities through digitalization with a potential for disruptive innovations.[2] The understanding is that new start-ups create digitally enabled business models to disrupt existing organizations in line with the analysis of Schumpeter (1942).

Gradual Improvements through Digitalization

There are two aspects of the process of digitalization (1) adding digital and connectivity functionalities to existing components of the value chains of production and services which would otherwise not have such features; (2) imbedding digital and connectivity functionalities during the design phase of a product.

Gradual innovation can be exemplified with electrical motors, which incorporate internal bearings that are prone to wear out over time and can cause the motor to break down unexpectedly. An imminent breakdown of the bearing is indicated by increasing vibrations. External sensors can be plugged onto the machine to send a warning to an external control unit to alert the operator. With this information, a planned interruption of the production process can be scheduled in order to replace the defective part before the breakdown will occur. Even more substantial benefits can be obtained when data is aggregated at a centralized database.[3] If the operator of the electrical motor is enabled to continuously collect operating data from a large number of existing installations, statistical data can be systematically collected to analyze critical patterns and improve products and services. In such manner even components which have initially not been equipped with technical networking functionalities can be integrated into the digital value chains.

As a second aspect, major benefits of digitalization can be achieved when digital and connectivity functionalities have already been implemented during the design phase. The advantage of this approach resides in the fact that increasingly new functionalities are embedded within software, not mechanical hardware. Implementing new functionalities through software integration is advantageous, since software can be updated and modified at comparably lower cost than upgrading hardware. The low cost of replacement is achieved due to the possibility of remote replacement (operation can be performed using ICT) and through economy of scale (copies of the software are produced at zero marginal cost). Thus, the functionality and flexibility of hardware is improved when embedded software can be upgraded in a flexible manner with low cost.

Disruptive Potential of New Digital Technologies

The digitalization of existing processes of production can be seen as a reactive approach to the potential of digitalization in line with the Kirznerian approach to incremental innovation. Contrary to the gradual approach, Schumpeterian style of innovations provoke the often-cited gales of creative destruction (Schumpeter 1942). Creative destruction is associated with the emergence of new modes of organizing markets and production while simultaneously destroying older ones. The flow of continuously upcoming innovative technologies and new ways of organizing business threaten existing business, often well-established firms with a strong foothold in their markets. For outsider firms seeking market entry, increasing digitalization presents opportunities to change the rule of the game and compete in new ways. Frequently, disruptive innovations are initiated by industry outsiders, who attack the market position of incumbents from below (Christensen 1997). Outsiders are often small start-ups or SMEs with resources that are too limited to attack the incumbent firm head-on. Instead, they try to find alternative ways to create new value that have potential to render the competitive advantages of established firms irrelevant. The creation of new markets and value networks frequently disrupts existing markets and displaces existing firms. For the market entrants to challenge existing processes of value creation, digital technologies and distributed computing provide opportunities for low-cost alternatives to existing processes of value creation that new entrepreneurial start-ups can profit from to overcome their limited resource base.

The success of entrepreneurial start-ups who build applications for mobile devices like Whatsapp or Viber can be traced back to Metcalfe's law. This law states that the value of a network increases proportionally to the square of the number of users (Hendler and Golbeck 2008). The more participants join the network, the more attractive membership becomes. With the upcoming IoT, an unlimited number of hitherto unconnected physical items is provided with digital functionalities to become part of a technical network. Networks of physical devices are linked to cloud computing platforms, in which data can be collected and aggregated, providing the basis for new innovative types of products, services and business models.

Digital intelligence is implemented into mechanical devices to provide connectivity and create network structures of things. New entrepreneurial opportunities will come from the possibility to create digital copies of existing physical devices. Emerging technologies for 3D scanning and printing cause marginal costs to diminish or even disappear. This will result in an abundance of new business model opportunities and will create potentials to disrupt existing firms and industrial structures. In the area of transportation systems it is already possible to observe that new business models disrupt established taxi companies. Vehicles with sensors and network connectivity can continuously send their operating data into the computing cloud. Real time aggregated data from a large number of vehicles are useful to detect upcoming dangerous situations or traffic congestions. Free transport capacity can be auctioned in real time, reducing the need for ownership of vehicles. Also, upcoming digital technologies allow for a better management of transportation capacities, including innovations like self-driving vehicles, resulting in energy savings, more secure operations and so on. Developments which are already becoming visible in the field of road traffic management are also taking place in the agricultural sector, health management, transportation, energy management, or home automation. These developments provide multiple opportunities for resource-constrained SMEs and entrepreneurial start-up companies who can capitalize on the new opportunities by linking into digital platforms which large technology-based firms provide.

3. Data Collection

The aim of this study is to investigate the nature of respective digital platforms and how large companies, the owners of these platforms, collaborate with SMEs and start-ups. In line with the aim of this study a sample of companies that play a role in the digital economy has been chosen. We spoke with representatives from the companies at the Industrial Fair of Hannover, in Spring 2016. The interviews were held in an open-ended and semi-structured style taking place at the respective locations of the trade fair booths. For analysis, secondary data, such as annual company reports to shareholders, as well as other third-party information, have been taken into consideration.

4. Siemens AG

General Characteristics of Siemens

Siemens is the largest engineering company in Europe with a presence in most countries in the world. The company has its activities in various industrial and technological sectors. The principal divisions are Industry, Energy, Health and Live Sciences and Public Infrastructures and Cities. One of the main competences of Siemens is in highly complex industrial systems and related services which are marketed on a global scale. Siemens expects the drive towards digitalization to be a major source of future growth. The company aims to leverage its size to achieve economies of scale by building technological platforms which can be implemented within different divisions. A technology which is developed once can subsequently be deployed in different areas, for example, facility management, production or health-care technologies. Siemens sees size as an advantage, when digital technologies can be replicated at negligible marginal costs over the entire range of its activities.

Siemens as a company fits neatly into the *Industry 4.0* paradigm, where the main emphasis rests on digitalization of existing industrial processes. To access industrial end customers, Siemens depends on internal sales force, as well as external partners. External relationships are long term in nature, these firms frequently employ academically trained technicians who are specialists in their field. Partner firms acquire their customers independently of Siemens and market themselves as providers of individualized adapted solutions which build on technologies provided by Siemens.

Siemens develops and commercializes virtualization technologies to create digital representations of physical production processes. This technology allows a production line to be tested in the virtual space before implementing it as a physical installation. This approach reduces development costs by eliminating errors in the virtual space before the actual physical implementation takes place. For example, virtual technologies are used for creating digital copies of oil production rigs, as they are used at offshore crude oil extraction. By using a digital representation of rigs, it becomes possible to train workers in a virtual reality. Once they have been trained, they can be productive from day one when they are deployed offshore. This saves significant costs, because training on the real oil rigs would be much more costly. Every day that an oil rig cannot be used in production causes a substantial financial loss because production cannot take place.

Industrial Platform and Ecosystems

Being broad in scope, Siemens AG tends to partner with technical consulting and engineering firms that are highly specialized and have already gained a solid position in their respective markets. Typically, partners of Siemens AG utilize the technology as a basis for their own products and technologies. Siemens draws on a network of smaller partner companies (SMEs) in the technology and software areas to complement its product and services. By collaborating with external partners, Siemens gains access to new technologies and business models. The focus rests both on advancing incremental as well as radical innovations.

To strengthen its market position Siemens has entered long term cooperation with other large multinational companies such as SAP and Intel. SAP has its expertise in ERP (enterprise resource planning) and specializes in providing administrative systems for larger companies. Collaborating closely with SAP, Siemens contributes industrial engineering know-how. In return, SAP contributes its knowledge as a large-scale software technology for management of administrative processes.

Collaboration with Intel, the US-based computer processes specialist, is another example. In this collaboration, Siemens draws on Intel's expertise in digital security systems to design their own products. Both companies combine their knowledge in industrial automation and cyber security to reduce risks and increase system efficiency. By simultaneously cooperating and competing with large firms, Siemens widens the technological scope of its own platform, which can indirectly benefit other smaller platform partners.

Although the main emphasis seems to be in engagement with larger firms, Siemens also fosters SMEs and start-ups (often in academic collaboration initiatives). Next24 (Siemens 2016b) is a Siemens platform, which can be presented as an outstanding example of how large companies utilize their resources to promote entrepreneurship and innovation in the era of digitalization. This platform acts as an incubator of innovations in diverse technological fields. Possessing technological know-how manufacturing capacities in more than 200 locations worldwide, Siemens is well positioned to promote collaboration between SMEs, venture capitalists, start-ups and research institutes and universities.

Siemens appeals to companies to join their platform, suggesting the following benefits: (1) access to global markets (connecting to Siemens´s customers) and commercial opportunities; (2) technological know-how and domain expertise; (3) fast prototyping; and (4) access to data to test algorithms. Such offerings are valuable propositions for SMEs, which are encouraged to join the platform and utilize the large company resources in order to achieve success in innovation activities. In this case, Siemens acts as a facilitator of collaborations in the given industrial ecosystem.

5. Intel Corporation

General Characteristics

Intel is a global technology company with headquarters in California. The company is a main player in the market for computer processors, which are used in desktop and mobile computers. At the moment Intel is directing its focus on IoT applications, as a response to the expected decline of the processor business and increasing market saturation of the PC market, as well as the shift towards mobile computing. Thus, Intel perceives a need to change its business model to find a favorable position to profit from the emergence of the IoT. On the global scale, Intel foresees a dramatic growth of connected devices from 15 billion to 200 billion until the year 2020 (Intel 2016). In parallel to the market of personal computers, Intel anticipates a decline in demand of powerful processors which are commonly used in network servers. Within the new IoT paradigm, large numbers of network servers with high performing processors are replaced by centralized cloud computing, for which demand for data storage is high but relatively less processor capacity is needed. Such *clouds* usually consist of large numbers of PCs with cheap standard technology that run Linux as the operating system, a free and open source-based technology.

Another process causing a decline in high-powered processors is the increased use of lightweight mobile devices. Intel anticipates an increased demand for processors with lower processing capacity and less energy consumption that will be needed to drive the large amount of distributed devices and sensors. Intel plans to capitalize on upcoming IoT-related opportunities by developing new energy efficient processors which are better suited to the requirements of the IoT, and software-based solutions to increase productivity and security. In general, the move towards the IoT will also increase the demand for sophisticated software, for example, in the field of security where Intel has developed specific competences. Examples of areas where Intel sees opportunities for enhancing productivity are conference systems, automated maintenance of mobile devices, technologies to improve manufacturing efficiency, and driver assistance systems.

Industrial Platform and Ecosystems

The value and promise of the IoT rest essentially on the possibility to collect and aggregate data, and then analyze them for different purposes to find ways to monetize the value which resides in the data. In the upstream part of the value chain which is part of Intel's framework, data from third parties are gathered. It is mainly in the downstream part of the IoT value chain where Intel sees ways to connect with internal partners as part of an ecosystem. In Intel's IoT framework, Intel itself is at the center by maintaining control, with external partners involved in a selective manner. Due to its central position in the microprocessor industry, Intel collaborates with a significant number of external partners. The major emphasis of Intel's platform building efforts seems to rest on new forms of collaboration with larger industrial players, although Intel also takes an interest in developing new start-ups with promising business models. Being a major technology company with a history of production of microprocessors, Intel has an interest to develop technologies for lightweight microprocessors to support the future IoT architecture. The focus of value creation is gradually shifting from hardware to software production. As functionality moves from hardware into software, the latter will increasingly become more important. Similar to Siemens, Intel seeks to incorporate other major firms into their new digital platform. For example, Intel works closely together with Siemens in the area of security-related software. Although Intel provides interfaces for collaboration with smaller SMEs and entrepreneurial start-ups, these initiatives do not seem to take first priority. However, it can be expected that smaller firms will at least indirectly profit from Intel's innovation in microprocessor chip design.

6. Huawei Technologies CO., LTD

General Characteristics

Huawei describes itself as a "leading global information and communications technology (ICT) solutions provider" (Huawei 2016). Huawei's core business is to be a supplier to telecom carriers and other network infrastructure firms in the sector. The Chinese firm claims to have built over 1,500 networks connecting a large part of the world population. From being a supplier of telecommunication equipment, Huawei has moved into the sector for mobile telecommunication handsets and aims to become a major supplier for IoT solutions by providing cloud computing services along with related services and products. To develop the industrial platforms, Huawei supports an annual developer conference, supports open source projects, and runs a so-called "Business Solution Alliance" to develop local/global partner networks to adapt and promote its technologies. Huawei claims that currently, they have developed more than 600 partner companies worldwide. Huawei runs a number of business start-up incubators in China, but also in other countries, such as Poland.

Industrial Platform and Ecosystems

In around 2010, coming from producing networking and telecommunications equipment, Huawei made the strategic decision to expand its activities from telecom equipment manufacturing into enterprise IT and consumer-oriented sectors. Huawei speaks of a "new digital world where every new business becomes digital business." Huawei predicts that digitalization will impact two thirds of the global economy in a fundamental way. Huawei envisions digitally enabled products and services which are connected to an underlying platform providing universal connectivity.

As a company, Huawei is in the process of transforming into a structure which Sany (2016) describes as an "L-Shape": on the vertical axis, Huawei runs a digital business corresponding to and emerging from Huawei's present market position as a supplier of networking solutions. On the horizontal axis, Huawei provides a digital backbone which serves as a platform for complementary systems. Substantial parts of Huawei's platform construct will consist of open source technologies as a viable alternative to commercial platforms. Huawei is contributing to the open source community with source code and other resources. What Huawei receives in return is up-to-date technical know-how.[4] The strategic intent of Huawei's industrial platform is not to provide specific products or services, but to be enabled to quickly identify an upcoming opportunity for an innovation (technological and/or business model) through the collaboration with the open source community. Then, the innovation will be promoted through the company's own cloud based infrastructure and be distributed worldwide through a network of partners.

7. Ericsson AB

General Characteristics

Ericsson (Telefonaktiebolaget L. M. Ericsson) is a multinational telecom equipment provider based in Sweden. The company has a global market share of about 35% in 2G, 3G and 4G technologies. Ericsson is heavily investing in development of 5th (5G) in order to prepare for the expected decline of demand in 4G technology as the technology reaches maturity phase, mobile data technology. Among Ericsson's most valuable assets is its base of intellectual property and related patents. Ericsson's intellectual assets are related to the field of technologies that are central links telecommunication networks. The company specializes in provision of information and communications technologies, related software and infrastructure for fixed and mobile broadband technologies, video technologies, etc. In addition, Ericsson licenses out technologies which are implemented in mobile devices. Ericsson states that it is a net receiver of royalties from licensing intellectual properties. Ericsson's two main areas of activity are "Radio, Core and Transmission," and related services. These central elements form the base for technologies in the areas of cloud computing and related operating systems, TV and media streaming, as well as other related products and services. As a network equipment producer for data connectivity, Ericsson's business has been transformed from being an equipment provider for voice transmission networks shifting towards a growing emphasis on mobile data transmission serving all major regions in the world. Ericsson focuses on mobile data network development, production, deployment and related services. While the main part of Ericsson's turnover is still based on hardware, the share of software and service based business is increasing, providing the company with more profitable margins. Technology is gradually moving from the current IPv4 standard with a limited number of available address spaces, and shifting towards the new IPv6 standard, which allows for addressing a virtually unlimited number of remotely connected devices. As a result, there will be a need for supporting network traffic generated by a very large number of devices, which includes the remote provision of energy for low-powered devices that are not connected to the energy grid.

Industrial Platform and Ecosystems

Ericsson runs a number of incubator projects. For example, in the so called "garage," young start-up entrepreneurs can receive support to develop new ideas and to create first working prototypes in a structured way. Apart from Kista in Sweden, Ericsson has launched a similar initiative in Hungary. Ericsson growth is driven by an increasing volume of data that is transferred in telecommunication networks. However, Ericson is aware that the company is not yet positioned to fully exploit future possibilities. In particular, there is no technology available yet to tap and analyze in real-time mode the enormous amounts of data that Ericsson's network routers are currently handling. If it were possible to extract valuable information residing in the data flow, it could be possible to identify communication patterns to predict upcoming developments. This information could be very valuable and be used as a basis for promising future business models. As technological and business opportunities are manifold, Ericsson needs to build up external partners to fully exploit the potential. Ericsson states that it has not yet constructed an industrial platform, but is working towards this direction by systematically building up a network of SMEs and start-ups as satellites to provide third party support to its technologies.

The other example of how large companies utilize their resources in order to attract SMEs for collaboration is "Ericsson Garage"(Ericsson 2016). This platform is provided as a network facilitator for SMEs and start-ups. Ericsson is also collaborating with other entities like the Swedish communication company Telia. Collaboration agreements exist with Intel, as well as with one of Sweden's largest incubators, "The Innovation GrowHouse Stockholm AB." This incubator supports entrepreneurs and innovators by providing them with commercial opportunities and access to customers, including the provision of venture capital.

Future opportunities for collaboration within the industrial platform reside in this area, since valuable information can be extracted from network flow data. As we pointed out above, for analysis of large amounts of data, sophisticated software is needed to extract information which can be used for trend analysis and other statistical methods. Ericsson supports open source communities which focus on software for complex real-time data analysis. Although such software already exists, it is not of much use: Ericsson compares the situation to a spreadsheet program without any data: it can only become useful if it is fed with purposeful information. There is a need for partners participating in the industrial platform for development of sophisticated algorithms so that extracted information can be made useful for new business opportunities. By developing complementary technologies, smaller partner companies could develop ways to connect and build on Eriksson´s technology by connecting to central communication nodes for channeling data and voice traffic.

8. Analysis

The major underlying driver causing the shift towards the IoT is the move of product and service functionalities from hardware towards software. The shift of product functionality from hardware to software and related services creates business opportunities to upgrade the existing value chain. The use of digital technologies has the potential to dramatically increase efficiency and create opportunities for rapid upscaling by taking advantage of network effects. IoT facilitates potential opportunities for new business models, which can have disruptive effects on existing industrial sectors. IoT based ecosystems create opportunities in two ways.

Potential or existing platform leaders seek ways to build or consolidate dominating positions in their respective industries. Even with sufficient resources it is a challenge to become a platform leader. Successful platform leadership implies the ability to involve third parties who are able to contribute different types of tangible and intangible variations of resources.

For an industrial platform to succeed, it is imperative to attract third-party firms who can bring in new technological and organizational innovation. In analogy to an ecosystem, a large and varied pool of genes will strengthen an ecosystem and improve resiliency. Therefore, existing or aspiring platform leaders need to attract third parties to become part of the system in analogy to ecosystems.

Secondly, platforms are attractive for smaller firms who are in general more resource-constrained than large firms that dominate an industrial sector. Industrial platforms create multiple opportunities for small and larger firms. For the latter, partnership offers the opportunity to overcome resource scarcity by gaining access to technology, information about market opportunity and social network contacts. By linking to industrial platforms, smaller firms which seek to secure growth but suffer from limited resources find new opportunities for future growth. Small firms profit from access to diverse types of resources. In consequence, association with industrial platforms generates opportunities for new approaches for creating value.

With regards to the firms analyzed in this article, all companies which we discussed here (Siemens, Intel, Huawei and Ericsson) have potential and show ambitions to take leadership in industrial platforms. Intel has already a tradition of platform leadership together with Microsoft in the sector for personal computing. Intel also provides high-power processors for IT network servers. As these areas are reaching maturity in the product life cycle, Intel needs to develop new opportunities. Faced by the decline of demand in high-performance but energy-hungry computer processors, Intel can profit from the shift to distributed computing by prioritizing low-powered but energy-efficient computer chips which are more adequate for distributed computing. Intel is also adapting to the increasing importance of software, where it can leverage specific competences, for example, in the field of security software. This fits well into the overarching paradigm of the IoT, where many devices are expected to be connected. In terms of industrial platforms Intel is about to profit from IoT advantages in multiple areas, basically everywhere their specific products can fit: smart cities, health care, energy management and generation, traffic management and so on. In all areas, Intel provides opportunities for potential platform partners, such as providing programming start-up kits which appeal to students and potential start-ups and supporting engineering consulting firms who can integrate Intel solutions into their own offering.

Coming from industrial engineering with competences in building up and managing large scale industrial installations, Siemens also aims to implement their solutions in a larger variety of industrial sectors. Similarly to Intel, Siemens moves into software-based solutions. However, their approach is different: profiting from competences in industrial installations and engineering, Siemens develops competences in digital-enabled design and management by creating digital mirror images of existing physical installations. The ability to "edit" physical production and infrastructure allows for fast development in the form of a digital mirror image, for prototyping, testing, training and so on. To subsume, both Siemens and Intel offer entry to potential network partners and new opportunities for existing platform partners. Intel provides the opportunity to build new products and services building on their platform. In turn, Siemens's existing and potential partners are typically engineering companies and consultants who implement Siemens's technology for their own clients. In this sense, Siemens´s IoT-related approach is to upgrade and extend existing value chains with digital functionality. The focus is rather on enhancing and strengthening existing business models. Intel's approach in turn is to provide a technological platform, both in terms of hardware and software, on which potential platform partners can build their own products and services, including creation of new business models. The examples of Siemens and Intel illustrate two different approaches with respect to the IoT. Siemens´s focus is mainly oriented towards the upgrading of existing supply chains. Thus the approach is towards gradual innovation. Intel's approach is to create hardware and software components to recreate the value chain. Thus, the approach corresponds to the notion of radical innovation. Both approaches cater to different sorts of potential third-party network partners. Siemens tends to aim for established partners to enhance established business models, thus following a gradual approach. Intel's predominant approach is to find potential partners who enter the market with business models that have a potential for disruption. Both Huawei and Ericsson have a background of providing network equipment that forms the nodes of telecommunication networks. They have in common that they take significant market share in the industrial sector in which both compete. Apart from this similarity, however, the companies have quite different backgrounds. Being a Swedish company, Ericsson has its origins in a small developed economy. In turn, Huawei is based in China, a developing economy with a large population. The approaches chosen by the two firms are quite different in particular from the perspective of technological scope. Ericsson focuses on the opportunities that the company perceives, resulting from the massive data flows which Ericssons' network routers are handling. At the present time, it is basically not possible to analyze the flow of data which is passing through telecommunication network equipment because it is technically not possible to extract the full value of the data. Ericsson states that it might be possible to store data in a database and then run queries on the data ex post. But Ericsson describes this approach as "naïve," since the data is still too large in quantity and complex in quality to be fruitfully analyzed with current technologies. The benefit derived from real-time data analysis, which is one of the main promises of the IoT, would be lost if data cannot be processed in real time. Thus, there is a significant need for new technology development, which Ericsson wants to achieve by collaboration with SMEs and entrepreneurial start-ups. To create the necessary tools for data analysis, Ericsson contributes to and collaborates with the open source community in a number of projects. Development of these technologies have already born fruits in forms of new software, but what is still needed are varied and sophisticated software algorithms. Specific business models need to be created to extract value from the data flows. Thus, there is a need for potential partners who can use Ericsson's industrial platform to monetize the benefits deriving from the large amounts of raw data. Ericsson offers collaboration and participation within their ecosystem. The potential for new applications in different industrial sectors is substantial, but the technological scope is relatively narrow as solutions are focused on Ericsson network equipment technologies.

Huawei takes an approach which is different from Ericsson's. Not neglecting the focus on its core business and related technologies, similar to Ericsson's approach, Huawei aims to open up many other opportunities. Huawei's approach is to support the open source community, just as Ericsson does. Huawei aims to establish cloud-based computing capacities on a large scale. The promise for Huawei's potential partners within the industrial platform is to create an IT-based solution (software- and perhaps hardware-based) which can be implemented in the computing cloud. Once installed and implemented, in conjunction with potentially promising business models, new technologies can be tested and adapted while Huawei provides backup support. Once the technology has proven to be viable, Huawei can rapidly spawn out and deploy the solution (followed by corresponding business models) on a worldwide scale. This approach is not costly and is open to trial and error, but once a solution proves to be successful, it can be multiplied immediately on a large scale due to the flexibility of the cloud computing environment. This approach leaves the door open to new opportunities as they come up. For a continuous supply of promising ideas, Huawei fosters large numbers of developers, in particular in China. For example, one way of supporting developers who want to participate in Huawei's ecosystem and perhaps become entrepreneurs is to organize large conferences and other events. Developers with interesting ideas can then use Huawei's technological platform to develop new technologies and business models. In this way, Huawei can profit from the large number of interested individuals in its own home market to create an industrial platform and a corresponding ecosystem.

9. Discussion

The analysis of the data presented in the cases describing how industrial platforms undertake their collaboration with their partners allowed us to identify and describe several aspects of collaboration between SMEs and large companies on their platforms in terms of their innovation and entrepreneurial attempts in Nordic countries. Below these aspects will be elaborated.

Digitalization and Innovation are Backed up by EU and National Level Programs

SMEs are recognized as one of the sources for economic growth and employment in the EU. It is expected that SMEs will advance entrepreneurship and innovation, while being responsive to the market and enhancing technological development. Therefore, a number of EU and national level initiatives have been initiated in order to promote SMEs' development, internationalization and globalization, enabling them to compete in a global marketplace. These initiatives are aimed to raise digital skills, technical expertise and organizational competencies such as market knowledge. Beyond technical skills, strategic management skills, operation management skills and business-related skills are on the agenda (DI Digital 2016).

Drivers and Motivations for SMEs

SMEs foster digitalization and collaboration with large companies on the basis of platforms aiming at both more efficient internal processes and market expansion. Platforms provide SMEs with relevant skills and digital technologies.

Frequently, the collaboration between large companies and SMEs is complemented by engagement of universities and scientific institutions on behalf of governments with the aim to strengthen cooperation and technological advances. By joining the platform, companies are saving on costs and can shorten the new product development cycle and accelerate their new product access to global markets. SMEs are learning new skills and technologies to make operations and processes more effective and reduce the cost of operations. Platforms equip SMEs and start-ups with the opportunity to rapidly test new ideas and prototype new products. Additionally, SMEs are provided with training digitals skills initiatives, sponsored by EU and national schemes.

Drivers and Motivations for Large Companies: Digital Disruption

Digitalization is predicted to change not only how a single company operates, but the whole industry. The digital disruption may have catastrophic consequences for existing conventional business; that is why companies should take steps to prepare. By establishing platform-based collaboration, large companies have the capacity to detect a potential disrupter and avoid the potential risks of disrupting. Using resources and sharing future technologies with flexible and innovative SMEs, large companies solidify their position. Moreover, peer-to-peer-based collaboration is a good mechanism for learning and enhancing research and development activities.

Nordic Models of Innovation and Entrepreneurship

Innovation and entrepreneurship through collaboration on the basis of industrial platforms in Nordic countries are characterized both by a science- and technology-based innovation (STI) approach and a pragmatic approach: "doing, using, interacting" (DUI) (Cooke 2016). Large companies, SMEs, entrepreneurial start-ups and scientific organizations join in a common effort on the basis of one digital platform.

Nowadays, increasing digitalization reduces the differences between large companies and SMEs in terms of opportunities for innovation and internationalization. Digital platforms reconfigure relationships between stakeholders and serve as attractive platforms for collaboration.

Nordic countries are characterized by a large-scope support for innovation and entrepreneurships from state and regional organizations. Science park "NOVI," situated in Northern Jutland, Denmark, can be presented as one such example. NOVI is a science park, which has been established with the aim to create an innovative business environment, where along with networking opportunities, other benefits are offered, such as co-financing and professional consultancy advising on establishing new enterprise. The park is facilitated by BOREAN Innovation—one of several state-certified innovation environments. BOREAN, together with other incubator initiatives (Pre-Seed Innovation, Syddansk Teknologisk Innovation and CAPNOVA), has been initiated and approved by The Danish Agency for Science, Technology and Innovation under the Ministry of Higher Education and Science as a part of a program of development knowledge-based innovative companies (BOREAN 2017).

Political and cultural specifics play a significant role in Nordic innovative systems. Firstly, there is a high level of labor force egalitarianism and a strong support for welfare. Public spending is at a high level, and while there is criticism that numbers of people are misusing welfare benefits, a notable amount of resources is used on retraining and requalification of workers to acquire skills and competencies needed for joining the labor force. Secondly, "networking"—as a feature of Nordic social economy (Cooke 2016)—is considered to be the main feature for well-functioning innovation processes. Openness, trust, reciprocity, collaboration and interaction are the sources of entrepreneurial success in the Nordic economies. Thirdly, northern European policymaking supporting entrepreneurs can be considered radical, with great effort and tremendous public resources devoted to the issue.

The data and discussion above regarding conditions and trends of Nordic innovative systems allow us to make the suggestion that this system is well positioned for the future, taking advantage of ICT and IoT trends, and presents a potential growth for Europe.

Barriers and Challenges

The digital transformation of European industry leads to important changes in the industrial environment, and therefore upcoming risk needs to be predicted and potential main challenges and barriers for future digital transformation need to be outlined. First of all, digitalization of industry will make many jobs disappear. The new task will arise in front of policymakers and companies: How to retrain the workforce and determine which skills and competencies are needed to re-employ people? Secondly, there are no clear understandings and solutions for data privacy and data security for the upcoming new products and services. Therefore, protection of property rights and know-how needs to be reinforced; security risks need to be forecast and actions need to be taken to avoid these risks. The response to new demand for data management systems will lead to ongoing development of a common European standardization system. This brings attention to the foregoing discussion and negotiations between large companies, SMEs and governmental institutions regarding national and EU standards and regulations.

10. Conclusion

In this contribution, we have provided a profound description and discussion of four digital industrial platforms. Furthermore, we have discussed how four large firms create and contribute to lead industrial platforms as ecosystems to which SMEs and start-ups can connect. With increasing digitalization, opportunities for creating new types of platforms will increase. Periods of change create challenges for established companies, translating into upcoming opportunities for new entrants and entrepreneurial start-ups. The main contribution of this article is to point to variations in building up industrial platforms as ecosystems, as well as different types of collaboration between large companies and SMEs and start-ups in Northern Europe countries. The analysis of the data revealed that political and cultural specifics of these countries, such as high levels of public spending and a "networking" culture, play an influential role in creating entrepreneurial successes for SMEs and start-ups. This contribution has the following managerial implications: (1) By describing and discussing platforms, information is provided for managers to make a decision for potential collaboration; (2) discussion of drivers and motivations, as well as information regarding existing EU and National support, helps to develop future strategies for SMEs and start-ups. Further investigation is suggested with the aim to understand how platform association impacts firm behavior such as innovation and internationalization strategies.

Notes

1 For example, computer code which has been developed for the UNIX computer system, initiated by the Bell Laboratories after 1969, still lives on in modern computer systems such as Linux or Android. Apple has adapted NetBSD, which is derived from the UNIX systems, for its own operating system, MAC OS X.
2 For example, whatsapp.com challenges the telecoms industry by disrupting a business model that relies on charging voice calls by the minute, uber.com disrupts the global taxi industry, while airbnb.com challenges the existing hotel industry with a new business model.
3 Such databases are now referred to as a *cloud*.

4 Huawei claims to be a major contributor to projects like Spark, Docker, Hadoop, or the OPNFV Summit, a conference platform for open source developers and other supporters.

References

Baldwin, Carliss Y., and Kim B. Clark. 2000. *Design Rules: The Power of Modularity. Volume 1.* Cambridge, MA: MIT press.

BOREAN. 2017. "Borean Innovation." www.borean.dk/en/about-borean. Accessed December 14.

Christensen, Clayton M. 1997. *The Innovator's Dilemma: When New Technologies Cause Great Firms to Fail.* Boston, MA: Harvard Business School Press.

Cooke, Philip. 2016. "Nordic Innovation Models: Why Is Norway Different?" *Norsk Geografisk Tidsskrift-Norwegian Journal of Geography*: 70(3): 190–201.

DI Digital. 2016. "Digital skills for SMEs." http://digital.di.dk/SiteCollectionDocuments/Publikationer/DigitalskillsforSMEs.pdf. Accessed December 17.

Ericsson. 2016. "Ericsson Garage." www.ericsson.com/innovation/ericsson-garage. Accessed December 16.

Hendler, James, and Jennifer Golbeck. 2008. "Metcalfe's Law, Web 2.0, and the Semantic Web." *Web Semantics: Science, Services and Agents on the World Wide Web* 6(1): 14–20.

Huawei. 2016. "Huawei Annual Report 2015." www.huawei.com/en/about-huawei/annual-report/2015. Accessed March 24.

Intel. 2016. "From the Backroom to the Boardroom: It Propels Intel to Insight and Excellence." Technical Report. www.intel.com/content/dam/www/public/us/en/documents/best-practices/intel-it-annual-performance-report-2015-16-paper.pdf. Accessed September 17.

Katsamakas, Evangelos. 2014. "Value Network Competition and Information Technology." *Human Systems Management* 33(1–2): 7–17.

Sany, Peter. 2016. "L-Shaped Telcos in a Co-Opetitive World." *Huawei*. www.huawei.com/minisite/has2016/l-shaped-telcos-in-a-co-opetitive-world.html. Accessed May 28.

Schumpeter, Joseph. 1942/1975. "Creative Destruction." In *Capitalism, Socialism and Democracy*, 82–85. New York: Harper.

Siemens. 2016a. "Industry 4.0": Seven Facts to Know About the Future of Manufacturing." www.siemens.com/innovation/en/home/pictures-of-the-future/industry-and-automation/digtial-factory-trends-industrie-4-0.html. Accessed March 15.

Siemens. 2016b. "Innovation Strategy." www.siemens.com/global/en/home/company/innovation/innovation-strategy.html. Accessed December 17.

Weiser, Mark. 1993. "Ubiquitous Computing." *Computer* 10: 71–72.

7 The Role of Auditing in Banks' Risk Assessment of SMEs

A Literature Review and New Venues For Future Research

Giulia Giunti and Tobias Svanström

1. Introduction

The overarching aim of this chapter is to contribute to research on the development of SMEs in Sweden and internationally by focusing on the topic of banks' risk assessment, which is an essential step in the growth and survival of a small firm. Further, the role of auditing in this process is to provide assurance to external parties, such as investors and creditors, and thereby facilitate national and international funding which would lead to the internationalization of the SME in question.

More specifically, the purpose of the chapter is to review the literature on this topic. The review does two things. Firstly, it presents and discusses existing research on the provision of advisory services to SMEs by banks and auditors, the loan assessment process for SMEs, and the importance of audited financial information and auditors' assurance in this process. Secondly, it highlights future venues for research in the field of SMEs and auditing.

The chapter is structured as follows. The first section explains when and why SMEs both need and use support/advisory services and what the most common sources of support are for SMEs. The second section provides an overview of the loan assessment process for SMEs and discusses the different factors that loan officers need to take into account. The third section presents and discusses the role of financial information in general and provides an overview of research relating to the value of auditor assurance in the credit granting context. The chapter concludes by highlighting which research areas should be explored in the future.

2. SMES and Their Need For Support/Advisory Services

Business advisory services are provided by both certified auditors and external accountants in the SME environment and these services have developed considerably in recent decades (Carey and Tanewski 2016). This does not mean that advisory services are a new phenomenon in the SME environment, but simply that external accountants have continuously expanded the services they provide (Carey and Tanewski 2016). Traditionally, the services relate to tax returns, statutory audits and the provision of annual updates to the corporate regulator. The main focus of these "traditional services" is usually on the preparation or interpretation of financial information following existing standardized formats (i.e. GAAP and IFRS). As the business environment has developed, the services that are provided have become more multi-disciplinary (Fogarty *et al.* 2006, Greenwood *et al.* 2002). Nowadays, audit firms market themselves as complete providers of business advice.

In their study, Bohman and Boter (1979) show that small companies require the services of external accountants. It is also common that such contact with an agency opens up an effective channel that allows a small firm to have continuous access to external advisory services with regard to taxation and contact with the authorities (Bohman and Boter 1979). The results of the survey conducted by the Swedish National Board for Industrial and Technical Development (NUTEK) confirm this early research (NUTEK 2000), namely that 46 percent of companies with 1–19 employees and 21 percent of companies with 20–49 employees engage the services of an external agency. It is also important to state that newly established small firms manage their bookkeeping with the aid of external agencies to a greater extent than older and larger companies because over time a company acquires more competence in this area (NUTEK 2000).

Despite the predominance and economic significance of SMEs in modern economies, the empirical evidence of large-scale growth in terms of the magnitude and range of advisory services by accountants has been almost exclusively researched for listed public companies (Carey and Tanewski 2016). The literature on SMEs is relatively unanimous in finding that these companies mostly use the professional services of certified auditors and external accountants (e.g. Bennett and Robson 1999; Berry *et al.* 2006; Blackburn and Jarvis 2010; Collis and Jarvis 2002; Curran and Blackburn 1994; Deakins *et al.* 2001; Kirby *et al.* 1998; Svanström 2008). Blackburn and Jarvis (2010) further stress that "research should be more precise when reporting on the size and type of advice provided in the relationship between external accountants and SMEs." They also suggest that in the context of the changing role of the external accountant, this aspect should be given special attention in further research (Blackburn and Jarvis 2010).

The NUTEK survey showed that 87 percent of SMEs regularly employed the services of auditors and that only 5 percent had never had any professional contact with this category of external expertise (NUTEK 2000). This result can be partially explained by the fact that at the time the survey was performed, the legislation required companies to have their annual accounts audited by an external auditor. However, this audit requirement was abolished for SMEs in 2011.[1] Up to August 2013, 52 percent of the companies that were exempted from the audit requirement (and had been formed before 1st November 2010) opted out of such an audit (Marténg 2013, 24–25). Crucial to the choice of commissioning an audit or not is whether the benefits exceed the costs. It should also be stated that such an assessment is significantly different between companies within the heterogeneous group.

Langli (2015) studied the various consequences of the abolished statutory audit requirement in Norway by analyzing the entire population of opt-out companies and comparing them with the companies that remained under audit. One of the themes for his analysis was whether firms had fewer options for external financing, or could only access such financing on worse terms after choosing not to be audited. Assuming that (audited) accounting information is valuable to creditors when they decide whether or not to approve a loan and how to price a credit, this could be the case. Opting out of auditing would then increase the risk and lead to lenders protecting themselves by refusing loan applications more often or by charging a higher interest rate as a way of compensating for taking on more risk.

However, Langli (2015) found no indication that opt-out companies had problems obtaining external finance as a result of opting out. Interest rates did not increase, and opt-out companies did not see a rise in payment remarks or increased problems with accessing loans from banks they had no prior contact with. Based on the findings of this study, the financing effects of opting out of auditing in Norway are none or very minor.

The lack of in-house expertise creates a need for owner-managers to use external service providers to guide them in their business process (Bennett and Robson 2005; Blackburn and Jarvis 2010; Dyer and Ross 2008; Smeltzer *et al.* 1991). Dynamic environments, complexity and new regulations to comply with are some of the factors that increase the demand for external service providers (Blackburn *et al.* 2006). A large number of support providers in Sweden offer advisory services to small firms (NUTEK 2000).[2] Among these, auditors and banks are the most frequently used channels for SMEs requiring advisory services (Svanström 2008; NUTEK 2000). It follows that when SMEs come in contact with banks and their lending officers, they are not only provided with a loan assessment, but also with support and advice (NUTEK 2000). Thus, the important role that banks and auditors play in the development of SMEs highlights the importance of knowledge about the loan assessment process.

3. SMES and the Process of Loan Assessment

As in other western countries, borrowing from banks is the most common source of external financing for SMEs in Sweden (Berggren 2002; Winborg and Landström 2001). However, SMEs generally find it difficult to obtain bank loans (Binks *et al.* 1992; Walker 1989). According to Sjögren and Zackrisson (2005), Sweden has a bank-oriented and relationship-based financial system in which banks play an important role in the financing of firms. Further, in Sweden, the individual lending officer is an important factor in the credit decision process. Bruns (2001) argues that compared to customer credit, business credit is a more manual and individual process in

Swedish banks. A bank's decision is a combination of the individual manger's analysis and the bank's formal decision-making system. Depending on the amount of money and risk involved, it is not uncommon for a final decision to be made higher up in the bank's hierarchy. Concerning the lending officer's credit decision-making with regard to SMEs, it would seem that banks place the strongest emphasis on the tangible accounting figures that SMEs present. Further, the general risk-taking inclination of the SME interacts with its financial position and the eventual collateral that is provided (Bruns and Fletcher 2008).

The supply of bank credit to SMEs differs from that to larger businesses (Armstrong *et al.* 2013). The differences can be grouped into three main aspects: (1) SMEs are riskier investments, in that they are often relatively new, have less collateral and a small market share, (2) SMEs are no longer required to report, which implies less information transparency and availability and (3) the collateral and/or assets used to secure the loans are often less liquid (Armstrong *et al.* 2013). When it comes to the second aspect of less information transparency and availability, privately held firms lack access to important financial instruments, such as issuing new public stock (Bruns and Fletcher 2008). Further, as owner-managed firms are less transparent, this information asymmetry can be used opportunistically by the borrower, which means that external financers such as banks may feel less inclined to invest in the business (Fiet 1995). In such cases, it is vital that banks properly evaluate the credit risk of a borrower.

The lending officer does not know ex-ante how likely an SME is to repay a loan and interest. Asymmetric information can lead to the well-known adverse selection problem, which in turn could manifest itself in opportunistic behavior and moral hazard (Stiglitz and Weiss 1981). Furthermore, although the owner-manager may reveal all the formal information that he or she has access to, this information may be incomplete or erroneous. Overall, two types of errors need to be considered in loan assessment. Type I errors rise when a loan officer denies a loan that has the potential to be paid back with the planned interests, implying a net loss for the bank. Type II errors occur if a loan is approved but is not repaid, resulting in a credit loss for the bank. Earlier studies suggest that loan officers tend to focus almost exclusively on reducing Type II errors due to bank regulations (i.e. Basel Accords) and the fact that this kind of error is detectable and directly traceable to the lending officer (Deakins and Hussain 1994a and 1994b; Wahlström 2009). The focus on the avoidance of Type II errors has also been confirmed by later studies on loan assessment for SMEs (e.g. Armstrong *et al.* 2013; Nilsson and Öhman 2012).

The information provided in a loan application can be divided into two categories: hard and soft (Nilsson and Öhman 2012). Hard information is quantitative in nature, while soft is qualitative. A large research stream argues that quantitative information, such as financial statements, collateral and cash flow forecasts, is the most important type for loan officers (e.g. Berry and Robertson 2006; Liberti and Milan 2009; Nilsson and Öhman

2012). However, a parallel line of research claims that relationship banking which relies on soft information and a tight bond between the SME and the bank is more likely to result in a successful application (e.g. Baas and Schrooten 2006; McMahon 1998). Here, the firm and the bank enter into a long-term relationship that ensures the firm's access to credit and the bank's access to information about the firm (e.g. Allen *et al.* 1991; Boot 2000). It is considered that soft information can enhance the nature of the business idea, the personal skills of the owner/manager and the conditions of the market (Mason and Stark 2004; Udell 2008).

However, this is contradicted by empirical evidence. On the one hand, Petersen and Rajan (1995) suggest that loan interest rates decline with relationship lending. On the other hand, Sharpe (1997) shows that relationship banking is more profitable (lower interest rates) for SMEs in the long term. In a theoretical paper, Baas and Schrooten (2006) suggest a model that shows that a lack of reliable information can lead to comparably high interest rates, even if a long-term relationship between borrower and bank exists.

Further, in an attempt to provide evidence of the relationship between personal commitment and the allocation of small business credit, Avery *et al.* (1998) reveals that personal commitment is an important aspect of the loan assessment process of SMEs. It also appears to function as a substitute for business collateral, at least for lines of credit (Avery *et al.* 1998). The results are based on the responses to two surveys conducted between 1987 and 1995.[3]

Against this background, it is reasonable to conclude that the lending mechanisms and characteristics of SMEs differ from those of larger listed companies. It is also clear that the relationship with the bank is important, even though this is not always tangible in terms of lower interest rates. At the same time, hard information is a predominant source of knowledge for loan officers in that it is relevant, correct and trustworthy.

In sum, bank loans are crucial for many SMEs. Alongside personal interviews, accounting information is an important source of information and influences a bank's credit decisions (Berry *et al.* 1993; Berry and Robertson 2006). Svensson (2003) reveals that in Sweden institutional creditors typically collect annual assessments of the creditworthiness of SMEs. Banks' credit decisions are primarily based on a company's profitability, financial stability, liquidity and collateral (Berry *et al.* 1993). A major problem associated with lending decisions to SMEs is the lack of sufficient equity capital and adequate profits (Hutchinson and McKillop 1992). Credible financial information is therefore important for creditors to monitor a company's performance.

4. The Value of Financial Information and Auditor Assurance

As presented in the previous section, loan officers rely heavily on financial information when assessing the credit risk of SMEs, because it allows capital providers to evaluate the return of different investment opportunities. In order for this financial information to serve as a valuable basis for valuation, it needs to be accurate and reliable (Beyer *et al.* 2010). Audited financial reports are expected to provide security for external parties such as shareholders, customers, public authorities, suppliers, and creditors. Therefore, one of the potential advantages of having an audit is easier access to credit and lower interest rates, since audited financial statements provide the bank with a higher level of assurance. Put simply, the bank will charge a rate of interest that is determined by three factors (Arens *et al.* 2014, 26): 1) risk-free interest rate, 2) business risk for the customer, and 3) information risk. Although the quality of financial statements and audit assurances has no effect on the risk-free interest rate or business risk, it may have a significant impact on the information risk.

The methodologies that are used to study the value of financial statement verification in the context of SMEs' access to credit and cost of debt vary. However, it should also be noted that the total number of studies on this is relatively limited. The most prominent example is the study conducted by Blackwell *et al.* (1998) in which the authors analyzed 212 revolving credit agreements of private or closely held firms and compared them to the loan files of six banks. The study revealed that, *ceteris paribus*, firms that are audited pay significantly lower interest rates than non-audited firms.

A second and slightly more common line of research concerns the impact of financial statement verification on the access to credit and the cost of debt (Allee and Yohn 2009; Cano and Alegria 2012; Hope *et al.* 2011; Kim *et al.* 2011; Lennox and Pitman 2011; Minnis 2011). Allee and Yohn (2009) document that the risk of a loan application being rejected decreases if the company has audited financial statements. Additionally, they determine the factors associated with the sophistication of financial statements. More specifically, they look at whether the financial information is compiled, reviewed, and/or audited by a professional accountant and whether the firm produces accrual-based financial statements. Finally, the potential benefits experienced by firms producing financial statements, having audited financial statements, and having accrual-based financial statements are studied. Allee and Yohn (2009) find that firms with audited financial statements have greater access to credit and that firms with accrual-based financial statements have a lower cost of credit.

Hope *et al.* (2011) provide evidence that firms presenting financial statements that have been reviewed by an external auditor experience significantly fewer problems in gaining access to external finance. The study considers a sample of firms across 68 countries and conducts a country-level analysis of the impact of the strengths/weaknesses of creditor rights on the effect of audited information. The results show that in countries with weaker creditors' rights, the value of auditing in facilitating access to credit is even more pronounced.

Kim *et al.* (2011) use a large sample of privately held Korean companies that are not required to have an external audit and examine the informational value of voluntary audits of financial statements in relation to the cost of debt. They find that private companies with an external audit pay a significantly lower interest rate on their debt than private companies without an audit.

Minnis (2011) examines how the corroboration of financial statements influences debt pricing in the context of privately held U.S. firms. The author finds that audited firms have a significantly lower cost of debt, and that accruals from audited financial statements are better predictors of future cash flows than unaudited financial statements. Together, the results indicate that audited financial statements are more informative and that this influences lenders' decisions.

Lennox and Pittman (2011) focus on the impact of the signaling effect of voluntarily choosing to be audited. The authors exploit the situation in the U.K., where voluntary audits have replaced mandatory audits for private companies. They analyze whether mandatory audits make it more difficult to know which types of company voluntarily choose to be audited and which do not. They focus on companies that are audited under both regimes in order to control for the assurance benefits of auditing and isolate the role that signaling plays. They find that these companies are characterized by improvements in their credit ratings, because they send a positive signal by submitting to an audit when this is no longer legally required. On the other hand, companies that cease to be audited suffer downgrades in their ratings, because avoiding an audit sends a negative signal and removes its assurance value.

Cano and Alegria (2012) investigate whether loan officers take auditor selection into account in the formation of the cost of debt in the Spanish context. The results show that private companies obtain a lower cost of debt when they are audited by a large audit firm, or so-called "Big N." This result indicates that loan officers may consider which type of auditor is hired for their loan decisions.

A final line of research consists of experimental or survey studies that investigate how lending officers use financial information and value audited figures (e.g. Gul 1987; Gul 1989; Wright and Davidson 2000). However, this research stream consists of older studies and confirms the need for new experimental or survey studies on these subjects. Gul (1987) conducts an experiment in order to investigate the lending officers' perceptions of risk. Further, he investigates the type of additional financial information that is required when reports receive a "subject to" audit qualification. The author finds that lending officers' risk perceptions and their need for additional information increase as a result of a "subject to" audit qualification. In a later study, Gul (1989) surveys a group of volunteer lending officers in New Zealand to test a series of hypotheses regarding how different factors (e.g. the presence of an audit committee, the client's financial condition, the provision of management advisory services, the size of the audit firm and competition) affect lending officers' perceptions of auditor independence. The

Table 7.1 Research on the Value of Auditing in Credit Granting

	Purpose	Data	Method	Results
Panel A				
Blackwell et al. 1998	Providing empirical evidence on the economic value of services provided by auditors in terms of reduced interest rates and credit agreements.	212 revolving credit agreements at the end of 1988 involving private firms. Six banks from two different holding companies gave access to their loan files. (Archival)	Multivariate regressions analyzing the relation between interest rates and the degree of auditor association with the financial statements provided.	*Ceteris paribus*, audited firms pay significantly lower interest rates than non-audited firms.
Panel B				
Allee and Yohn 2009	Examining the potential benefits afforded by firms producing financial statements, having audited financial statements, and having accrual-based financial statements.	Data from 4,240 firms representing 6.3 million of profit, nonfinancial, non-farm, non-subsidiary small businesses in the United States with fewer than 500 employees. (Archival)	Stratified sample design as well as the multiple imputations for missing values.	Firms with audited financial statements benefit in the form of greater access to credit and firms with accrual-based financial statements benefit in the form of a lower cost of credit.
Kim et al. 2011	Finding empirical evidence on the value of an external audit per se using a large sample of private Korean companies.	Sample of private Korean companies over the 16-year period of 1987–2002, which includes 1997, the year in which the Asian (and Korean) financial crisis took place. (Archival)	Assessing the interest rate differentials between private companies with voluntary audits and those with no audit. Investigating whether voluntary audits by Big 4 auditors are associated with lower borrowing costs than those by non–Big 4 auditors	Private companies with voluntary audits pay significantly lower interest rates on their debt than do private companies with no audit.

Minnis 2011	Examining how verification of financial statements influences debt pricing.	The data is supplied by Sageworks, Inc., a company that collects private firm data and develops financial analysis tools, primarily for accounting firms and banks. (Archival)	Regression analysis	Audited firms have a significantly lower cost of debt, and lenders place more weight on audited financial information in setting the interest rate.
Cano and Alegria 2012	Comparing the value of audit quality, proxied by the selection of a big N auditor, to the external claimholders of private and public companies. Analyzing if banks and lenders take into account auditor selection in the formation of the cost of debt.	The data for private companies is from the Sistema de Analisis de Balances Ibericos (SABI) database (Iberian Balances Analysis System database). The financial data for companies reported in SABI are gathered from the Spanish Mercantile Registry. The data for the public companies have been obtained from the Comision Nacional del Mercado de Valores (CNMV) database. (Archival)	Regression analysis	Only private companies obtain a lower cost of debt when they are audited by a high-quality auditor.
Hope et al. 2011	Testing three hypotheses: (1) financial reporting credibility reduces financing constraints; (2) the ability of financial reporting credibility to reduce financing constraints increases when a controlling owner exists; (3) the joint	Data from the World Bank's Enterprise Surveys (Archival + Survey)	Regression analysis	For the sample of firms across 68 countries, firms with greater financial reporting credibility experience significantly lower perceived problems in gaining access to external finance. Further, the impact of financial credibility

(Continued)

Table 7.1 (Continued)

	Purpose	Data	Method	Results
	role (interaction effect) of financial reporting credibility and a controlling owner in reducing financing constraints in countries with weaker creditor rights.			in reducing financing constraints in the presence of a controlling owner is more pronounced in countries with weaker creditor rights.
Lennox and Pittman 2011	Analyzing whether imposing audits takes away valuable information about the types of companies that would voluntarily choose to be audited.	The sample is from the Financial Analysis Made Easy (FAME) database. (Archival)	They isolate the role signaling plays by focusing on companies that are audited under both regimes. These companies experience no change in audit assurance, although they can now reveal for the first time their desire to be audited.	Companies attract upgrades to their credit ratings because they send a positive signal by submitting to an audit when this is no longer legally required.

Panel C

	Purpose	Data	Method	Results
Gul 1987	Investigating the perceptions that lending officers in Singapore have of risk and the additional information required when a client's financial reports receive a "subject to" audit qualification.	31 lending officers in Singapore (Experiment)	Experiment, Repeated-measurements ANOVA design	The lending officers' perceptions of risk and their demand for additional information required both increase as a result of a "subject to" audit qualification.

Gul 1989	Investigating factors affecting lending officers' perception of audit independence.	A group of 64 volunteer lending officers in New Zealand (Experiment)	Survey, regressions.	MAS and competition had positive effects on auditor independence while size had a negative effect.
Wright and Davidson (2000)	Investigating whether the level of attestation affects the credibility perceived by lending officers, or contrariwise, the relative amount of ambiguity of the financial statements presented by management.	75 lending officers from a number of different banks (Experiment)	Between subjects experiment, ANOVA	Results indicate that only tolerance for ambiguity significantly affects the risk-assessment judgment.

results show that advisory services and competition have positive effects on auditor independence, while size has a negative effect.

Wright and Davidson (2000) conducted an experiment with creditors in six financial institutions in Canada. The authors assumed that the financial information used in a commercial loan application could either be fully audited or reviewed or prepared only by management. The underlying argument of the paper is that the level of attestation should affect the perceived credibility, or contrariwise, the relative amount of ambiguity of the financial statements presented by management. Consequently, tolerance for ambiguity should have an impact on how ambiguity is handled. They tested this argument in an experiment by manipulating the level of attestation in a between-subjects experiment with commercial loan officers. The results indicated that only tolerance for ambiguity significantly affected the risk-assessment judgment.

Collectively these results show that external audits have economic value and that companies should consider this when deciding whether or not to be audited. However, it is important to stress that the benefits of voluntarily choosing to be audited vary across firms. Furthermore, even though there is compelling evidence of the importance of audited financial information in the credit procedure, we still do not know how, when and to what extent this affects loan officers' processes for decision making. Research has so far neglected the perspective of creditors in the context of loan assessment for SMEs. Thus, there is a need to investigate how lending officers value auditing and other types of assurance services. It is important for SMEs to know how and whether audits matter when it comes to loan applications.

Table 7.1 on page 120 (Panel A, B and C) shows a summary of the studies presented in this section. Panel A presents the line of research with access to actual revolving credit agreements. Panel B summarizes the studies investigating the impact of financial statement verification on firms' cost of debt. Finally, Panel C summarizes the studies using experimental methods or surveys.

5. The Role of Audited Financial Information In Credit Granting Decisions: A Fruitful Venue for Future Research

This chapter has provided an overview of the relevant research on the multifaceted topic of credit granting and SMEs. This final section discusses fruitful venues for future research in two main areas.

The first area is the need to investigate and understand lending officers' use of financial information when assessing the credibility of SMEs and comparing it to auditors' (materiality) judgments. Materiality and risk are central concepts in the auditing process and form the basis for many auditors' judgments, even though they are often difficult to interpret. Further, materiality is applied differently in practice by audit firms and individual auditors (Carpenter *et al.* 1994; Estes and Reames 1988; Libby and Kinney

2000; Messier *et al.* 2005; Nelson *et al.* 2005). In the context of the financing of SMEs, important questions are: what is considered as a material amount in a credit evaluation (in different situations), are some individual accounts considered more important than others, and is there a lower tolerance for errors/misstatements? Previous research in this area is mostly based on experiments with university students as participants (Fisher 1990; Haka *et al.* 1986; Tuttle *et al.* 2002). The findings in this area may have implications for whether auditors do too much or too little (in relation to what users expect).

There is a general need to empirically explore the views of lending officers and auditors by means of semi-structured interviews, which is a way of gathering data that has been somewhat neglected in the literature. Important research questions that need to be addressed are: *What does the risk assessment process of creditors look like, and what type of (materiality) judgments are critical when evaluating SMEs? How do creditors' and auditors' perceptions differ concerning material amounts and accounts in the financial statements of SMEs? How do creditors value audits and alternative types of assurance services in the risk assessment process of SMEs?*

The second area relates to whether auditing is the most effective way of checking the reliability of content of SMEs' annual reports and financial information or whether there are alternative ways of doing this. The audit of the financial statement provides a high, although not absolute, level of assurance and should be conducted in accordance with the International Standards on Auditing (ISAs) regardless of firm size. There are alternatives to full audits, and these services are likely to evolve in a market in which auditing is voluntary. Internationally, a "review" is an established alternative service to full audits. Although the costs of a review are lower than the cost of a full audit, the downside is the lower level of assurance. Following the long tradition of statutory audits for all limited liability companies in Sweden, there is very little experience of audits alternatives. In other words, in the past banks could rely on audited financial information for all limited liability companies without exception and without any extra costs. The situation is now different with regard to small companies in that they still have to present annual reports, but do not need to be audited.

However, a recent phenomenon in the Swedish market is the existence of "disclosure assurance" (Sw. *bokslutsintyg*), which is usually issued by a certified accounting consultant (not an auditor) with a lower level of assurance relative to the audit. Existing research on the differences between an audit and a review is relatively old and based on studies in Anglo-Saxon countries (e.g. Johnson *et al.* 1983), which means that there is no clear guidance when it comes to Swedish creditors' preferences. As yet, no empirical studies have been conducted on how creditors value and distinguish between services with different levels of assurance in the context of SMEs.

Finally, bank loans are an important source for financing of SMEs and from that perspective, it is important for managers to gain a good understanding of how auditing and assurance services may affect both the possibility of getting a loan and the loan's conditions. Growth and internationalization of SMEs involve challenges and hindrances related to profitability (We and Beamish 2006) and require significant access to financing and relevant expertise in various areas. Thus, if managers are aware of what determines bankers' loan assessments and the potential role of accountants and auditors in this process, managers' decisions on the desirable level of assurance (and auditor choice) can become more relevant and accurate. To motivate SMEs in this regard, future research could devote more attention to how banks and auditors can assist managers in the growth and internationalization processes.

Notes

1 Companies exceeding two of the following size criteria are exempted from the statutory audit requirement: three employees, a balance sheet total of 1.5 million SEK (approx. 158,227 Euro) and a turnover of 3 million SEK (approx. 316,456 Euro). 1 Euro = 9.48 as of August 16, 2016.
2 The Nutek report (2000) presents the following list of support providers: Almi Business Partner, Nutek, Swedish Trade Council, Euro Info Centres, Chamber of Commerce, Local Employment Office, County Administrative Board, the municipality, universities, science parks, banks, auditors, legal advisors and business associations.
3 The primary data source is the National Survey of Small Business Finance (NSSBF), available for the years 1987 and 1993. The authors also use data from the Survey of Consumer Finances (SCF) for the years 1989, 1992 and 1995, which includes details about the finances of small business owners and whether or not they have made pledges of personal wealth in their business arrangements.

References

Allee, Kristian D., and Teri L. Yohn. 2009. "The Demand for Financial Statements in an Unregulated Environment: An Examination of the Production and Use of Financial Statements by Privately Held Small Businesses." *The Accounting Review* 84(1): 1–25.
Allen, Linda, Anthony Saunders, and Gregory F. Udell. 1991. "The Pricing of Retail Deposits: Concentration and Information." *Journal of Financial Intermediation* 1(4): 335–361.
Arens, Alvis A., Randal J. Elder, and Mark S. Beasley. 2014. *Auditing and Assurance Services: An Integrated Approach* (5th Global ed.). London, UK: Pearson Education.
Armstrong, Angus, Philip. E. Davis, Iana Liadze, and Cinzia Rienzo. 2013. "An Assessment of Bank Lending to UK SMEs in the Wake of the Crisis." *R40 National Institute Economic Review* 225, August: 39–51.
Avery, Robert B., Raphael W. Bostic, and Katherine A. Samolyk. 1998. "The Role of Personal Wealth in Small Business Finance." *Journal of Banking & Finance* 22: 1019–1061.
Baas, Timo, and Mechtild Schrooten. 2006. "Relationship Banking and SMEs: A Theoretical Analysis." *Small Business Economics* 27(2/3): 127–137.

Bennett, Robert J., and Paul. J.A. Robson. 1999. "The Use of External Business Advice by SMEs in Britain." *Enterprise and Regional Development* 11: 155–180.

Bennett, Robert J., and Paul. J.A. Robson. 2005. "The Advisor-SME Client Relationship: Impact, Satisfaction and Commitment." *Small Business Economics* 25(3): 255–271.

Berggren, Björn. 2002. "The Demand of Stakeholder Competence and Capital for the Development of SMEs." PhD diss., Uppsala University.

Berry, Aidan J., Sue Faulkner, Mark Hughes, and Robin Jarvis. 1993. "Financial information: The banker and the small business." *British Accounting Review* 25: 131–150.

Berry, Aidan J., and Jenny Robertson. 2006. "Overseas Bankers in the UK and Their Use of Information for Making Lending Decisions: Changes from 1985." *The British Accounting Review* 38(2): 175–191.

Berry, Anthony J., Robert Sweeting, and Jitsu Goto. 2006. "The Effect of Business Advisers on the Performance of SMEs." *Journal of Small Business and Enterprise Development* 13(1): 33–47.

Beyer, Anne., Daniel A. Cohen, Thomas Z. Lys, and Beverly R. Walther. 2010. "The Financial Reporting Environment: Review of the Recent Literature." *Journal of Accounting and Economics* 50: 296–343.

Binks, Martin R., Christine T. Ennew, and G.V. Reed. 1992. "Information Asymmetries and the Provision of Finance to Small Firms." *International Small Business Journal* 11(1): 35–46.

Blackburn, Robert, William Eadson, Rock Lefebvre, and Philip Gans. 2006. "SMEs, Regulations and the Role of Accountant." ACCA.

Blackburn, Robert, and Robin Jarvis. 2010. "The Role of Small and Medium Practices in Providing Business Support to Small- and Medium-sized Enterprises." Information paper April 2010, International Federation of Accountants. www.ifac.org/sites/default/files/publications/files/the-role-of-small-and-mediu.pdf.

Blackwell, David, Thomas Noland, and Drew Winters. 1998. "The Value of Auditor Assurance: Evidence from Loan Pricing." *Journal of Accounting Research* 36: 57–70.

Bohman, Håkan, Håkan Boter, and Ulrika Liljeberg. 1979. "Hur styrs mindre och medelstora företag?" Småföretagsprojekten, 99–0182460–5 Stockholm Arbetslivscentrum Libris.

Boot, Arnoud W.A. 2000. "Relationship Banking: What Do We know?" *Journal of Financial Intermediation* 9(1): 7–25.

Bruns, Volker. 2001. "A Dual Perspective on the Credit Process Between Banks and Growing Privately Held Firms." PhD diss., Jönköping International Business School.

Bruns, Volker, and Margaret Fletcher. 2008. "Banks' Risk Assessment of Swedish SMEs." *Venture Capital* 10(2): 171–194.

Cano, Manuel Rodrigez, and Sanchez Santiago Alegria. 2012. "The Value of Audit Quality in Public and Private Companies: Evidence from Spain." *Journal of Management and Governance* 16: 683–706.

Carey, Peter, and George Tanewsky. 2016. "The Provision of Business Advice to SMEs by External Accountants." *Managerial Auditing Journal* 31(3): 290–313.

Carpenter, Brian W., Mark W. Dirsmith, and Parveen P. Gupta. 1994. "Materiality Judgments and Audit Firm Culture: Social Behavioral and Political Perspectives." *Accounting, Organizations and Society* 19(4): 355–380.

Collis, Jill and Robin Jarvis. 2002. "Financial Information and the Management of Small Private Companies," *Journal of Small Business and Enterprise Development* 9(2): 100–110.

Curran, James, and Robert Blackburn. 1994. *Small Firms and Local Economic Networks: The Death of the Local Economy?* London: Paul Chapman/Sage.

Deakins, David, and Guhlum Hussain. 1994a. "Financial Information, the Banker and the Small Business: A Comment." *British Accounting Review* 26(1): 323–335.

Deakins, David, and Guhlum Hussain. 1994b. "Risk Assessment with Asymmetric Information." *The International Journal of Bank Marketing* 12(1): 24–31.

Deakins, David, Alana Morrison, and Laura Galloway. 2002. "Evolution, Financial Management and Learning in Small Firms." *Journal of Small Business and Enterprise Development* 9(1): 7–16.

Deakins, D., D. Logan, and L. Steele. 2001. "The Financial Management of the Small Enterprise." ACCA Research Report No. 64, London: The Association of Chartered Certified Accountants, Certified Accountants Educational Trust.

Dyer, Linda M., and Christopher A. Ross. 2008. "Seeking Advice in a Dynamic and Complex Business Environment: Impact on the Success of Small Firms." *Journal of Developmental Entrepreneurship* 13(2): 133–149.

Estes, Ralph and D.D. Reames. 1988. "Effects of Personal Characteristics on Materiality Decisions: A Multivariate Analysis." *Accounting and Business Research* 18(72): 291–296.

Fiet, James O. 1995. "Risk Avoidance Strategies in Venture Capital Markets." *Journal of Management Studies* 324(4): 551–575.

Fisher, Marguerite H. 1990. "The Effects of Reporting Auditor Materiality Levels Publicly, Privately, or not at All in an Experimental Setting." *Auditing: A Journal of Practice & Theory* 9 (Supplement): 184–223.

Fogarty, Timothy J., Vaughan S. Radcliffe, and David R. Campbell. 2006. "Accountancy Before the Fall: The AICPA Vision Project and Related Professional Enterprises." *Accounting, Organizations and Society* 31(1): 1–25.

Greenwood, Royston, Roy Suddaby, and C.R. (Bob) Hinings. 2002. "Theorizing Change: The Role of Professional Associations in the Transformation of Institutional Fields." *Academy of Management Journal* 45(1): 58–80.

Gul, Ferdinand A. 1987. "The Effects of Uncertainty Reporting on Lending Officers' Perceptions of Risk and Additional Information Required." *Abacus* 23(2): 172–181.

Gul, Ferdinand A. 1989. "Bankers' Perceptions of Factors Affecting Auditor Independence." *Accounting, Auditing & Accountability Journal* 2(3): 40–50.

Haka, Susan, Lauren Friedman, and Virginia M. Jones. 1986. "Functional Fixation and Interference Theory: A Theoretical and Empirical Investigation." *The Accounting Review* 61(3): 455–447.

Hope, Ole-Kristian, Wayne Thomas, and Dushyantkumar Vyas. 2011. "Financial Credibility, Ownership, and Financing Constraints in Private Firms." *Journal of International Business Studies* 42: 935–957.

Hutchinson, R.W, and Donald G. McKillop. 1992. "Bank and Small to Medium Size Business Financing in the United Kingdom: Some General Issues." *National Westminister Bank Quarterly Review*, February: 84–95.

Johnson, Douglas A., Kurt Pany, and Richard White. 1983. "Audit Reports and the Loan Decision: Actions and Perceptions." *Auditing: A Journal of Theory and Practice* 2(2): 38–51.

Kim, Jeong-Bon, Dan A. Simunic, Michael T. Stein, and Cheong H. Yi. 2011. "Voluntary Audits and the Cost of Debt Capital for Privately Held Firms: Korean Evidence." *Contemporary Accounting Research* 28(2): 585–615.

Kirby, D.A, Najak, B., and Greene, F. 1998. *Accounting for growth: Ways accountants can add value to small business.* The Research Board, ICAEW, London.

Langli, John Christian. 2015. "Evaluering av unntak fra revisjonsplikt for små aksjeselskaper." Handelshøyskolen BI, 625.

Lennox, Clive S., and Jeffrey A. Pittman. 2011. "Voluntary Audits Versus Mandatory Audits." *The Accounting Review* 86(5): 1655–1678.

Libby, Robert, and William R. Jr. Kinney. 2000. "Does Mandated Audit Communication Reduce Opportunistic Corrections to Manage Earnings to Forecast?" *The Accounting Review* 75(4): 383–404.

Liberti, Jose M., and Atif R. Milan. 2009. "Estimating the Effect of Hierarchies on Information Use." *Review of Financial Studies* 22(10): 4057–4090.

Lu, Jane W., and Paul W. Beamish. 2006. "Estimating SME Internationalization and Performance: Growth vs. Profitability." *Journal of International Entrepreneurship* 4(1): 27–48.

Marténg, Charlotta. 2013. "Tuff Match för Revisorn att behålla kunderna—Men Jönköping och Norrbotten går mot strömmen." *Balans* nr 9–2013: 24–25.

Mason, Colin, and Matthew Stark. 2004. "What Do Investors Look for in a Business Plan? A Comparison of the Investment Criteria of Bankers, Venture Capitalists and Business Angels." *International Small Business Journal* 22(3): 227–248.

McMahon, Richard G.P. 1998. "Putting SME Financial Reporting Into Theoretical and Practical Perspective." *Small Enterprise Research* 6(2): 80–88.

Messier, William F., Nonna Martinov-Bennie, and Aasmund Eilifsen. 2005. "A Review and Integration of Empirical Research on Materiality: Two Decades Later." *Auditing: A Journal of Practice & Theory* 24(2): 153–187.

Minnis, Michael. 2011. "The Value of Financial Statement Verification in Debt Financing: Evidence from Private Firms." *Journal of Accounting Research* 49: 457–506.

Nelson, Mark W., Steven D. Smith, and Zoe-Vonna Palmrose. 2005. "The Effect of Quantitative Materiality Approach on Auditors' Adjustments Decisions." *The Accounting Review* 80(3): 897–920.

Nilsson, Anders, and Peter Öhman. 2012. "Better Safe than Sorry: Defensive Loan Assessment Behavior in a Changing Bank Environment." *Qualitative Research in Accounting & Management* 9(2): 146–167.

NUTEK. 2000. *Support Services to SMEs: Analysis of Support Services in the Context of the Working Group on the Visibility and Quality of Support Services.* Stockholm: Närings- och teknikutvecklingsverket.

Petersen, Mitchell A., and Raghuram G. Rajan. 1995. "The Effect of Credit Market Competition on Lending Relationships." *The Quarterly Journal of Economics* 110(2): 407–443.

Svanström, Tobias. 2008. "Revision och Rådgivning. Efterfrågan, Kvalitet och Oberoende." ["Auditing and Advisory Services; Demand, Quality and Independence."] PhD diss., Umeå University.

Sharpe, Steven A. 1997. "The Effects of Consumer Switching Costs on Prices: A Theory and Its Application to the Bank Deposit Market." *Review of Industrial Organization* 12(1): 79–94.

Sjögren, Hans, and Marcus Zackrisson. 2005. "The Search for Competent Capital: Financing of High Technology Small Firms in Sweden and USA." *Venture Capital: An International Journal of Entrepreneurial Finance* 7(1): 75–97.

Smeltzer, Larry R., Berry L. Van Hook, and Roger W. Hutt. 1991. "Analysis of the Use of Advisors as Information Sources in Venture Startups." *Journal of Small Business Management* 29(3): 10–20.

Stiglitz, Joseph E., and Andrew Weiss. 1981. "Credit Rationing in Markets with Imperfect Information." *The American Economic Review* 71(3): 393–410.

Svensson, Birgitta. 2003. "Redovisningsinformation och bedömning av små och medelstora företags kreditvärdighet." PhD diss., Uppsala University.

Tuttle, Brad, Maribeth Coller, and David R. Plumlee. 2002. "The Effect of Misstatements on Decisions of Financial Statement Users: An Experimental Investigation Auditor Materiality Thresholds." *Auditing: A Journal of Practice & Theory* 21(1): 11–27.

Udell, Gregory F. 2008. "What's in a Relationship? The Case of Commercial Lending." *Business Horizons* 51(2): 93–103.

Wahlström, Gunnar. 2009. "Risk Management Versus Operational Action: Basel II in a Swedish Context." *Management Accounting Research* 20(1): 53–68.

Walker, David A. 1989. "Financing the Small Firm." *Small Business Economics* 1: 285–296.

Winborg, Joakim and Hans Landström. 2001. "Financial Bootstrapping in Small Businesses: Examining Small Business Managers' Source Acquisition Behaviours." *Journal of Business Venturing* 16, 235–254.

Wright, Michael E., and Ronald A. Davidson. 2000. "The Effect of Auditor Attestation and Tolerance for Ambiguity on Commercial Lending Decisions." *Auditing: A Journal of Practice & Theory* 19(2): 67–81.

Part III

Industrial Networks Development

8 Nascent Entrepreneurial Teams Managing In Networks

Mobilization, Utilization and Saturation

Thommie Burström, Jussi Harri and Timothy Wilson

1. Introduction

This book takes a dynamic perspective in studying the collaborative efforts of SMEs. With such interest in mind it is inevitable that one thinks of the development of networks as an essential element in collaboration. This chapter therefore describes the dynamics of network development in the very early phases of venture creation. It is a matter of fact that minimal attention has been paid to understanding how networks change over time in business networks (Gedajlovic *et al.* 2013). Yet, research has also established that changes in business networks are necessary (Slotte-Kock and Covielly 2010).

In this regard, Shipilov (2012) suggested that network relationships are traditionally described as simple and non-problematic. Nevertheless, network relationships do contain complexity. Shipilov (2012) illustrates that researchers typically ignore that each stage of organizational development carries unique challenges and that contents of interactions tend to change. Additionally, it has been proposed that studies should be concerned with the early phases of entrepreneurship when entrepreneurs are less experienced and their companies less mature (Kamm and Nurick 1993). These "early" phases have been described as 1) the emergence of the firm, 2) the newly established firm and 3) the mature firm. In this regard, start-up firm activities relate to the first two phases of venture development. It follows that there is a need for more studies illustrating how entrepreneurial networks change as evolving resource needs change over time. This chapter is therefore based on the research question: How do networks evolve in the early phases of venture creation?

The study derives from entrepreneurial team networks in Finland, and the connection to network literature acknowledges the dynamics of networks. A team perspective is used and an objective is to build a dynamic conceptual model illustrating how the networks of novice entrepreneurial teams change over time. By taking this approach this chapter contributes to existing literature by extending process based network theory (cf. Reynold and Miller 1992). This study presumes that the conditions for building and maintaining networks are "contingent upon spatial proximity and the presence of social settings that enable individuals from diverse circles to meet and interact" (Stam 2010, 628). That is, the character of fundamental networking elements is context dependent. Furthermore, an evolutionary perspective on networks is taken, assuming that entrepreneurial teams are *not* managing networks; they are rather managing *in* networks (Freytag and Ritter 2005). Networks are also seen as fluid systems in which relationships can/should change in content and strength (Slotte-Kock and Coviello 2010). Finally, it is accepted that changes in networks can take place through a punctuated equilibrium model where more or less goal-oriented behavior follows a discontinuous change pattern (Kilduff and Tsai 2003, 115). Interpretation draws from Reynolds and Miller (1992) who describe the first phase of venture development as *conceptualization*; secondary adaption follows Evald *et al.* (2006) who define the second phase of venture creation as a firm being *newly founded*, and the third phase is defined as *newly established*.

2. Background

This subsection discusses venture processes and the dynamics related to such processes.

Processes

This study extends research that focuses on understanding the dynamics of processes related to establishing a venture (cf Bygrave and Hofer 1991; Gartner 1985; Shane and Venkatamaran 2000). Particular interest is associated with the process of developing business-related networks (Greve and Salaff 2003) in the very early phases of venture creation. Participants in this field of research have found it plausible to describe the process of network development as going through different phases (cf Katz and Gartner 1988; Kamm and Nurick 1993). For example, Slotte-Kock and Coviello (2010, 50) describe a dynamic process of firm development from birth to exit where organizations and networks are proposed to co-develop. Network development would in that case move through a life-cycle characterized by (1) variation (new ties added more or less intentionally), (2) selection (ties that are contributing something) and (3) retention (embeddedness and transformation of ties). Expressively, it is suggested that these phases are interwoven and involve unexpected events. Finding inspiration from Slotte-Kock and Coviello, who studied mature firms, this book chapter is instead dedicated to studying network development in early phases of venture creation since the content provided by various network contacts not can be taken as a given (cf Batjargal 2003).

A Dynamic Approach to Ties

The relationship among actors in a network is commonly referred to as ties. Researchers traditionally discuss the role of strong and weak ties following Granovetter (1973, 1361), who seminally defined the strength of a tie as "a (probably linear) combination of the amount of time, the emotional intensity, the intimacy (mutual confiding), and the reciprocal services which characterize the tie." Nevertheless, other studies follow a more dynamic network approach and even suggest that the number of ties, or the strength of ties, are of remote interest; it is rather what entrepreneurs can access from ties that is of significant importance—the content. Nonetheless, changes in networks are common and network membership is not infinite; actually members come and go (Greve and Salaff 2003), consequently there are reasons to believe that content provision would also change in the networks.

The Content of Ties

From the preceding it follows that the content provided by various network contacts is of central interest for any entrepreneur. It can also be understood that there is an intimate relationship between processes, network contacts and content. This relationship will be further discussed below. First, it is reasonable to assume that the creation of a content providing network has a starting point. Drawing on Greve and Salaff (2003), the starting point herein is referred to as "mobilization." That is, during the mobilization process entrepreneurial teams create the necessary contacts needed to initiate the business venture. These content-providing contacts tend to be very few and come naturally in the form of friends, family members and work-related ties (Elfring and Hulsink 2003; Jonsson 2015; Renzulli et al. 2000). Still, this study proposes that mobilization is not a "one-time" occasion. Reasonably, all network contacts cannot be identified at once, and the need for different kinds of content cannot be understood at once. Rather network contacts should be mobilized at various points of time, and different kinds of content would also be received at various points of time. This view of network development seems plausible since characteristically, as teams go about venture creation, they commonly find that resources that are required cannot be provided by pre-existing contacts (cf Ruef et al. 2003; Semrau and Werner 2014). The reason behind the mismatch between venture needs and content provided by network contacts can be explained through the ongoing changes of the business plan (Delmar et al. 2003; Zahra et al. 2009). Thus, there is a need to search for resource complementarities (Vissa 2011). Consequently, some researchers (Newbert and Tornikoski 2012; Stam et al. 2014) emphasize that the content of a tie should be addressed. Newbert et al. (2013) suggest that resources should be acquired from numerous sources, and it is also proposed that entrepreneurs should tailor their network to the task at hand

(Vissa 2011). That is, the contents achieved from various contacts are of a different kind and of a different value to nascent[1] entrepreneurs (Anderson *et al.* 2010). Some of the content may be of an emotional value, while some may be of a more tangible value (Newbert and Tornikoski 2012).

The question is of course how nascent entrepreneurs should go about getting access to various content-rich contacts through meaningful network activities (cf. Gronum *et al.* 2012). Stam (2010) finds that event participation is beneficial for network development. Other researchers illustrate the importance of being a member of a business network as, for example, the Lions, Rotary or Chamber of Commerce in order to develop social capital (Davidsson and Honig 2003). Additionally, Sullivan and Ford (2014) propose that it would be expected that different experts are added to the network in early phases of network development when entrepreneurs conceive their first service or product offerings. Finally, Watson (2007) proposes that it can be beneficial to network for advice in the early phases of venture creation; in the later stages of venture development, such networking instead can hamper growth of the firm. Still, whatever measures are being taken, nascent entrepreneurial teams are expected to change both the business plan and strategic intentions more than once. Thus, network activities will change as well. Nevertheless, in-depth studies of such changes are lacking. More specifically, it is proposed that dynamic network development will follow some kind of an *s*-curve development (Jacobsson and Wilson 2014). Apart from knowing that processes start with mobilization activities, little is known of what the rest of such development processes would look like.

Finally, the knowledge about the evolution of entrepreneurial networks is limited and has at large focused on individual networks; there is actually a need to learn more about team network development (Arenius and Laitinen 2011; Jack *et al.* 2008). This need becomes even more emphatic when considering that the lion's share of entrepreneurial team studies has neglected the issue of network development in earlier phases of venture creation (Cooney 2005). See Cooney (2005) and Harper (2008) for a good summary of team entrepreneurship research. Consequently in this research, the nascent entrepreneurial team was used as an analytical unit for studying network development in early phases of venture creation.

3. Method

This study was carried out in Finland in 2015. The sample consisted of seven case companies and 23 respondents in total. An abductive approach (Orton 1997) was applied as a research approach, and a qualitative method (Hoang and Antoncic 2003) was used in analysis. A purposive selection method (cf Patton 2015) was used when deciding on the sample of firms. That is, companies in the sample shared three criteria (1) it was the first experience for entrepreneurs of starting a venture (2) respondents were also the founders of the firm (3) companies were not active for more than five years. It turned out that all of the respondents were younger than 35 years. On average, firms were 3.7 years old and represented the clothing, furniture, internet secondhand retailing, mobile games (2), software development and textile design sectors.

This research captured the process of venture development through documenting a retrospective story told by the respondents. Team-based interviews, which lasted at least an hour (average ~ 1.22 hr.), were used as the main data collection method, and at least two respondents were present for each firm. This method is considered one of the best ways of understanding why humans take certain actions. The strength of the group interview is that it helps in distinguishing between shared and variable opinions. As regards this, the researcher needs to create an environment supporting a healthy discussion climate. In our case, as recommended by Kreuger and Casey (2014), the interviewer took a moderating role, nurturing the discussion with various questions. Thus, team members were allowed to give voice to contradictory opinions and openly discuss various interpretations of the networking processes that they tried to describe. Moreover, in order to capture process development from a retrospective perspective, visualizing techniques were also used. The teams were asked to create network maps in order to capture network evolution over time. Teams described the role and value of network contacts during each phase of development. Subsequently each network contact was also color coded so that growth patterns could be identified and discussed.

Nonetheless, Hines (2000) reports a risk of one team member dominating the discussion. No such domination was observed; rather team discussions were open and vivid; there is therefore small reason to believe that there was an impact of group think. We found that participants, as illustrated by Frey and Fontana (1991), normally "corrected" each other, thus creating a form of intersubjectivity.

Interviews were semi-structured (cf. Easterby-Smith *et al.* 2012) and were based on an interview guide that was divided into two basic themes: background and networking activities. Data analysis was performed in five steps. First the transcribed interviews and network illustrations were studied. Then, categories of network contacts were divided into three segments; first tier (close to the core business and having good insight into business activities), second tier (further from the core business and having limited insight into business activities) and third tier hubs (distant from the core business and having limited insight into business activities). Next, a cross-case analysis was performed in order to create consistent categories. This categorization guided us in defining actors in networks. As a second step, the type of benefit nascent entrepreneurs achieved from various network contacts was analyzed. The third step of analysis compared results with previous theory. In the fourth step, additional networking dimensions (mobilization, utilization, saturation) were developed in order to explain the dynamics of network development. In the fifth step findings were integrated in order to create a holistic picture of network development, whose synthesis is reported here.

4. Empirics

The nature of findings shows that different phases of venture development called for different needs of parallel organizational and network development. In short, the teams mobilized networks, utilized networks and experienced network saturation during the early phases of venture creation.

Phase 1: Conceptualization

Throughout the Conceptualization phase, mobilization and utilization of the network was typically performed in an iterative manner. The teams did not exactly know how to benefit from various contacts in the value network since the business model was vague; there was uncertainty in how to follow through on doing business; the market to serve was not identified; there was a lack of precision in activities, and the business offer was inexact. Teams were generally aiming at establishing a business plan robust enough to enable them to move forward to the next phase of development. In this phase of development, all teams said that the networks had to be developed further in order to reach the next level of venture creation; in regard to content, networks could not provide enough support to enable business leverage. The main task in this phase can therefore be described as defining the business and building absolutely necessary infrastructure. The most relevant role was played by the family who provided psychological support, advice and a helping hand. The teams described a situation with high levels of trust and generally claimed that easy access was the reason they turned to the family for help.

> "I believe that the family is the most important. They are there in every single way and encourage one to keep on fighting even when the whole thing feels very hard."
>
> (Co-founder and designer at furniture design shop)

Friends also played a central role during this phase. Their role was also complex, but less intense. Personal support such as encouragement was typically described as the most important type of support. Beside this, teams emphasized that friends often took on a role as feedback providers. All teams actively consulted their friendship circle before founding the company, e.g. getting advice about a new product or service before deciding to launch it to the market. Due to different kinds of expertise, friends could indicate whether there would be an interest in and a need for a product/ service on the market. This, in turn, affected the very foundation of the company. It was also common that friends could help with work tasks.

For about half of the teams, previous coworkers and mentors also brought support. They largely acted as network providers and advisers, providing business contacts and market intelligence. At this point in time other relationships played a lesser role. Only three teams said that they had used collaboration partners during this very early phase of venture creation. These partners had special industrial contacts that could be utilized by the teams. They also participated actively in product development activities, and helped in marketing the firms. Two of the companies also had contact with producers. This type of contact mainly fulfilled one role, namely product supplier. The content in ties with customers could purely be described as money.

Finally, another prominent role was played by the university contacts. All seven teams said that the university had an important role during the first phase, which was to function as a resource provider, e.g. with networks, advice, work tools and work spaces. These resources were especially used during the first phase when the teams had not yet acquired their own business tools and work spaces. Four of the teams identified Fairs & Events as important. These teams were aware of the networking possibilities during such occasions. Thus, although not having a business plan or products to offer, these teams still found it valuable to attend. The teams described the value of participation as identifying potential retailers, investors and customers. They could also start making a name for themselves, creating awareness about the firm-to-be, and gaining knowledge about how business was conducted in the industry.

Phase 2: Newly Founded

At this point in development a basic version of the business model was developed, the team was determined to follow through in doing business; the market to serve was to some extent identified, there was still a lack of precision in business activities but the business offer was at large developed and more distinct. When entering the phase of Newly Founded, network roles and value output in some cases remained the same, but there were also some significant changes in terms of role performance; value output and new contacts were added to the network. In this phase, team activities changed from thinking about, and planning business activities, to actually performing business activities such as making the first sales. There was therefore also a need to create a functional chain of logistics. The network also had to be renewed in order to fit the more complex task environment. This meant a new phase of mobilization of network contacts, but also new ways of utilizing network contacts.

Relationships with the family still played an important role when it came to personal support, but the advising role was reduced. Instead families typically took the role as resource providers and in several cases also functioned as a workforce. Family members were typically happy to help the teams when it came to smaller services e.g. transportation, relocation assistance and renovation work without charging the teams for these services. It was also possible to use family venues for storage and office activities. In a similar manner the role of friends also changed, it actually grew bigger. One observation is that as the friendship circle were much larger than the family; thus, teams also could get access to a bigger variety of resources from friends. One team, for example, made use of a friend being a good photographer.

> "All models we use are taken form the friendship circle. Several friends also offered their help if there was anything that we needed. One friend made e.g. a video about our pre-launch evening, totally free of charge, which was like a big deal for us at that time and the video then turned out to be very useful. There have been a lot of smaller things too. If we e.g. need help during an event there is always a bunch of friends lined up to help us. Even if it is just about pouring some bubbly at the events this help has been very important for us".
>
> (Co-Founder of internet second hand shop)

Just as in the case with families, friends helped out with smaller services such as transportation, relocation assistance and renovation work without charging the teams for these services. But friends also often acted as active marketers of the company. All teams specifically mentioned the important role that the friends had when it came to word-of-mouth marketing and creating visibility for the company. Beside this marketing role, several of the teams also received their first customers through friends.

The role of previous workmates also changed. Teams said that they still appreciated advice from previous workmates, who still provided the network with new contacts. However, the supporting role diminished and instead, the use of mentors became more common (5/7 teams). In general, at this stage of business development mentors took the advising role rather than family and friends. The teams stated that they especially appreciated the mentors' industrial specific knowledge. That knowledge helped the teams to fine-adjust their business models so that they with higher precision could focus their business activities.

In this phase both investors (2 teams) and accountants (4 teams) were added to the network. Both types of contacts brought new content to the teams. Investors were experienced and could provide large international networks; they also knew how to make entry into new markets. Investors played a role of providing financial support, giving business advice and offering new network contacts. Teams also suggested that the accountant, besides taking care of accounting activities, had been very helpful in advising the teams about everyday business activities, providing administrative efficiency and knowledge.

It was observed that the importance of some business relationships increased significantly as teams entered the Newly Founded phase. Six of the companies had at least one collaboration partner at this stage. These contacts were all mentioned as an important part of the value network and were collaboration partners of different kinds. Teams collaborated with both startup firms and already established firms. It was a matter of drawing benefits of any contact that could be established. Through this collaboration new contacts could be made, work processes could be performed more efficiently and the collaboration also worked as a marketing effort making the teams better known in the business community. The number of customers, producers and retailers in the networks also increased, but these relationships remained transaction based and simple in their character.

There were also other significant changes in the networks. Incubators took over the role as the main network hub and there was a slight decline in the role of the Universities. Six out of the seven teams in this stage participated in incubator activities, which provided resources, networks and advice. It was mostly common that the teams participated in an incubator directly after entering this phase of the entrepreneurial process. There was also a significant increase in the interaction with Civil service departments (5/7 teams and Fairs & Events (6/7 teams). The content in the ties with these contacts at large stayed the same. However, one team even went so far that they organized an international event of their own together with a large firm in the telecommunication industry.

"We realized that events are a great place to network. You can quickly schedule meetings with different people that you otherwise would never find under the same roof. We have participated several times e.g. in Slush [International technology- and startup event] and during our second year we already created a lot of new contacts. On Slush, 2011, we met our Russian investors. Through this event we were able to arrange a meeting with them, which then later led to our second round of financing. They on the other hand then helped us to gain a lot of contacts in Russia which had for us been some sort of a 'black box' until then".

(Co-founder and CTO at software co.)

At this phase of development, one of the teams also had joined an industry-specific association in order to build a broader value network, hopefully providing them with more industry-specific information and knowledge. They succeeded in their intention and the association played a role in advising, marketing and providing a network. Meanwhile, the content provided through Social media did not change during this phase. In contrast, the role of Media changed significantly. Most teams (6/7) mentioned media as having an important role during the second phase. It was a big difference to the first phase where only one company mentioned such support. The most important role for Media contacts was to function as a marketing tool, providing brand awareness.

Just as in the first phase of development, mobilization and utilization of the network was typically done in an iterative manner. Nevertheless, the teams had developed better capabilities of managing in networks. They could more intentionally search for contacts and draw benefits from various contacts in the value network. During this phase, teams generally aimed to establish more advanced business activities; thus, the network also in general was of a more professional character. Still, there was need for additional parallel organizational and network development before reaching the stage of being Newly Established.

Phase 3: Newly Established

At this point of development, the business model tended to be well developed; i.e., the teams were expanding their market, there was a clear understanding of what market to serve, business routines had been developed and the business offer was more precise. Thus, upon entering this phase, changes in networks continued, but with less intensity. In this phase teams' activities developed a character of fine-tuning. Most of the necessary business routines had been created and the focus was on increasing sales and expanding business. Consequently, the network was renewed in order to fit a somewhat more complex task environment, but with an aim to gain higher efficiency and effectiveness.

In this phase, the role of the family was significantly reduced. The need for resource provision and free labor was reduced because the teams had gained their own resources by practicing business. The family only provided personal support in the form of encouragement and thus created a sense of safety. The role of friends and workmates followed a similar change pattern. While the advising role diminished among family, friends and workmates, teams instead turned to mentors for advice. Most teams (5/7) utilized mentors in this phase of venture development since they possessed specific industrial knowledge and could be used as support when teams wanted to expand their business nationally or internationally. The role of investors also changed, usually to that of advisor. Significantly, three out of seven teams were in contact with investors; the remaining four teams believed that creating investor relationships would probably be the next step in the evolution of their value network. Whereas the role of the investors changed, the role of the accountants stayed the same. Accountants were not seen as a critical resource.

The roles of collaboration partners, customers, producers, retailers and banks remained the same as in the previous phase of venture development. The only significant difference was that the number of customers increased. However, the content in the tie stayed the same—money. But there were other more drastic changes in the networks. For example, the importance of incubators decreased significantly. Teams indicated that it was natural to let go of these ties. Three of the teams still utilized these ties but were also planning to finalize this relationship. Thus, the role for incubators remained the same, but the contact became of less value. The role of the universities also changed. They were reduced to the role of resource providers. The teams utilizing this resource also indicated that this contact would be almost terminated if no new collaborative needs appeared. The importance of the civil service department contact was also somewhat reduced. The teams described the support that they initially had from such contacts as very good for getting business started, but they had reached a point where they should care more about customers. However, teams were also keen to point out that this type of contact could become more critical in the future in case of the need for product or business innovation. All teams emphasized the need to continue participation in fairs and events. Nonetheless, they also pointed out that they were more careful in choosing events. Through experience they had learned what events were important for marketing purposes, knowledge, or meeting with collaboration partners or customers. In this phase yet another team established membership with a branch specific association. The roles of the associations were described as advisers, network providers and marketing resources. The two teams asserted that they could learn about events and visit fairs together with other members. The role of social media and other media increased to some extent in this phase. The reason for this increase was related to the connection with fairs and events. The teams had discovered that being seen through various media coverage during fairs and events was beneficial for business. Just as in previous phases, mobilization and utilization of the network was typically performed through iterations. However, the teams had developed better capabilities in managing within networks. They were more competent in evaluating contacts and they also terminated contacts. The network became more professional, and as a consequence the value output from various contacts changed, with the role of especially first-tier relationships changing significantly.

5. Analysis and Discussion

The research question in this study was "How do networks evolve in early phases of venture creation?" and this book chapter describes nascent entrepreneurial team network development during three phases of venture expansion: Conceptualization, Newly Founded, and Newly Established. More specifically, this chapter analyzes the initiation of and changes in early network development.

Conceptualization—Business Planning

Clearly, in the very early stages of venture development, nascent entrepreneurial teams mobilized and utilized a variety of network contacts. By the end of this phase, teams knew roughly in which direction they were heading and why. Still, both the organizations and their networks had to be further developed. This situation is here described as when teams reached a level of network saturation, the networks in their current configuration could not bring the teams to the next level. Thus, there had to be a new round of mobilization and utilization of network contacts.

Previous research suggests that nascent entrepreneurial teams commonly change both the business plan and strategic intentions more than once (Delmar *et al.* 2003; Zahara *et al.* 2009). This was also the case in this study. The business plan and the strategy had to be developed, and so did the network. Therefore, teams typically spent time thinking of/planning plausible future business activities. Consequently, as described by Vissa (2011), there was a need to create a better match between business activities and network resources. The needs of the teams were of a basic nature, and the tasks performed by the teams concerned mobilization and utilization of resources that matched the foundations of early strategic intentions. Vissa (2011, 138) describes this situation as teams searching for significant task complementaries. Research also suggests that there are typically few network contacts in early phases of venture creation (Elfring and Hulsink 2003; Jonsson 2015; Renzulli *et al.* 2000). This was also the case in this study. Only three network contacts were mobilized and utilized by all teams: family, friends and university. Still, overall, thirteen different network contacts were identified as content providers. Most contacts provided more than one type of content.

Significantly, four teams already in this early stage of venture creation mobilized and utilized fairs and events as hubs for networking. This observation is to some extent in line with Stam (2010), who studied the value of event participation for established firms. Nevertheless, this finding is somewhat surprising, since only one team had something to offer customers at this stage of venture creation. Furthermore, Newbert and Tornikoski (2012) propose that network resources may be of different types. Previous researchers have proposed that networking not only relates to gaining access to physical resources but also relates to acquiring skills and information, learning the trade of the business, finding employees, obtaining financial support and finding buyers (cf. Anderson *et al.* 2010; Jack *et al.* 2010). As suggested by Newbert and Tornikoski (2012) some of the content was of an emotional kind, while other content was of a strategic kind.

Newly Founded: Business Becomes Real

As newly founded teams moved on into the phase of ventures there was also an increase in the intensity of mobilizing and utilizing network contacts. As a consequence, networks grew larger and were also diversified. However, as will be discussed below, there were also already signs of de-mobilization of established network contacts, and consequently a change in content provision. These changes of the network relate to what Vissa (2011) describes as creating a match between offered resources and resource requirements. Contacts were added in first-, second- and third-tier business relationships. The most significant change among the first-tier business relationship was that investors and accountants came into play. However, mobilization and utilization of mentors and previous workmates also increased among teams. It is proposed that mobilization of these new contacts came for different reasons. The mobilization of accountants, especially, was in some sense necessary due to legal requirements and could be seen as mobilization of expertise (Sullivan and Ford 2014). The entrance of investors indicates that some ventures had matured to such a state that they attracted external interest. Thus, it should be understood that significant contacts can appear during any phase of early venture creation.

In this phase, more teams also mobilized and utilized collaboration partners, customers and producers. Also retailers and banks were mobilized. This could be expected since it is common that ventures try to acquire financial recourses (Anderson *et al.* 2010; Jack *et al.* 2010). Generally, what did change was that there was an overall increased mobilization and utilization of incubators, civil service departments, fairs and events and media. Thus, there was a change in terms of both network size and network diversity. More specifically, there was a transformation in the network in which private ties were exchanged for professional ties. This increase of professional ties is interpreted as being caused by a professionalization of the venture activities. This need for professionalization is what causes the dramatic change in the network when crossing the knowledge boundary between the phase of Conceptualization and the phase of being Newly Founded. As in the case when moving from the Conceptual phase to the Newly Founded phase, both the organizations and their networks had to be further developed. Thus there had to be a new round of mobilization and utilization of network contacts.

Newly Established: Running A Sustainable Business

At this stage of development each team had developed and tested the business plan and their respective business model. Thus, the teams had left a phase of attempting to do business and instead initiated a phase of venture development where they would run a sustainable business. This phase of venture development was therefore significantly different in character from the Conceptualization phase. Tasks were largely routine, and teams focused on mobilizing contacts in the customer base. The development of networks in this phase shows that the value of networks cannot be taken for granted (cf Batjargal 2003). For example, observations suggested that family, friend and previous workmate contacts were de-mobilized. It was as if parts of the network had reached a level of saturation. It does not mean that these contacts were not seen as important by the teams, but their value-adding capability had become circumscribed. This example of de-mobilization is in line with the findings of Vissa (2011) who indicated that network contacts rarely are optimal. On the other hand, in this phase of development teams focused on mobilizing customers and, when found necessary, other contacts in the supply chain (producers, retailers). Commonly, the content from these business relationships did not change. It seems that the benefit of utilizing these network actors in order to extend networks was very limited. Somewhat surprisingly, it was only collaboration partners that contributed to network extension. This situation indicates that teams had a transaction-based relationship with most contacts. Thus, even though ties with some of these actors would be considered strong, they failed to produce additional network contacts. Still, these network contacts were vital for creating a healthy financial flow in the firms.

There were also signs of de-mobilization of other contacts. This change concerned incubators and university contacts. Incubator contacts were in some cases terminated, and the university contact was only used for cost reduction purposes. Teams here showed evidence of being able to make assessments of what activities were more meaningful than others (cf. Gronum *et al.* 2012). The next stage of venture development for the nascent entrepreneurial teams in this study would be to enter the phase of being established on the market. In that phase of development, the characteristics of the firms would change again. In that phase they would leave the intensive work of mobilizing, utilizing networks and experiencing network saturation. As established firms they would instead perform networking activities as described by Slotte-Kock and Coviello (2010). That is, when firms are mature it could be expected that teams would make more informed decisions and also be more selective about the network connections that they make. Such luxury is rarely found among nascent entrepreneurial teams.

Managing in Networks

This study relates to the call from Cooney (2005) to connect the knowledge of team entrepreneurship with network development in early phases of venture creation. Typically, when nascent entrepreneurs are occupied in creating a product, they know very little of the market. Nevertheless, as a network gets mobilized and utilized, the level of experienced knowledge increases. As a consequence, the structure of the network will be clearer, and the roles of contacts in the network will be more understood. However, as nascent entrepreneurs enter a new process of venture development (Newly Founded), new knowledge gaps are experienced as they try to solve new problems. This means that some parts of the network will be changed and new content will be added in order to create task/role congruence. Subsequently, as the venture reaches the level of being Newly Established, new knowledge gaps will be revealed, and a new phase of network mobilization will begin. Thus, the network is developed in waves.

Figure 8.1 on page 147 illustrates the process of managing in networks. We see it as a sequential process where the individual steps are characterized by s curves (cf Jacobsson and Wilson 2014). During each phase of development, the network is managed through subprocesses of mobilization, utilization and saturation in each phase of development. Just as Kilduff and Tsai (2003) noted, this paper finds that changes in networks can take place through a punctuated equilibrium model where more or less goal-oriented behavior follows a discontinuous change pattern. In line with Slotte-Kock and Covielly (2010, 47) it is also found that entrepreneurial teams are enacting their environment through more or less purposeful activities.

A significant observation in the study is that although all teams agreed on the fact that networks are essential for business development, none of the firms utilized a strategic network plan. The lack of a network plan leads us to propose that networks unfold as businesses develop. That is, as nascent entrepreneurial teams realize the importance of networking, they also see multiple opportunities for networking, but they do not really know how to maneuver in the network. On an aggregated level, it is shown that each entrepreneurial phase is based on three complementary sub-processes: mobilization, utilization and saturation. These sub-processes are intimately related. Mobilization of one contact can be ongoing at the same time as some other contacts are being utilized; meanwhile teams might experience that a third contact has reached a level of saturation (no essential content). When the network at large is characterized by saturation, the current configuration cannot provide sufficient support to achieve leveraged firm performance. In such situations there is a need for network renewal. This renewal implies a change in relative positions and network configuration.

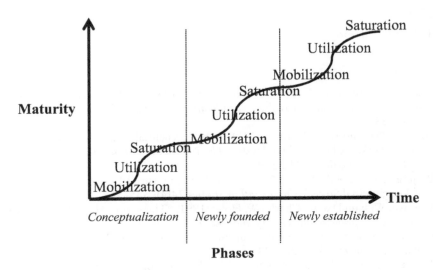

Figure 8.1 Managing in Networks

148   *Thommie Burström* et al.

6. Conclusions

This book takes a dynamic perspective on studying the collaborative efforts of SMEs. Responding to the call of Cooney (2005) this chapter in particular makes a contribution by providing explanations of how networks evolve in early phases of venture creation. This chapter more specifically poses the research question "How do networks evolve in early phases of venture creation?" Using seven nascent entrepreneurial teams as a base for the research, a three-phase process was studied: Conceptualization, Newly Founded and Newly Established. The development of the value network in each phase can be understood as an ongoing modification of three networking processes: network mobilization, network utilization and network saturation. That is, the value network changes character as business matures. It was found that the content provided by different contacts in the venture networks change as the venture develops. The study makes a connection to network literature that acknowledges the dynamics of networks (Cooney 2005; Hoang and Antoncic 2003; Shane and Venkatamaran 2000) and contributes an extension of process-based network theory (Evald *et al.* 2006; Reynold and Miller 1992). Limitations are acknowledged insofar as only new ventures in Finland were represented and a qualitative method was used. Consequently, generalizations are problematic. Still, the paper suggests an understanding of the early phases of venture creation. Nevertheless, venture creation by nascent entrepreneurial teams should be further studied, especially those teams that are offsprings of established firms. Reasonably, they would already have a large network; thus, the early phases of venture creation would look significantly different from the firms in this study.

Note

1 That is, entrepreneurs within the earliest phases of new venture formation.

References

Anderson, Alistair R., Sarah D. Dodd, and Sarah Jack. 2010. "Network Practices and Entrepreneurial Growth." *Scandinavian Journal of Management* 26(2): 121–133.

Arenius, Pia, and Katja Laitinen. 2011. "Entrepreneurial Teams and the Evolution of Networks: A Longitudinal Study." *The International Journal of Entrepreneurship and Innovation* 12(4): 239–247.

Batjargal, Bat. 2003. "Social Capital and Entrepreneurial Performance in Russia: A Longitudinal Study." *Organization Studies* 24(4): 535–556.

Bygrave, William D., and Charles W. Hofer. 1991. "Theorizing About Entrepreneurship." *Entrepreneurship Theory and Practice* 16(2): 13–22.

Cooney, Thomas. 2005. "What Is an Entrepreneurial Team?" *International Small Business Journal* 23(3): 226–235.

Davidsson, Per, and Benson Honig. 2003. "The Role of Social and Human Capital Among Nascent Entrepreneurs." *Journal of Business Venturing* 18(3): 301–331.

Delmar, Frédérik, Per Davidsson, and William B. Gartner. 2003. "Arriving at the High-Growth Firm." *Journal of Business Venturing* 18(2): 189–216.

Easterby-Smith, Mark, Richard Thorpe, and Paul R. Jackson. 2012. *Management Research*. Thousand Oaks, CA: Sage.

Elfring, Tom, and Willem Hulsink. 2003. "Networks in Entrepreneurship: The Case of High-Technology Firms." *Small Business Economics* 21(4): 409–422.

Evald, Majbrit R., Kim Klyver, and Susanne G. Svendsen. 2006. "The Changing Importance of the Strength of Ties Throughout the Entrepreneurial Process." *Journal of Enterprising Culture* 14(1): 1–26.

Frey, James J., and Andrea Fontana. 1991. "The Group Interview in Social Research." *The Social Science Journal* 28(2): 175–187.

Freytag, Per V., and Thomas Ritter. 2005. "Dynamics of Relationships and Networks—Creation, Maintenance and Destruction as Managerial Challenges." *Industrial Marketing Management* 34(7): 644–647.

Gartner, William B. 1985. "A Conceptual Framework for Describing the Phenomenon of New Venture Creation." *Academy of Management Review* 10(4): 696–706.

Gedajlovic, Eric, Benson Honig, Curt B. Moore, Tyge G. Payne, and Mike Wright. 2013. "Social Capital and Entrepreneurship: A Schema and Research Agenda." *Entrepreneurship Theory and Practice* 37(3): 455–478.

Granovetter, Mark S. 1973. "The Strength of Weak Ties." *American Journal of Sociology* 78: 1360–1380.

Greve Arent, and Janet W. Salaff. 2003. "Social Networks and Entrepreneurship." *Entrepreneurship Theory and Practice* 28(1): 1–22.

Gronum, Sarel, Martie-Louise Verreynne, and Tim Kastelle. 2012. "The Role of Networks in Small and Medium-Sized Enterprise Innovation and Firm Performance." *Journal of Small Business Management* 50(2): 257–282.

Harper, David A. 2008. "Towards a Theory of Entrepreneurial Teams." *Journal of Business Venturing* 23(6): 613–626.

Hines, Tony. 2000. "An Evaluation of Two Qualitative Methods (Focus Group Interviews and Cognitive Maps) for Conducting Research into Entrepreneurial Decision Making." *Qualitative Market Research: An International Journal* 3(1): 7–16.

Hoang, Ha, and Bostjan Antoncic. 2003. "Network-Based Research in Entrepreneurship: A Critical Review." *Journal of Business Venturing* 18(2): 165–187.

Jack, Sarah, Sarah D. Dodd, and Alistair, R. Anderson. 2008. "Change and the Development of Entrepreneurial Networks Over Time: A Processual Perspective." *Entrepreneurship and Regional Development* 20(2): 125–159.

Jack, Sarah, Susan Moult, Alistair R. Anderson, and Sarah D. Dodd. 2010. "An Entrepreneurial Network Evolving: Patterns of Change." *International Small Business Journal* 28(4): 315–337.

Jacobsson, Mattias, and Timothy L. Wilson. 2014. "Partnering Hierarchy of Needs." *Management Decision* 52(10): 1907–2017.

Jonsson, Sara. 2015. "Entrepreneurs' Network Evolution—The Relevance of Cognitive Social Capital." *International Journal of Entrepreneurial Behavior & Research* 21(2): 197–223.

Kamm, Judith B., and Aaron J. Nurick. 1993. "The Stages of Team Venture Formation: A Decision-Making Model." *Entrepreneurship Theory and Practice* 17: 17–17.

Katz, Jerome, and William B. Gartner. 1988. "Properties of Emerging Organizations." *Academy of Management Review* 13(3): 429–441.

Kilduff, Martin, and Wenpin Tsai. 2003 *Social Networks and Organizations.* Thousand Oaks, CA: Sage.

Kreuger, Richard A., and Mary Anne Casey. 2014. *Focus Groups: A Practical Guide for Applied Research.* New Delhi: Sage.

Newbert, Scott L., and Erno T. Tornikoski. 2012. "Supporter Networks and Network Growth: A Contingency Model of Organizational Emergence." *Small Business Economics* 39(1): 141–159.

Newbert, Scott L., Erno T. Tornikoski, and Narda R. Quigley. 2013. "Exploring the Evolution of Supporter Networks in the Creation of New Organizations." *Journal of Business Venturing* 28(2): 281–298.

Orton, James D. 1997. "From Inductive to Iterative Grounded Theory: Zipping the Gap Between Process Theory and Process Data." *Scandinavian Journal of Management* 13(4): 419–438.

Patton, Michael Q. 2015. *Qualitative Research and Evaluation Methods: Integrating Theory and Practice.* Beverley Hills, CA: Sage.

Renzulli, Linda A., Howard Aldrich, and James Moody. 2000. "Family Matters: Gender, Networks, and Entrepreneurial Outcomes." *Social Forces* 79(2): 523–546.

Reynolds, Paul, and Brenda Miller. 1992. "New Firm Gestation: Conception, Birth, and Implications for Research." *Journal of Business Venturing* 7(5): 405–417.

Ruef, Martin, Howard E. Aldrich, and Nancy M. Carter. 2003. "The Structure of Founding Teams: Homophily, Strong Ties, and Isolation Among US Entrepreneurs." *American Sociological Review* 68(2): 195–222.

Semrau, Torsten, and Arndt Werner. 2014. "How Exactly Do Network Relationships Pay Off? The Effects of Network Size and Relationship Quality on Access to Start-Up Resources." *Entrepreneurship Theory and Practice* 38(3): 501–525.

Shane, Scott, and Sankaran Venkataraman. 2000. "The Promise of Entrepreneurship as a Field of Research." *Academy of Management Review* 25(1): 217–226.

Shipilov, Andrew. 2012. "Strategic multiplexity." *Strategic Organization* 10(3): 215–222.

Stam, Wouter. 2010. "Industry Event Participation and Network Brokerage Among Entrepreneurial Ventures." *Journal of Management Studies* 47(4): 625–653.

Stam, Wouter, Souren Arzlanian, and Tom Elfring. 2014. "Social Capital of Entrepreneurs and Small Firm Performance: A Meta-Analysis of Contextual and Methodological Moderators." *Journal of Business Venturing* 29(1): 152–173.

Sullivan, Diane M., and Cameron M. Ford. 2014. "How Entrepreneurs Use Networks to Address Changing Resource Requirements During Early Venture Development." *Entrepreneurship Theory and Practice* 38(3): 551–574.

Susanna Slotte-Kock, and Nicole Coviello. 2010. "Entrepreneurship Research on Network Processes: A Review and Ways Forward." *Entrepreneurship Theory and Practice* 34(1): 31–57.

Vissa, Balagopal. 2011. "A Matching Theory of Entrepreneurs' Tie Formation Intentions and Initiation of Economic Exchange." *Academy of Management Journal* 54(1): 137–158.

Watson, John. 2007. "Modeling the Relationship Between Networking and Firm Performance." *Journal of Business Venturing* 22(6): 852–874.

Zahra, Shaker A., Igor Filatotchev, and Mike Wright. 2009. "How Do Threshold Firms Sustain Corporate Entrepreneurship? The Role of Boards and Absorptive Capacity." *Journal of Business Venturing* 24(3): 248–260.

9 SME-MNE Cooperation in a Regional Cluster

Zsuzsanna Vincze[1] and Peter Zettinig

1. Introduction

Industrial clusters are agglomerated configurations of companies and institutions with positive externalities of specialized labor, productive inputs and knowledge (Lorenzen 2005). They exist because they represent a relatively efficient or competitive form of economic organization. Maskell and Lorenzen (2004) suggested that each cluster, as a unique configuration, influences the organization of the market. According to Porter (1998), the cluster's key role is to foster entrepreneurship and economic competitiveness by means of concentrations of interconnected companies, specialized suppliers, service providers, training institutions, and support organizations formed around a technology or an end product within a geographically defined region.

In the literature in economic geography, international business in relation to innovation is replete with conceptual frameworks and models in which the primary focus is on the influencing factors and consequences of different types of cluster structures. The subject in these frameworks is either a core firm, or the wider cluster ecosystem and the local and regional society at large (Bell *et al.* 2009; Coenen *et al.* 2012; Ketels 2003; Krugman and Venables 1995; Malecki 1983; Maskell 2001; Peterson 2011). In terms of cluster change, economic geography literature tends to focus on the formation of clusters, which are seen as emergent. Firms find themselves benefiting from such agglomeration. Firms are, however, not only passive beneficiaries; they also make strategic decisions to become participants (Jenkins and Tallman 2010). In parallel, International Business (IB) researchers have been long interested in and have analyzed the organization of multinational enterprises (MNE) and their networks. These networks also consist of small and medium-sized firms (SME), some of which are entirely focused on their regional or local markets. Recent research in IB focuses on understanding how firm organization facilitates the exploitation of knowledge assets between locations (Dunning 2009; Beugelsdijk *et al.* 2010). However, the general critique of these IB approaches is that they often treat location synonymously with a country market without providing any real differentiation or nuanced examination of internal locational features (Beugelsdijk *et al.* 2010). Further, MNEs are studied in geographical space as independent units agglomerating in certain locations, treating the nature of interaction between places and "spaces" as black box.

Despite voluminous extant literature on clusters in economic geography and IB, the MNE's strategy and structure within the context of its locational embeddedness has not received sufficient attention. In order to understand how and why economic clusters change, integrating the MNEs' organizational issues with the characteristics of the sub-national region is essential for better understanding the interplay between the MNE and its spatial environment (Buckley and Ghauri 2004; Beugelsdijk *et al.* 2010), especially SMEs, which are often displaying entrepreneurial behavior and mindsets. In this paper, we follow these interactions between MNEs and local/regional entrepreneurial SMEs, as one important dimension influencing change. We aim to explain the dynamics and focus on the change and development of the cluster during structural changes originating in ownership and structural changes within a large lead firm, which had become part of an agglomerated globally acting MNE. Although it can be assumed that various mechanisms are at play simultaneously, in this study we focus on interplay between MNEs' global strategies and local/regional entrepreneurship in SMEs as important mechanisms of cluster change.

The paper commences with the proposal of a typology in relation to exploration and exploitation of new knowledge (March 1991) and a means of balancing these processes (March 1991; Zettinig and Vincze 2012). The typology itself is for differentiating between the domain (use of knowledge) of managers and entrepreneurs. Here, we incorporate the framework of "prediction and control" suggested by Wiltbank *et al.* (2006, 983). This framework distinguishes among the ways different actors compute their environment, and conceptualizes fundamental differences in the way the nature of the environment is viewed and processed by entrepreneurs and managers (Zettinig *et al.* 2017). In agreement with Beugelsdijk *et al.* (2010), we believe that this approach has potential for opening the black box containing the organizational and knowledge relationships which mediate and facilitate the links between place and space. This in terms of theoretical contribution means that we aim at developing explanations of cluster transformation so that we bring together IB's knowledge of MNEs' organizational issues with entrepreneurial coordination issues inherent in most SMEs because of their active role in changing the knowledge base and relationships within a cluster.

Next, from the resulting typology we derive propositions that may explain how clusters transform with special emphasis on the changes around events of MNEs leaving and joining a cluster mostly consisting of SMEs. The subsequent sections are developed for employing this synthesised framework to analyse a longitudinal single case of a cluster transformation during a period of about ten years, when one MNE decided to divest from a cluster, a phase of re-orientation until a new MNE decided to acquire the cluster's lead firm.

The first section will explain our methodological choices. Next we describe the selected case, the biorefinery cluster in Örnsköldsvik (Övik), Sweden. The case description and the further analysis involve both firm and cluster levels, but will especially focus on the cluster's lead firm Domsjö Fabriker (DF), its changing ownership and the consequences in explaining cluster evolvement and consequences for SMEs. In order to develop our theoretical framework (typology), we contrast this case with the theoretical propositions (analysis section). The paper ends with a discussion and the drawing of conclusions. This final section also sets out the limitations of the study, the theoretical and managerial implications, and gives suggestions for future research.

2. Theoretical Framework

In explaining how and why industrial clusters change, what we should better understand is how new types of companies, institutions and externalities coming in and leaving from the cluster, through their interactions, bring about qualitative changes in such areas as knowledge base, structure, business model, identity, mindset and behavior, and subsequently create new developmental trajectories of a cluster. In the literature, we often find examples about the triggers of changes. These are characterized as exogenous or endogenous factors (Lorenzen 2005). Change may come about by changes in cost structures and technologies that apply across geographical space. Cluster change can be explained by changes in trade flows. Political powers and trade regimes may lock regions into particular trade and development patterns and they may change as a result of MNEs' global movements. The institutional tradition offers various explanations for change based on the differences among institutional infrastructures. Clusters' capacity for change may be explained by their social capital, entrepreneurs, or strategic political alliances that are opting for collective efficiency. Entrepreneurship is essentially linked to cluster development in respect to evolutionary and constructive forces (Sölvell *et al.* 2003), as the role of entrepreneurs is to advance the coordination of activities in the complex economic system (cf., Casson and Della Guista 2007).

Typology of Knowledge Development and Managerial-Entrepreneurial Computation of the Environment

In order for a cluster to transform, the knowledge base should evolve through innovation. Innovation instills spill-overs and interactions of ideas leading to new resource combinations with new value propositions to stimulate development among firms within the region, and migration of knowledge flows between regions through the active intervention of MNEs (Jenkins and Tallman 2010). This, however, is not simple. Location-based determinism for the knowledge attributed to a particular region can make changes difficult to pursue (Pouder and St. John 1996). Isomorphic pressures (Damanpour 1991) may lead to knowledge convergence among the firms in a region, leading to the tendency for the focus of innovation to narrow over time, thereby resulting in a move away from more radical breakthrough innovations. March (1991) argued against convergence-type learning in organizations. According to his well-accepted argument, the essence of exploration is experimentation with new alternatives. Its returns are uncertain, distant and often negative. Thus, the distance in time and space between the locus of learning and the locus for the realization of returns is generally greater than in the case of exploitation, as is uncertainty. This leads to the problem, the tendency to emphasize exploitation of known alternatives and "neglect" the exploration of the unknown, i.e., to increase the reliability of performance rather than its means.

In addition to March's (1991) work, Wiltbank *et al.* (2006, 983) provides us with another framework of behavior and mindset distinguishing between the "construction of reality," which arguably is archetypically entrepreneurial behavior, often prevalent in SMEs, and with "positioning within an organizationally accepted reality," which could be interpreted as managerial behavior, which is more typical for globally integrated firms. If we accept this distinction of fundamentally different behaviors and mindsets, and the fact that there are preferences in regard to comfortable levels of prediction concerning future outcomes, then we can also accept that organizational behaviors might vary. In a typology, there are those who follow in their behaviors entrepreneurial mindsets of (1) visionary approaches (e.g. Hamel and Prahalad 1991); or (2) transformative approaches (e.g. Sarasvathy 2001) to construct their realities. The first case (1) means that the organization would be able to construct a desirable future and put in place means and exercise influence on its stakeholders to attain it, thus increasing the probability for its realization. The second entrepreneurial case (2) does not rely on "guessing what the future shall bring" but on influencing parts of the stakeholders in their task environment to increase their repository of resources and capabilities. These processes subsequently lead to constructed convergence and evolving agreement concerning the common organizational objectives leading to potential "new market creations" (cf Sarasvathy and Dew 2005, 943), which will be illustrated in this case.

For the managerial mindset the typology distinguishes between (3) an adaptive behavior to the changes in the environment (e.g. Teece *et al.* 1997), or (4) traditional planning and strategic positioning cycles (e.g. Ansoff 1979; Porter 1980). The first one, based on flexible enough organiational structures, focuses on behavior to de- and reintegrate resources and capabilities depending on detected changes in the external environment. The latter approach, ascribed to strategic planning, follows from management's *belief* in extant knowledge being continuous, which is influencing their strategic positions and spurring them to act upon them by extrapolating knowledge to be applicable in future.

The typology in Table 9.1 (page 155) generates two important utilities: First, it takes the well accepted generalizations concerning exploitation and exploration of March (1991) and reflects on it on a mid-range theory level (compare Pinder and Moore 1979) to differentiate between differences in mindset and actions, which influence the way cluster members might interact with each other through their cooperation.

The typology provides us with new and more precise boundary conditions related to the processes of exploitation, exploration and balancing in March's original concept. It allows us to distinguish between different actors' mindsets and their associated effects in terms of dealing with uncertainties, their assumptions about the environment and their behavioral choices leading to focus on exploring and exploiting. It also gives us a better understanding of the role of balancing, which is, in our opinion, critically important to the nature of change processes in its own right because it can explain why certain decisions or action paths are easier for some to engage

Table 9.1 Typology of Different Mindsets and Behaviors Affecting Cluster Development

	Planning Type	*Adaptive Type*	*Transformative Type*	*Visionary Type*
Exploitation	Main Process	Gradually adjusting to environmental changes	Exploration of own possibilities	Focused on constructing knowledge of a viable future
Exploration	Minimal and limited to external certainties	Ad hoc; little pressure for long-run exploration	Exploration of integrating own with others' opportunities	Focused on convincing others to adapt their vision
Balancing	Less important and mainly favoring exploitation	Less important	Main process in order to find and build a viable opportunity	Control over others' beliefs creates basis for exploitation
Perception of the environment/ coping mechanisms	Certainty seeking	Uncertainty avoidance through continuous adaptations	Certainties creation through control of own resources and stakeholders' quasi-internalization	Uncertainties are small due to strong belief in a future state that can be obtained through stakeholder influence

in than is the case for others (Zettinig and Vincze 2012). Secondly, the typology (Table 9.1) creates the opportunity to look at firm level mindsets and behaviors and propose how changes in the constellation of firms drive the development of a cluster. Thus, we can investigate how different cluster participants, with a diversity of mindsets (Wiltbank *et al.* 2006), act, interact and influence the changes happening in a cluster over time.

The Framework Applied to a Cluster of Lead-Firms

Clusters can be understood as organizations that are generated through quasi-internalization of independent legal and organizational entities (i.e., quasi-internalization is defined here as control without ownership). What we need to do is to investigate how the theoretical types (Table 9.1) apply to such "supra-organizations" as clusters. In order to fulfil the requirement to create current viability, or present revenues that result from exploiting given knowledge, the role of lead organizations must be critical. The role of lead organizations is to provide the whole cluster with viability through existing external relationships manifesting a value chain that organizes the transformation of inputs derived from suppliers and auxiliary organizations (cf. Porter 1998) into outputs for which current markets exist. A lead organization creates sufficient revenues to satisfy their own stakeholders (e.g. the HQ for a MNC) and to provide the legitimacy to the cluster as a whole and to associated firms, i.e. regional SMEs which are members in it. Relating these requirements of a lead organization to the typology developed in Table 9.1 it can be suggested that two types are well suited to take on this role.

On the one hand, the *planning type* seems predestined to serve such a role through the focus on exploitation of given knowledge and its strong need to seek certainties that are required for its realization. On the other hand, the *adaptive type* may take on such a role by providing less of a focus on prediction of where such certainties can be harvested and on planning towards meeting them, but instead having structural flexibility combined with a strong sense of changing environments and capabilities to continuously rearrange its resource base to meet new requirements posed by its task environment. The implications for the cluster may differ depending on what type of lead organization the cluster has. While the planning type reaps strategic certainties, the adapting type creates structural flexibilities. Either type may find its strengths in differently natured environments. The planning type prospers best in stable environments due to the need to plan, which requires facts. The adaptive type has advantages in moderately dynamic environments where they can rearrange resources in pace with environmental change. The cluster is affected by the planning type in that it provides other firms with security and viability on the cluster level, which may enable other firms to engage in more exploration types of approaches (e.g. by raising risk capital or subsidies for research and development). The adaptive type as lead organization is able to deal with more dynamic environments through its flexible capabilities, having a similar effect on the cluster to provide viability that may enable exploration-focused cluster members to substitute for a lack of current viability.

On the cluster level the type of lead organization has implications for how balancing is attained. The planning type will require other cluster members to create certainties for them, for instance, by providing them with needed services as inputs for their own business (e.g. research-focused cluster firms may also offer services in order to generate some revenues). The adaptive lead firm may look at other cluster firms as potential resource pools that can be tapped in case changes in the environment require the integration of their resources. The implications for balancing are that a planning lead firm may create some restrictions on the exploratory nature of the other firms in the cluster by using their productive capacities in exchange for legitimacy and a degree of current viability. The adaptive type may not affect other cluster firms that strongly until perceived changes in the environment may require them to more strongly bind other firms to their own business.

3. Methodology

In this paper, we focus on the lead company in the bio-refinery cluster of Övik and subsequently shed light on the implications for SMEs. It is approximately a ten-year period we investigate, during which one foreign MNE decided to divest from the cluster's lead firm (DF), followed by an intermediate period in which local/regional ownership was in control, until 2011 when another foreign MNE acquired the lead firm. Our aim is to understand with the help of the framework (Table 9.1) how these ownership changes impact the mindset and behavior of the lead firm and how these changes have affected the closely connected firms on the cluster level.

We have selected the Övik case based on theoretical considerations and due to the opportunity we had through primary data collection to follow different firms' and the cluster's development since 2008, having access to different key players within the cluster. The case has significant research coverage (e.g. Arbuthnott et al. 2010; Petersen 2011; Coenen et al. 2012), which provided us with useful secondary data, although the authors of those studies develop different perspectives. The choice of a single case study at this stage is justified because the objective of this research is to understand why and how clusters generate new trajectories in their developmental paths through lead firms' mindsets and behaviors and due to the complexities found in one cluster and its constituting parts (e.g., Nicol 2013). To strengthen this argument further, the single case approach applied provides us with the opportunity to study complex cluster change on the firm level and provides us with implications concerning the changes that unfold on cluster level (Yin 1994; Siggelkow 2007).

We considered this particular cluster suitable because the wider changes having taken place over one-and-a-half centuries are extensively documented.

The corporate and cluster data are accessible and transparent to the extent that they enhance rich case descriptions (Eisenhardt and Greabner 2007; Langley 1999, 2009; Pettigrew 1997), which is essential for theory development. The data available is both historical and also primary, as the authors have been following the cluster and its firms over the past eight years. From August 2008 onward, we collected retrospective and real-time data for the longitudinal case study. We obtained rich secondary data through the central cluster-management firm and other sources (i.e. cluster company websites, industry analysts, business historians, journalists and works of other researchers as mentioned above). We had access to documented events and to meetings between key individuals in the cluster, and attended and took notes at public presentations. We were able to benefit from observations that had been made at various points in time.

However, the most important data is comprised of the ten intensive formal and informal interviews (in 2008, 2009, 2012 and the latest in May 2016) with numerous informants, and a focus-group session (March 2009) with key decision makers from various cluster organisations. The interviews with many individual informants helped in terms of triangulating and assigning meaning to the different objective and subjective realities that influence cluster development. The wealth of data allowed us to write rich chronologies of the case and apply various theoretical lenses for understanding the changes in the lead firm and the unfolding cluster development process. Additionally, the rich data was critical in terms of understanding the context of the cluster environment in which the lead firm is embedded.

4. Case Description

The bio-refinery cluster in Övik in Northern Sweden was formally established in 2003 by a group of companies originating from the MoDo paper and pulp industry conglomerate. The longer history of the site, connected not only to paper and pulp industry but also more generally to its roots in chemistry (Coenen *et al.* 2012; Peterson 2011), is important because some traditions evolved over the long history of this industrial site which have transformed into powerful institutional forces in the region over time (Arbothnott *et al.* 2010; Vincze and Teräs 2016; Zettinig and Vincze 2012). While focusing on the recent developments and transformations in the cluster (i.e. the period 2003–2012) we will refer to these forces systematically.

Domsjö Fabriker (DF) can be characterized as the lead actor because it controlled the main industrial process, thus giving the firm much of the developmental and strategic weight in this cluster; and therefore DF constitutes the focus firm in this paper. However, as the lead actor it is developing in a symbiotic way with other local and regional SMEs (e.g., Sekab, Övik Energi, Akzo Nobel, MoRe). DF is engaged in the fractionation processes and others cooperating with them create a variety of marketable new products.

"*Without Domsjö there is nothing, because that is the key process. The wood comes in and it makes the fractions that all the other firms use. Domsjö has no available additional resources at the moment to make anything other than pulp and ligno-sulphonate—other products are made by other firms*" (Original comment by a chemical scientist, 2008).

Moreover, as one of Övik's managers stated in 2009, "*Fossil refinery and bio-refinery, they are producing a similar range of chemical products!*" Therefore, this bio-refinery cluster may contribute to generating many solutions that will be globally relevant in the decades to come.

DF as the lead firm in the cluster has a very interesting recent history. Between 2001 and 2003 it was owned by a Finnish pulp and paper MNE which divested from DF in order to focus on the dominant paper production technology (KRAFT). Kraft technology is economically superior in the production of paper, but has fewer productive opportunities than the sulphite process used at DF. DF has been taken over by local/regional investors (entrepreneurs and institutions) with strong loyalty to their home region to develop its own technology into new products. By using the method of dissolving cellulose, DF was starting to enter new value chains for which they saw good potential based on the advantages of their production approach. Resulting from this effort, four main product categories had been developed, with some of them having viable markets, while others were searching for technological and economic solutions to their challenges. To drive this process further, the cluster as a whole, dominantly driven by DF, founded a coordinating firm for the cluster called Processum. Established in 2003 with the purpose of coordinating old and new economically viable trajectories for the cluster and its firms (cf Peterson 2011), Processum started to raise funds and developed common research projects among member firms to transform into a bio-refinery cluster with viable solutions for a more sustainable economy with strong focus on the use of the combined local resources.

The 2008 economic crisis has been threatening to the most viable of all the businesses of DF, dissolving of cellulose, and it has also taken a toll on other firms (Coenen *et al.* 2012, 13). The crisis—while short-lived for DF, as its markets recovered quickly and a new boom started in 2009—has made management realize the vulnerabilities in financing its growing business. This set in motion an effort to strengthen the financial basis of the firm by preparing a public offering. In that process an Indian conglomerate MNE (Aditya Birla) with strong interests in the pulp and fibre industry started to pay attention to DF and its capabilities. This resulted in the takeover of DF, with the change of the firm's ownership to the hands of a foreign MNE in 2011, this time one from a developing country. This created interesting interactions between the lead firm and the wider cluster, mostly consisting of smaller firms with a regional and national orientation.

5. Analysis

The Lead Firm Under Control of Certainty Seeking Ownership

The Finnish multinational which acquired MoDo Paper group in 2000 divested from the DF plant in 2003. As we interpret this move, the Finnish multinational would rather rely on the certainties (Kraft technology), concluding that they know best, than to invest too heavily in exploration. Their behavior can be seen as 'internalization' of technologies that have a known viable market (Kraft) and an understood value chain, instead of pursuing a technology which may have many productive opportunities with many potential innovations, but in the uncertain future. Internally, the brief period when the MNE has owned DF has been characterized by a strong planning approach focusing on the pulp and paper business, an area that the MNE knows best. The MNE did not really access the location-tied knowledge of acidic processes for paper production. It did not integrate nor reconfigure that knowledge to leverage its own firm-specific advantages as extant IB theory would suggest. The Finnish MNE chose the Kraft process as the most viable technology for paper production (keeping other manufacturing sites which rely on that process) and decided to exit from the Övik site. This MNE's move out can also be explained by the fact that its main motivation is strategic asset seeking (e.g. Dunning 1988) and Övik did not fit into its integrated global strategy providing the needed degree of certainty that this type requires. The divestment of DF indicates the strong preferences of the planning type for perceived certainties. It goes to the extent that clear alternative opportunities are neglected because they do not corroborate with the management's understanding of its environment and because only minimum levels of exploration are tolerated (e.g. they slashed the large research unit of MoDo, cf Peterson 2011). When the Finnish multinational left Övik, the cluster's competitive base rested on a technology that was only partially commercially viable. This required the lead organization, DF, to find alternatives, including the alternative to the typical planning-type behavior.

Shifting to an Adaptive Mindset

DF, since then, has started generating revenues based on the advantages of cellulose production using the sulphite process that preserves wood structures, while at the same time keeping all options open to develop new businesses in liaison with other firms, many of those being small and reliant on the larger industrial processes to feed off or contribute to. DF, after the MNE's exit, could be classified as the archetypical adaptive firm, able to sense changes in the environment and rearrange its resource base to focus on newly emerging certainties in its task environment. This behavior is extraordinary since the core technology the firm is using is an extensive chemical process in huge industrial installations, which poses many engineering and science-related challenges. Throughout its history DF, and earlier the MoDo conglomerate, has proved to be able to rely on location-based advantages and to leverage them with deep scientific knowledge about acidic (sulphite) processes. This relates to the technology and knowledge at the very core of the firm (exploitation), while at the same time it is flexible enough to allow for newly emerging technologies to be recognized and subsequently integrate new knowledge into its processes (exploration), very often in concert with local SMEs, which were often brought in by other firms (see below the role of the cluster management organization) and scientists. Exploration enabled DF to shift from an inferior paper production technology to divert its attention to a broader spectrum of cellulose products and opened up many new opportunities to develop potentially viable businesses. By 2008 the most promising technology categories the firm developed were besides dissolving cellulose (e.g. for textile production which can substitute cotton) a new technology to produce a ligno-sulphate (e.g. as an additive for the cement industry) and new trajectories to develop ethanol from a side product of dissolving cellulose (e.g. to develop automotive bio-fuels). It also developed gasification technology which converts the remainder of the 60% of input materials (wood) to an energy product satisfying local energy and environmental sustainability demands. While dissolving cellulose is a product, strongly dependent on global market fluctuations, as the crisis commencing in 2008 had shown, it was becoming a very profitable product in 2009 with strong viabilities in a booming market. At the same time, the other technologies started to provide evidence that they would have viable markets sooner or later. By 2009, however, the owners of DF realised that their financial capacities were not enough to really benefit from these developments, especially not for capturing the booming dissolving cellulose market (i.e. textile substitutes for cotton). Up to that point in time local ownership had engaged in an adaptive approach. It was based on balancing exploration and exploitation by focusing on detected realities in the environment and their sensed apparent changes and by adjusting internal resource configurations and subsequent actions accordingly. This means that exploitation of given certainties are constantly and gradually being changed according to new understanding of the unfolding environment, thus reducing far-reaching exploration pressures to a minimum, since incremental adaptation takes care of maintaining current and future viability of the firm. The organizational knowledge is constantly being developed and updated according to the emerging realities, keeping uncertainties at a minimum, and making balancing processes the main driver for learning.

The takeover event in 2011 changed the approach of DF once again. It is now again part of a MNE, which demands to exploit the certainties of the MNE (to dissolve cellulose for cotton substitution), while technologies which were not yet fully self-sufficient businesses (e.g. gasification) are scrutinized, in turn causing uncertainties in the smaller cluster firms.

Balancing Exploration with the Certainties
Within a Defined Global Value Chain

On the cluster level the implications of these shifts of the lead firm from a planning type to an adaptive type and potentially back has systemic implications for other cluster members. A major MNE exiting the cluster threatened the very existence of a cluster environment of SMEs, endangering the well-being of a whole region. This behavior is rather characteristic for the archetypical planning type since its business is focusing on exploiting its own knowledge base and improving its efficiencies in a managerial manner (cf March 1991). On the other side it forced the lead firm to find new opportunities and to develop an adaptive approach, which more closely adapts to new emerging realities while they happen—making them also open to understanding extant new opportunities in concert with local and regional SMEs. While this is providing the lead firm and the cluster as a whole with current viability, in parallel, it gives space to develop new knowledge (research unit of DF and other cluster members) that may materialize in capturing future markets.

The role of the cluster coordinating firm (Processum) is also interesting, as it is a result of the phase when adaptive behavior was driving outcomes, when the uncertain space forces small and large firms to find synergies across their overall operations. It changed the cluster because it affects the perceived boundaries of cluster firms, not only from a firm's but also from the outside perspectives. It set in motion processes that enable a balance between those who can provide viability through exploitation of knowledge-generating revenues and those developing a number of new trajectories exploring new knowledge for future opportunities. This behavior is clearly explained through the entrepreneurial process of effectuation as proposed by Sarasvathy and Dew (2005), creating convergence of cluster-level objectives, while quasi-internalizing the resource pools of small and large cluster firms and beyond. The transformative type puts minimal emphasis on predicting the future but structures its activities around the creation of certainties obtained through the control of important parts (stakeholders) in its constructed task environment with many SMEs. The focus of this type of firm is to involve stakeholders in a process of effectuation (Sarasvathy and Dew 2005), involving among others the firms in a cluster to iterate a process that will gradually expand this type's resource pool while a negotiated common view emerges on what the objectives of their business may be. This type influences the balance of the cluster most in that it takes an active role in transforming its environment, in this case its cluster environment, to merge opportunities derived from exploitation activities with possible future opportunities developed in exploration activities.

While this approach appears to work well at the moment, utilizing the efficiencies provided by DF's main business while creating new opportunities with other cluster firms, it may also create new tensions. These tensions may be between DF as an important part of the MNE's global value chain and the MNE's efforts to develop new viable businesses that emerge from cooperative actions in the cluster. DF may need to defend its innovation activities to an owner who requires a strong focus on the certainties provided by their global value chains, with a major focus on generating efficiencies to feed the MNE's own internal value chains. However, our recent data (2016) on the acquirer (AB) as an emerging market multinational (EMNE), even if it is considered a planning type according to our typology, shows considerable differences from owner/acquirers of developed market multinationals. Consequently, we can expect different interactions between AB and the local/regional SMEs and changes in the cluster, overall. These preliminary insights are supported by upcoming discussions on EMNEs' strategies and behavior in the most recent IB literature. EMNEs' motives to expand abroad are fundamentally different from those of developed economy firms (DMNE) (e.g. Madhok and Keyhani 2012; Ramamurti 2012). The main motive of DMNEs is to exploit firm-specific advantages. EMNEs transfer advantages *from* the target rather than *to* the target (Morresi and Pezzi 2014). EMNEs acquire not only because of what they know they can access or learn, but also because of the opportunity to create advantage and potential contribution to the capability building and transformation processes *even beyond what can be known or predicted ex ante* (Madhok and Keyhani 2012). EMNEs focus more on long-term performance. Indian acquisitions are often the examples of softer and more gradual integration processes, which is argued to create more successful knowledge transfer and favor access to emerging new opportunities.

The motives of AB to acquire DF were clearly strategic. It wanted to improve its global competitive advantage, with international (global) extension geographically, a mix of resource and market-seeking motives. Similarly, as other Indian and Chinese conglomerates, it is active in large-scale acquisitions in order to secure material resources needed for growth and to access Western technologies. As innovation is also more and more a focus of AB, it also needs to acquire research capacities. Beyond the motive of securing raw material, DF, with its proven technology for specialty pulp and bio-refinery, is one example to the point.

"*The acquisition of Domsjö Fabriker, a world-class company, with the most environmentally-friendly technology, marks a significant milestone for our Pulp & Fibre business. Its cutting-edge technology and production process coupled with a state-of-the-art bio-refinery add significant value to our Pulp & Fibre operations. Its high-quality pulp will enable us to enhance the supply of top quality premium VSF to our customers.*" (Press Release, 9. April, 2011).

One interpretation of this acquisition is certainly that AB is interested in DF's production capacities to contribute to the internal value chain. All other things that DF is involved in (exploration) are supported by AB because of economies of scope for the cellulose operations.

On the other hand, the key criterion was the extent of strategic interdependence; the need for transfer or share of capabilities (technology) and resources (manufacturing facility) in order to capture value. This value in the case of the DF acquisition could be captured almost purely through the ownership of assets and probably integration of some organizational systems (financial), but not all. There was a need for organizational autonomy because the acquired firm had distinct culture, was at a geographical distance and performed at a high level.

AB's preservation strategy towards DF (Haspeslagh and Jemison 1991) is important to follow in the future to better understand not only EMNEs internationalization behavior but also their effects on cluster transformation and how they affect local and regional small and medium-sized firms.

6. Discussion and Conclusions

Depending on the firms in a cluster, their assumed roles and influences, the implications for the development of a cluster are far reaching and require further conceptual development through in-depth study of different clusters.

A beginning has been made to better understand how firms' behaviors and cluster development may interact depending on the typology developed, from integrating March (1991) an organizational approach to understand the long-term effects of different types of knowledge and the insights brought from entrepreneurship literature (e.g. Sarasvathy and Dew 2005) and its clarifications concerning how they relate to the better understood managerial approaches (Wiltbank *et al*. 2006). Integrating these approaches has provided us with a conceptual framework that enables us to take these concepts and project them onto the cluster level to show that many different mindsets and roles exist and how they can shape the behavior of firms, leading to cluster development trajectories. In order to develop this framework further, more clusters and their change processes resulting from the activities of cluster members should be studied and compared in order to evaluate what kind of processes are at play.

While the Övik cluster is just one example of a cluster, it provides us with some insights for the development of our conceptual framework. In this paper, we have focused on the level of the cluster's lead firm, the changes that happen to it with changing ownership and integration into a MNE's value chains, and how that creates the task environment for partially highly dependent local and regional firms. It shows how clusters transform when the lead firms shift between the managerial approaches that either focus on strategic planning and the exploitation of knowledge or shift to a more adaptive approach once the MNE does not provide the certainties of established markets and value chains.

However, we have to be careful in generalizing and would suggest reflecting further on the boundary conditions each type of behavior poses and what they mean for defining conceptual boundaries in explaining the development of clusters. In the end, each cluster is different and the interactions between the lead firms and smaller firms create unique settings, especially when they are tied to the scientific and technological bases they are using for exploiting old and developing new opportunities.

The implications are multifaceted. For instance, looking at the effects of MNEs on integrated local/regional cluster firms, we see that MNEs may provide clusters and their SMEs with current viability, which not only creates paths to achieve a MNE's objectives, but is also critical for small and medium-sized firms' survival. However, there is some evidence and also concern that MNEs may be too focused on dealing with perceived certainties within their own focus areas, which may reduce the ability to develop new opportunities and innovations that may serve other SMES in the cluster and a region and an economy in the wider sense and longer run. MNEs' behavior, explained with the help of our integrated framework, is to exploit and move on to new locations rather than making a commitment to specific locations. They rather optimize and differentiate their work within their own value chains, which may not always be as beneficial to the development of a regional economy and dependent SMEs.

The impact of MNEs on local/regional firms belonging to a cluster should be further studied if one wants to reap benefits beyond the MNE level and create new opportunities for SMEs. We think that more research should follow up on how MNEs affect clusters' small and medium-sized firms, how they alter processes between these firms, and how they affect roles within the cluster and behaviors and mindsets within the firms they invest in.

Such an understanding may provide us with the means to improve the management of clusters and also benefit the strategic orientations of small and medium-sized firms. We may develop ways to use coordinating actors in clusters more effectively, in order to create a long-term balance between the viabilities of current and future businesses. To conclude, we know very little about how clusters change, but an effort in understanding the mindsets and behaviors of different cluster firms may help us to better understand what drives cluster dynamics.

Note

1 Acknowledgement: This work was supported by the Academy of Finland, Project No: 138835.

References

Ansoff, H. Igor. 1979. *Strategic Management*. London: Palgrave Macmillan.

Arbuthnott, Andrew, Jessica Eriksson, and Joakim Wincent. 2010. "When a New Industry Meets Traditional and Declining Ones: An Integrative Approach Towards Dialectics and Social Movement Theory in a Model of Regional Industry Emergence Processes." *Scandinavian Journal of Management* 26(3): 290–308. doi:10.1016/j.scaman.2010.05.001.

Bell, Simon J., Paul Tracey, and Jan B. Heide. 2009. "The Organization of Regional Clusters." *The Academy of Management Review* 34(4): 623–642.

Beugelsdijk, Sjoerd, Philip McCann, and Ram Mudambi. 2010. "Introduction: Place, Space and Organization—Economic Geography and the Multinational Enterprise." *Journal of Economic Geography* 10(4): 485–493.

Buckley, Peter J., and Pervez N. Ghauri. 2004. "Globalisation, Economic Geography and the Strategy of Multinational Enterprises." *Journal of International Business Studies* 35(2): 81–98.

Casson, Mark, and Marina Della Guista. 2007. "Entrepreneurship and Social Capital: Analysing the Impact of Social Networks on Entrepreneurial Activity from a Rational Action Perspective." *International Small Business Journal* 25(3): 220–244.

Coenen, Lars, Jerker Moodysson, and Hanna Westendorf. 2012. "Bridging Science and Traditional Industry: Institutional Change for Emergent Biorefinery Technologies." Paper presented at the AAG *Annual Meeting* New York, US, February 24–28.

Damanpour, Fariborz. 1991. "Organizational Innovation: A Meta-Analysis of Effects of Determinants and Moderators." *Academy of Management Journal* 34(3): 555–590.

Dunning, John H. 1988. "The Eclectic Paradigm of International Production: A Restatement and Some Possible Extensions." *Journal of International Business Studies* 19(1): 1–31.

Dunning, John H. 2009. "Location and the Multinational Enterprise: A Neglected Factor?" *Journal of International Business Studies* 40(1): 45–66.

Eisenhardt, Kathleen M., and Melissa E. Greabner. 2007. "Theory Building from Cases, Opportunities and Challenges." *Academy of Management Journal* 50: 25–32.

Hamel, Gary, and C.K. Prahalad. 1991. "Corporate Imagination and Expeditionary Marketing." *Harvard Business Review* 69(4): 81–92.

Haspeslagh, Phillippe C., and David B. Jemison. 1991. *Managing Acquisitions— Creating Value Through Corporate Renewal*. New York: Free Press.

Jenkins, Mark, and Stephen Tallman. 2010. "The Shifting Geography of Competitive Advantage: Clusters, Networks and Firms." *Journal of Economic Geography* 10(4): 599–618.

Ketels, Christian H.M. 2003. "The Development of Cluster Concept—Present Experiences and Further Development." In *Publication of the Institute for Strategy and Competitiveness*. Harvard Business School Press.

Krugman, Paul, and Anthony J. Venables. 1995. "Globalization and the Inequality of Nations." *Quarterly Journal of Economics* 110(4): 857–880.

Langley, Ann. 1999. "Strategies for Theorising from Process Data." *Academy of Management Review* 24(4): 691–710.

Langley, Ann. 2009. "Studying Processes in and Around Organizations." In *The Sage Handbook of Organizational Research Methods*, edited by David A. Buchanan and Alan Bryman, 409–429. London: Sage.

Lorenzen, Mark. 2005. "Why Do Cluster Change?" *European Urban and Regional Studies* 12(3): 203–208.

Madhok, Anoop, and Mohammad Keyhani. 2012. "Acquisitions as Entrepreneurship: Asymmetries, Opportunities, and the Internationalization of Multinationals from Emerging Economies." *Global Strategy Journal* 2(1): 26–40.

Malecki, Edward J. 1983. "Technology and Regional Development: A Survey." *International Regional Science Review* 8(2): 89–125.

March, James G. 1991. "Exploration and Exploitation in Organizational Learning." *Organization Science* 2(1): 71–87.

Maskell, Peter. 2001. "Growth and the Territorial Configuration of Economic Activity." Paper presented on the *DRUID Summer Conference*, Aalborg, Denmark, June 12–15.

Maskell, Peter, and Mark Lorenzen 2004. "The Cluster as Market Organization." *Urban Studies*, 41(5–6): 975–993.

Morresi, Ottorino, and Alberto Pezzi. 2014. *Cross-Border Mergers and Acquisitions, Theory and Empirical Evidence*. New York: Palgrave Macmillan.

Nicol, Cristopher G. 2013. "Change in the Cage, Exploring an Organisational Field: Sweden's Biofuel Region." PhD diss., Umeå University.

Peterson, Christer. 2011. "Sweden: From Large Corporation Towards a Knowledge-Intensive Economy." In *Nordic Capitalism and Globalization: New Forms of Economic Organization and Welfare Institutions*, edited by P. Hull Kristensen and Kari Lilja, 183–219. Oxford: Oxford University Press.

Pettigrew, Andrew M. 1997. "What Is a Processual Analysis?" *Scandinavian Journal of Management* 13(4): 337–348.

Pinder Craig C., and Larry F. Moore. 1979. "The Resurrection of Taxonomy to Aid the Development of Middle Range Theories of Organizational Behaviour." *Administrative Science Quarterly* 24(1): 99–118.

Porter, Michel E. 1980. *Competitive Strategy: Techniques for Analysing Industries and Competition*. New York: Free Press.

Porter, Michel E. 1998. "Clusters and the New Economics of Competition." *Harvard Business Review* 76(6): 77–90.

Pouder, Richard, and Caron H. St. John. 1996. "Hot Spots and Blind Spots: Geographical Clusters of Firms and Innovation." *Academy of Management Review* 21(4): 1192–1225.

Ramamurti, Ravi. 2012. "What Is Really Different About Emerging Market Multinationals?" *Global Strategy Journal* 2(1): 41–47.

Sarasvathy, Saras D. 2001. "Causation and Effectuation: Toward a Theoretical Shift from Economic Inevitability to Entrepreneurial Contingency." *Academy of Management Review* 26(2): 243–263.

Sarasvathy, Saras D., and Nicholas Dew. 2005. "Entrepreneurial Logics for a Technology of Foolishness." *Scandinavian Journal of Management* 21(4): 385–406.

Siggelkow, Nicolaj. 2007. "Persuasion with Case Studies." *Academy of Management Journal* 50(1): 20–24.

Sölvell, Örjan, Göran Lindquist, and Christian H.M. Ketels. 2003. *The Cluster Initiative Greenbook*. Sweden: Ivory Tower AB.

Teece, David J., Gary Pisano, and Amy Shuen. 1997. "Dynamic Capabilities and Strategic Management." *Strategic Management Journal* 18(7): 509–533.

Vincze, Zsuzsanna, and Jukka Teräs. 2016. "Mechanisms of Innovation-Based Cluster Transformation." In *Innovation Drivers and Regional Innovation Strategies*, edited by Davide M. Parrilli, Rune Dahl Fitjar, and Andres Rodriguez-Pose, 85–104. New York: Routledge.

Wiltbank, Robert, Nicholas Dew, Stuart Read, and Saras D. Sarasvathy. 2006. "What to Do Next? The Case for Non-Predictive Strategy." *Strategic Management Journal* 27(10): 981–998. doi:10.1002/smj.555.

Yin, Robert K. 1994. "Case Study Research, Design and Methods." In *Applied Social Research Method Series*. Thousand Oaks, CA: Sage.

Zettinig, Peter, Birgitta Sandberg, and Sasha Fuerst. 2017. "Value Creation During Different Development Stages: What Changes When an Entrepreneurial Firm Transforms into a Multinational Corporation?" In *Value Creation in International Business: An SME Perspective*, edited by Svetla T. Marinova, Jorma Larimo, and Niina Nummela, 109–130. London: Palgrave MacMillan.

Zettinig, Peter, and Zsuzsanna Vincze. 2012. "How Clusters Evolve?" *Competitiveness Review: An International Business Journal* 22(2): 110–132.

10 Straight Ahead or Wandering Through the Woods?

Decision-Making in Entrepreneurial Internationalization

Niina Nummela,[1] *Leila Hurmerinta, and Eriikka Paavilainen-Mäntymäki*

"The future depends on what you do today."
Mahatma Gandhi, Indian politician and philosopher, 1869–1948

1. Introduction

Extensive earlier research confirms that internationalization is a complex, time-based process which is not merely a set of separate decisions but a series of heavily context-embedded discontinuities (Welch and Paavilainen-Mäntymäki 2014). Internationalization does not simply happen to a firm; rather, the process is orchestrated by managers who actively respond to changes in the company's internal and external context (Liesch *et al.* 2011). The decisions behind the managers' actions form a pattern which can be labeled the internationalization strategy (cf Minzberg and Waters 1985). Even after decades of rigorous inquiry into internationalization, though, we do not know how these decisions evolve. Understanding this is of the utmost importance and would allow us not only to draw appropriate managerial implications but also to support the efforts of internationalizing firms. Studies focusing on decision-making in internationalization are few, and their findings are scattered and inconclusive. Furthermore, the great majority of these studies focus on managerial intentions or whether strategies are planned or emergent. Studies on the actual, tangible decision-making as it happens in practice are rare.

Already, in an early literature review, Cavusgil and Godiwalla (1982) identify two distinctive decision-making styles—formal and structured vs. disjointed and incremental—and point out that internationalizing firms are likely to move towards more formal decision-making as their level of organizational hierarchy and formalization increases. Features of rational decision-making among the firms at the most advanced level in internationalization are also found by Bilkey and Tesar (1977). Despite neglect of this seminal notion work on the aspect of decision-making in internationalization research, the past decade has seen growing interest in the theme (e.g. Ahi *et al.* 2017; Crick and Spence 2005; Spence and Crick 2006).

More recent studies on entrepreneurial decision-making in internationalization report contradictory results. For example, Collinson and Houlden (2005) find that decision-making is opportunistic and unstructured, whereas Perks and Hughes (2008) highlight that the decision-making is more strategic than expected. These contradictory findings may be due to different focuses of study. Some studies concentrate on analyzing a single decision (typically first entry into international markets), while other researchers have an interest in a series of decisions made by the company (cf Welch and Paavilainen-Mäntymäki 2014).

To fill the gap in the existing research, this paper focuses on the entrepreneurial decision-making of internationalizing firms. We are especially interested in whether the decision-making style of the firm changes as it advances in its internationalization process. We seek to answer two research questions: (1) how does decision-making change during internationalization, and (2) what is the role of networks in the entrepreneurial decision-making of internationalizing firms? Here, we adopt the view of the key decision-maker, namely, the entrepreneur.

Our study can be considered to be a contribution to a long set of Nordic studies on SME internationalization. The small, open economies of the Nordic countries effectively push companies to international markets, but the pull factors in these countries are also considerable due to the knowledge base and favorable attitudes of decision makers (e.g. Luostarinen 1979). Therefore, Nordic scholars, unsurprisingly, are active contributors to internationalization theory (e.g. the Uppsala internationalization process model, Johanson and Vahlne 1977). At the same time, they are also decisive contributors to the industrial network perspective, which links the company to international markets via the company's relationships in its business networks (Björkman and Forsgren 2000). This study builds on both approaches to deliver novel insights into the decision-making in entrepreneurial internationalization.

2. Literature Review

Decision-Making and Entrepreneurial Internationalization

Internationalization is generally understood as the evolutionary process of a company's adaptation to the international environment (e.g. Calof and Beamish 1995). The traditional models view internationalization as a step-by-step process in which the separate phases can be distinguished (for a review of process models, see, e.g., Leonidou and Katsikeas 1996; Welch and Paavilainen-Mäntymäki 2014). The different phases can be identified by various changes in, for example, operation modes, information acquisition and transition, attitudes towards internationalization and level of export involvement. In the majority of these models, companies progress from one phase to another without an explicit strategy despite making important decisions, such as the adoption of a more complex operation mode in international markets.

International entrepreneurial decision-making suffers from lateral rigidity, namely, the decision makers' limited understanding of the environment and relevant factors (Luostarinen 1979). In a way, decision makers act as a barrier between the environment and its effects on the organization and consequently have more impacts on the decisions made than the environment (Weick 1979). Good decisions, though, cannot be made without appropriate knowledge, which has a dual role in decision-making. First, it decreases the degree of uncertainty and the associated risks, thereby increasing the decision-maker's willingness to make an affirmative decision. This line of thinking is generally accepted in the literature on the internationalization of the firm and has roots in the Uppsala internationalization model (Johanson and Vahlne 1977). Second, decision-making may also be easier if the decision-maker possesses experiential knowledge of internationalization— whether business, institutional or internationalization knowledge (Fletcher and Harris 2012)—which enables better predictions of the future and reduces uncertainty. The company's business network may be an important source of the knowledge needed in decision-making related to internationalization (Evers and O'Gorman 2011; Schweizer *et al*. 2010; Yli-Renko *et al*. 2002).

However, it is not clear how the network is utilized in decision making during firms' internationalization process. It can be assumed that the roles of different actors in the network vary throughout the process (Coviello and Munro 1995; Coviello 2006; Ruokonen *et al*. 2006). In the pre-export stage of internationalization—when the firm is still searching for information and considering the possibility of entering international markets—most challenges are related to a lack of various resources. Small companies might turn to public and semi-public actors for assistance (cf. Fletcher and Harris 2012; Ojala 2009) or to their social networks for knowledge of markets and international business (Bonaccorsi 1992). This pattern is supported by a recent study by Galkina (2013) finding that, when international new ventures are formed, friends, former colleagues and family are important, but when product commercialization becomes the dominant goal, more active creation of an international network begins, and individual-level contacts are replaced with company-level contacts.

When a small company is already involved in international operations, it faces competition and environmental turbulence in the market. These new circumstances create novel needs, and the company's interests relate to different network actors, such as customers and suppliers (Nummela 2010). Galkina and Chetty (2015) suggest that, during intensive international growth, small, entrepreneurial companies focus primarily on maintaining existing relationships, and their network development is organic, for example, through recommendations. It is also suggested that, when the company grows, its management of its network becomes more calculated and intended (Jack *et al.* 2008; Slotte-Kock and Coviello 2010). Recent studies, however, indicate that, instead of following either calculated or intended network-management strategies, internationalizing entrepreneurial companies use a balanced combination of causal and effectual networking (Nummela *et al.* 2014). The inconclusiveness of existing research on decision-making in entrepreneurial internationalization suggests the need to search for additional insights in the entrepreneurship literature.

Entrepreneurial Decision-Making

Internationalization is an entrepreneurial process (Jones and Coviello 2005); therefore, the literature on entrepreneurial decision-making is relevant to this study. In general, entrepreneurship research is dominated by studies that presume rational decision-making based on neoclassical economic theories (Perry *et al.* 2012). These studies assume that internationalizing firms follow a deliberate, perhaps even "über-rational" decision-making logic in which intertwined cognitive stages follow each other (cf. Baum and Wally 2003). A number of studies, however, take an alternative approach and assume that firms' decision-making is more intuitive and a-rational (Barnard 1938; Baum and Wally 2003). Given the limited empirical studies on the question, we cannot draw any conclusions which is more probable. Nevertheless, Schweizer's (2012) study indicates that a firm's decision-making style may develop over time, and thus, a firm is not bound to a single decision-making style throughout its history.

The most popular theory in studying entrepreneurial decision-making from the past decade is effectuation theory (Sarasvathy 2001), which seems to have offered a potential explanation for the decision-making of internationally entrepreneurial firms (e.g. Andersson 2011; Evers and O'Gorman 2011; Nummela *et al.* 2014). The previously described rational logic can be labeled *causation* in Sarasvathy's terms and should be extended by adapting it, with effectuation logic, (Sarasvathy 2001) to fit the context of the strategic decision-making of internationalizing firms. Causation-based decision-making is characterized by predetermined goal-setting, intentionality, planning and systematic information-gathering (Chandler *et al.* 2011; Fisher 2012; Sarasvathy 2001). Instead of leveraging opportunities, the company efficiently exploits its existing resources and knowledge (Perry *et al.* 2012). *Effectuation* means that, under high levels of uncertainty—a condition of international market entry—decision makers focus more on affordable losses, act opportunistically and follow feelings and intuition rather than make rational calculations. Effectuation logic thus helps the entrepreneur convert uncertainty into opportunity (cf. Sarasvathy *et al.* 2008). These two decision-making logics are not the opposite ends of the same continuum, as mistakenly assumed. Instead, they are two distinct approaches to decision-making, well illustrated by Sarasvathy's (2008) metaphors of the jigsaw puzzle and patchwork quilt. This difference is especially important for measurement, and previous research does indicate that causation and effectuation are distinct constructs (Chandler *et al.* 2011).

Regarding networks, the literature on causation and effectuation is quite unsatisfactory. Although networks are addressed as an important element in effectuation (Sarasvathy 2001), the literature on their role is not very specific. Indeed, the discussion seems to focus on the actors in the networks—"who I know"—instead of the content, dynamics, interchanges or strength of the relationships in the network. Additionally, the descriptions of the network-related characteristics of effectuated behavior are slightly confusing. For example, the use of pre-existing knowledge is identified as a characteristic of causation and the use of partnerships as a characteristic of effectuation—but what if the knowledge is possessed not by the decision-maker but by the network partners and/or is embedded in the network interaction? In sum, numerous open questions remain, and the central concepts still offer room for improvement.

Studies on causation and effectuation among internationalizing firms are not many, and their findings are quite inconclusive, so they do not offer much of a foundation on which to build. Most studies concentrate on the early phases of internationalization, particularly the firm's entry into international markets. These studies indicate that effectuation-based logic might facilitate rapid internationalization, especially when supported with strong business networks through which the company obtains helpful information (Andersson 2011; Evers and O'Gorman 2011). Evidence on the role of context is inconclusive. Mainela and Puhakka (2009) find that effectual decision-making is preferred in markets with high uncertainty, but Chetty *et al.* (2015) report that, in such an environment, companies prefer to base decisions on causation.

Unfortunately, the findings of studies that take into account the entire process of internationalization are contradictory. For example, Harms and Schiele (2012) argue that experienced entrepreneurs tend to use effectuation rather than causation, whereas other studies (Gabrielsson and Gabrielsson 2013; Kalinic *et al.* 2014; Schweizer 2012) suggest that, in the course of internationalization, decision-making develops to favor causation-based decision. The latter view is in line with Sarasvathy's (2001) original argument that effectual logic is typical in the early stages of new venture creation when uncertainty is the greatest. In a recent study, Galkina and Chetty (2015) challenge this line of thinking, arguing that environmental conditions, such as high market uncertainty, are more decisive than the phase of internationalization in determining the use of effectual logic. Changes in the external and internal environments, as well as other triggers, may explain why some studies find evidence that SMEs are not bound to one type of decision-making, but, instead, their decision-making logic varies between causation and effectuation (Chetty *et al.* 2015; Nummela *et al.* 2014).

In sum, the findings from earlier research are inconclusive and partly contradictory and often based on qualitative, context-embedded case studies.

However, they do indicate a possible link between decision-making and phase of internationalization as over time, decision makers behave more rationally (Schweizer 2012). Therefore, we propose that, over the course of internationalization, the characteristics of entrepreneurial decision-making decreases, and companies tend to use more causation-based decision-making logic.

> Proposition 1. Causation-based decision-making logic increases over the course of internationalization.

As a company progresses in internationalization, the decisions it has to make become more complex. Therefore, it is probable that the decision-maker increasingly needs network support for decision-making. Our knowledge about the role of various networks in the internationalization process, though, is limited (Musteen *et al.* 2010).

From the entrepreneurship literature, we know that the personal social network is the new firm's greatest resource (Johannisson 1988), and entrepreneurs commonly begin networking with people they already know (Engel *et al.* 2017; Sarasvathy 2001). These interpersonal relationships are helpful for opportunity exploration, but interorganizational networks are also needed for opportunity exploitation (Eberhard and Craig 2013). Especially if the internationalizing firm seeks access to resources, internationalization requires insidership in relevant networks (Johanson and Vahlne 2009), which can be found in the home market, target market or a third market (Hewerdine *et al.* 2014). In general, we can expect that, over time, the decision-maker turns to more specialized and sophisticated relationships in the network for assistance (Galkina 2013; Nummela 2010). Therefore, we propose that, over the course of internationalization, the company not only expands its network, but the nature of the network also changes.

> Proposition 2a. Utilization of the firm's network to support decision-making increases over the course of internationalization.
> Proposition 2b. The network utilized to support the firm's decision-making becomes more specialized over the course of internationalization.

The expected increase in the size and professionalism of the network over the course of internationalization gives the entrepreneur access to information which can be utilized in decision-making (Child and Hsieh 2014). It can be also anticipated that the decision-maker not only obtains more useful information from the network but also becomes better able to absorb and utilize it.

> Proposition 2c. The perceived network-based benefits for decision-making increase over the course of internationalization.

Next, we empirically test our propositions with data from internationalizing companies from Finland.

3. Research Design

Research Setting

Following Michailova (2011), we agree that contextualization is extremely important in international business research. From the contextualization perspective, it is crucial to understand both the inner and outer context of a phenomenon (Pettigrew 1987). Here, *inner context* refers to the internationalization process of the firm, while *outer context* denotes the external environment in which this process occurs, in this case, the Finnish food industry. To examine entrepreneurial decision-making skills, we consider it essential that the context of the study be a country in which SMEs are compelled to expand their operations to international markets. As a country, Finland provides a suitable background for this study due to its small, open economy. The selection of the food industry as the study focus provides the required variation in internationalization. This industry is highly conservative, is domestic-market-based and only recently has started to see internationalization as an attractive growth strategy. Consequently, companies in the industry range from domestic micro firms to large multinationals (Finnish Food Industry 2012).

Data Collection and Respondents' Profile

We collected quantitative data from 160 companies operating in the Finnish food industry. The population of interest was defined as Finnish companies operating in the food industry. Unfortunately, due to the unsuitability of standard industry classification codes, no single, up-to-date sampling frame was available. The names and contact information of companies, therefore, were sought from multiple sources, including the ProFinder and Asiakastieto databases, industry associations, governmental registers and professional magazines. A total of 2875 companies were identified, but valid e-mail addresses were acquired for only 2135. At this point, another seven companies were found to be ineligible for the study. A web-based, structured questionnaire was sent by e-mail to 2128 entrepreneurs and managing directors in autumn 2011. After a month, 150 companies were reminded by telephone, with the aim to ensure the representativeness of the sample (e.g. in company size and industry category). In this phase, nine companies had to be excluded from the dataset due to inadequate responses to the questionnaire, while 24 potential respondents refused to participant.

Altogether, 160 companies responded, yielding a response rate of 7.5%. Although regrettably low, the rate can be considered to be adequate as the questionnaire was extensive, and the respondents were mostly managing directors and entrepreneurs with busy schedules. Furthermore, the nature of the industry itself produced challenges in reaching respondents; typically, the companies and their managers work 24/7 (e.g. in the bakery and dairy industries), and especially in the smallest companies, the entrepreneur is involved in operational activities.

The demonstrated respondent bias is also notable. We compared the respondents and non-respondents by company size (number of employees), industry category and company location. The statistical analysis revealed that the data were clearly biased towards larger firms, and in particular, the share of bakeries in our dataset was smaller than in the whole population (26% vs. 33%). Although both shortcomings are understandable—a study focusing on internationalization is unlikely to attract the interest of the smallest, micro-sized and domestic-market-oriented firms—they were taken into account in the analysis and when drawing the conclusions.

Despite the bias towards larger firms, the companies in the dataset were quite small. The average revenue of the participating companies stood at 5.4 million euros, and their small size was also indicated in their number of employees: 73% employed ten or fewer full-time personnel. The median value for year of founding was 1991, indicating that the companies participating in the present study were relatively old, 30 years on average. The basic information on the companies is summarized in Table 10.1 on page 176.

Given the small size of the respondent companies and the subjective, cognitive nature of the entrepreneurial decision-making process (cf Perry *et al.* 2012), it was decided that focusing on a single decision-maker, typically the entrepreneur or managing director, is sufficient for the study purposes. This choice naturally raises the question of single informant bias. Although this decision can be considered to be a shortcoming, we should keep in mind that in SMEs, decision-making related to internationalization is heavily centralized in the key persons (e.g. Lloyd-Reason and Mughan 2002; Reid 1981). Therefore, from the decision-making perspective, the informants can be expected to provide a fairly accurate picture of the phenomenon.

Although many companies were relatively long established, the majority (72.5%) ran no international operations, in line with the general situation in the industry in Finland (cf Finnish Food industry 2012). On average, the firms that operated internationally had done so for a decade, and their lack of experience in international business was also reflected in the share of exports, quite low for most respondents (see Table 10.2 on page 177). Most companies (65%) focused their international operations on three or fewer international markets.

Table 10.1 Profile of the Respondents (n = 160)

	Mean	Median	Std Deviation	Minimum	Maximum
Revenue in 2010 (€ million)	5.4	0.55	18.39	0*)	191
Number of Employees in 2010	22	6	73.20	0*)	800
Establishment Year	1981	1991	29.25	1857	2011*)

* If a firm was established in 2011, there was no revenue or employees in 2010.

Table 10.2 Profile of Respondents with International Experience (n = 44)

	Mean	Median	Std Deviation	Minimum	Maximum
Exports Share in 2010	18.95	7.00	26.65	0	97
Start Year of International Operations	1998	2001	13.22	1948	2010

Measure Development

Causation-Based Decision-Making

Empirical studies on causation and effectuation are rare, and it is argued that one reason is the difficulty to develop appropriate measures (Perry *et al.* 2012). This difficulty might arise as the few empirical studies on causation and effectuation treat them as "two sides of the same coin" when, in fact, they are distinct constructs (Chandler *et al.* 2011). Based on earlier studies, we developed a measure for causation-based decision-making. To evaluate the respondents' causation-based decision-making, they were asked to reflect on statements based on earlier research. The respondents rated their agreement with each item using a 7-point Likert-type scale.

To test whether the measure also works within our data set, we conducted rotated factor analysis of eight items. The factor analysis produced two factors, of which one confirmed our literature-based measure of causation-based decision-making. It showed extremely high loadings for and high correlation among all four variables (see Tables 10.3 and 10.4 on page 178).

In addition, the goodness-of-fit test showed that the factors did not deviate significantly from the original correlation matrix for each individual variable (X^2 = 16.867; df = 13, p = .205). To assess internal consistency among the variables in the summed variable, we used Cronbach's alpha based on the rationale that the individual items of the scale should all measure the same construct and thus be highly intercorrelated. In this case, the scale showed high reliability (.828), clearly exceeding the lowest acceptable limit of .70 (cf Hair *et al.* 2010, 125). A summated scale was calculated for the variable "causation-based decision-making" based on the average of each item.

Utilization of Network in Decision-Making

In our analysis of network utilization, we aimed to take into account both social and business ties. The respondents were asked to report on how many (1) family members and friends, (2) external experts and (3) business contacts (e.g. suppliers, distributors) they had consulted to support their

Table 10.3 Items Used to Describe Causation-based Decision-making in This Study (cf Chandler *et al.* 2011; Fisher 2012; Harms and Schiele 2012; Perry *et al.* 2012; Sarasvathy 2001).

Items	Factor loading
Our company applies analytic tools (e.g. computer-based programs) to important production-, market- or economics-related decisions.	.627
Our company utilizes external experts.	.652
Our company gathers systematically information on new supply, investment and market opportunities.	.888
Company management discusses systematically new solutions in their think tank sessions.	.809

Table 10.4 Correlation Matrix for Items Used to Describe Causation-based Decision-making in This Study (cf. Chandler *et al.* 2011; Fisher 2012; Harms and Schiele 2012; Perry *et al.* 2012; Sarasvathy 2001).

Item	Q1	Q2	Q3	Q4
Our company applies analytic tools (e.g. computer-based programs) to important production-, market- or economics-related decisions.	1	.494**	.540**	.470**
Our company utilizes external experts.	.494**	1	.734**	.500**
Our company gathers systematically information on new supply, investment and market opportunities.	.540**	.734**	1	.581**
Company management discusses systematically new solutions in their think tank sessions.	.470**	.500**	.581**	1

** Correlation is significant at the 0.01 level (two-tailed).

decision-making during the past half-year. The respondents were then summated to test the size of the network utilized to support decision-making. This absolute number was used for the analysis of P2a.

Next, the role of each type of network ties was evaluated. Network ties were labeled as personal ties, professional ties and business ties, and the sum of each type was calculated. Then, they were compared to the size of the network utilized to assess the relative share of each type of network ties. This relative share was used for the analysis of P2b.

Finally, the network-based benefits for decision-making were measured with nine benefits: related to firm development (four items), new customer contacts (two items) and market entry (three items) (cf. Ostgaard and Birley 1996). Each benefit item was evaluated with a 7-point Likert-type scale to assess the degree to which the respondent perceived the benefit to be realized through network consultation. The summated assessment as a measure of network-based benefits was used for the analysis of P2c.

Internationalization

For our analysis, we also needed a measure indicating companies' phase of internationalization. The phases of internationalization were taken from earlier research (Reid 1981) and validated in numerous studies. Respondents indicated whether they considered their companies to be (1) not interested in foreign markets (N = 72), (2) interested in foreign markets but not internationalised yet (N = 44), (3) experienced in sporadic exports (N = 18) or (4) conducting regular exports or sales abroad (N = 26). The answers were further controlled by another question regarding the exports' share of total revenue, and any inconsistency between the answers was further checked by phone. Due to the small number of export firms, the two last groups were combined into one. The resulting three groups were labelled as domestic firms (N = 72), potential exporters (N = 44) and exporters (N = 44) and were considered to indicate the internationalization phases of the responding companies in this study.

4. Findings and Discussion

First, we investigated whether the companies' decision-making logic in the various phases of internationalization differs from each other. In line with the measure used, causation-based decision-making refers to the systematic use of analytic tools, information collection, external experts and regular discussions in decision-making. A one-way analysis of variance (ANOVA) showed that the group means differ significantly; in other words, there was a clear deviation in decision-making logic related to internationalization ($F_{2,142}$ = 24.465, ***p < 0.001). Figure 10.1 (page 180) further illustrates the linear relationship between the internationalization phase and decision-making logic: the more internationalized the company is, the more likely it is to apply causation-based logic in its decision-making. Thus, *proposition 1 is supported.*

The network is an important source of knowledge and resources for the entrepreneur; therefore, we proposed that the utilization of network to support decision-making increases over the course of internationalization (P2a). We classified network relationships into three categories: family members and friends (personal ties), external experts (professional ties) and business contacts (business ties). To test P2a, we calculated each respondent's total number of contacts with network actors. We then conducted ANOVA to study whether the mean of contacts differs among groups of firms or, in other words, over the course of internationalization (Figure 10.2 on page 180).

Although Figure 10.2 seems to show clear differences in network size between firm groups, the difference is only marginal (e.g. between domestic

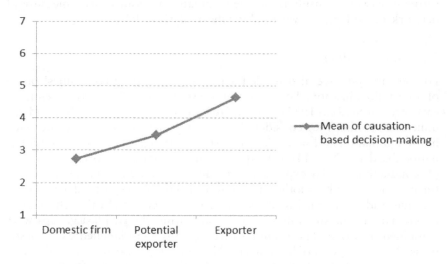

Figure 10.1 Causation-based Decision-making According to a Firm's Phase of Internationalization (scale 1 = not at all; 7 = very much)

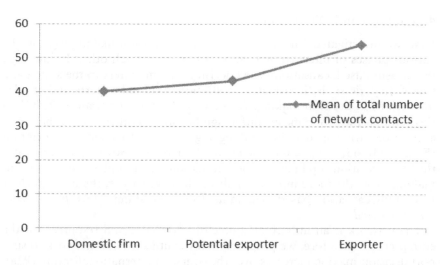

Figure 10.2 Size of Network (Measured with Number of Contacts with Network Actors) According to a Firm's Phase of Internationalization

firms and potential exporters), and no significant correlation was found ($F_{2,149}$ = .760, p > 0.1). Thus, the utilization of network to support decision-making does not increase over the course of internationalization, although a difference in network utilization seems to exist between exporters and other firm types. *P2 is not supported.*

Next, to study changes in networks, we performed ANOVA to study whether the mean (average share of all network ties) of each category deviates among firm groups (Figure 10.3, page 181).

First, business ties are notably the most extensive network for every group of firms. According to the above, the emphasis on the closest surrounding contacts, such as family and friends (i.e. personal ties) significantly diminishes along with the firm's internationalization ($F_{2,148} = 7.328$, ***$p = 0.001$), while the role of network members in the business environment increases almost at the same rate ($F_{2,148} = 3.231$, *$p < 0.05$). However, the role of experts external to the firm (i.e. professional ties) remains at a relatively same level regardless of the level of the firm's internationalization, indicating no significant correlation ($F_{2,149} = .931$, $p > 0.1$). Thus, the network utilized to support decision-making becomes relatively more sophisticated and specialized over the course of internationalization, as proposed. Therefore, we can conclude that *proposition P2b is partially supported.*

To study the network-based benefits perceived by respondents, we conducted ANOVA to study the summated mean of all nine benefit items and whether it deviates among firm groups (see Figure 10.4 on page 182).

Network-based benefits vary slightly but significantly according to phase of internationalization ($F_{2,153} = 3.383$, *$p < 0.05$). A closer look shows that the most significant differences appear in the benefits of gaining market knowledge ($F_{2,145} = 10,711$, ***$p < 0.001$) and finding new business contacts ($F_{2,149} = 5,791$, **$p < 0.01$), thus, in outwards-based, market entry benefits. To conclude, the perceived network-based benefits for decision-making

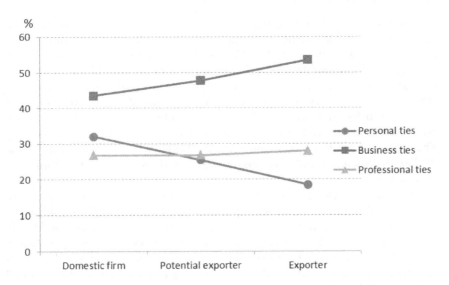

Figure 10.3 Average Share of Different Network Ties According to a Firm's Phase of Internationalization

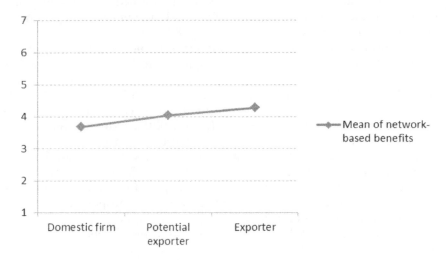

Figure 10.4 Average Benefits of Networks According to a Firm's Phase of Internationalization (scale 1 = not at all; 7 = very much)

seem to increase over the course of internationalization. *Proposition P2c is slightly supported.*

5. Conclusions and Future Directions

The findings point to interesting themes for discussion as they partly confirm but also complement the findings of earlier studies in a number of ways. In line with prior studies (Ahi *et al.* 2017; Bilkey and Tesar 1977; Cavusgil and Godiwalla 1982; Schweizer 2012), we found that entrepreneurial decision-making is more rational and formal among firms that already have international experience. These firms also seem to rely more on causation-based decision-making logic than the firms that are in the early phases of internationalization or have not entered international markets. Thus, the quantitative study confirmed the findings of prior qualitative case studies (Gabrielsson and Gabrielsson 2013; Kalinic *et al.* 2014; Nummela *et al.* 2014).

The findings also confirmed that, over time, the network utilized in decision-making becomes more sophisticated. We also provided additional information on how and why this happens. In line with Eberhard and Craig (2013), we found that firms use interpersonal networks for opportunity exploration, but these networks are not sufficient in the later phases of internationalization. When SMEs grow, whether in age, size or international coverage, their stakeholder base increases, broadens, deepens and becomes more formal, which usually creates more rigidity, demands, responsibilities and hierarchy in firms and decreases effectual, entrepreneurial behaviour. For example, financiers take more interest in how and what decisions are made as the stakes are higher. There are more employees to take care of, and rapidly making very risky decisions seems more difficult as the results of bad decisions affect more people. As well, the number of people making decisions can increase, requiring "longer negotiation" than the entrepreneur exclusively deciding an issue then and there (e.g. Paavilainen-Mäntymäki 2009).

As the network expands and becomes more sophisticated, the perceived network-based benefits for decision-making increase, especially in market knowledge and new business contacts (see, e.g., Nummela 2010). Therefore, internationalizing firms utilize their networks for market entry purposes. Thus, this result supports the idea of decreased 'liability of outsidership' in internationalization (cf. Johanson and Vahlne 2009)—to internationalize, firms need to have access to relevant networks.

However, our findings also question some claims made in earlier research. For example, professional ties with other companies, consultants and professional service providers are argued to be of importance, especially for companies still aiming to enter international markets (e.g. Fletcher and Harris 2012). Our data set does not confirm this hypothesis, possibly for multiple reasons. First, the partners with professional ties are a very heterogeneous group, which might be one factor confusing the results. Second, the short-term nature of these relationships might also influence the findings; only strong network ties might be important (on strong and weak ties, see Granovetter 1973). Finally, it has to be kept in mind that both the experiential learning and the capabilities of the decision-maker increase during the internationalization process, reducing the need and thus the importance of professional ties in the network. For professional practitioners, however, this study indicates that professional services, when targeted and specified properly, are useful in every phase of internationalization.

The reader should keep in mind that this study is cross-sectional in nature and provides only a snapshot view of firms' activities. Internationalization should be understood in the contexts of the industries, companies and people involved (Boter and Holmqvist 1996), and we know that the industrial context does make a difference when studying decision-making and network attachment in internationalization (Child and Hsieh 2014). Therefore, we cannot draw very strong conclusions about the (causal) relationships between the constructs in our model. In particular, the research setting does not permit explaining the development of decision-making logic in the internationalization process as we do not have process data but variance-type data at hand (cf Langley 1999). Additionally, this is a single-country, single-industry study, and the propositions should be more rigorously tested using several samples and a longitudinal research design.

We did not study the influences of decision-making styles on firm performance, which could be an avenue for future research: if effectuation decreases along with internationalization, what are its consequences for internationalization performance? Is development towards causation-based decision-making necessary for an internationalizing, growing firm, or does such a firm have more options (cf Ahi *et al.* 2017)? Accordingly, research on the decision-making style of networks is needed: can networks operate effectually, and where in the networks does decision-making take place?

Finally, recent research demonstrates the linear, sequential and stages models of internationalization not to be accurate. Instead, a more complex, nonlinear progression is found to be closer to the reality of internationalization (e.g. Hurmerinta *et al.* 2016; Welch and Paavilainen-Mäntymäki 2014) and the entrepreneurial decision-making process embedded in the internationalization process. Therefore, the interplay between causation and effectuation and their influences on firm performance should be opened to more in-depth research.

Note

1 Acknowledgment: This work was supported by the Estonian Research Council's grant PUT 1003.

References

Ahi, Ali, Gianpaolo Baronchelli, Olli Kuivalainen, and Mariella Piantoni. 2017. "International Market Entry: How Do SMEs Make Decisions?" *Journal of International Marketing* 25(1): 1–21.
Andersson, Svante. 2011. "International Entrepreneurship, Born Globals and the Theory of Effectuation." *Journal of Small Business and Enterprise Development* 28(3): 627–643.
Barnard, Chester I. 1938. *The Functions of the Executive.* Cambridge, MA: Harvard University Press.
Baum, J. Robert, and Stefan Wally. 2003. "Strategic Decision Speed and Firm Performance." *Strategic Management Journal* 24(11): 1107–1129.
Bilkey, Warren J., and George Tesar. 1977. "The Export Behavior of Smaller-Sized Wisconsin Manufacturing Firms." *Journal of International Business Studies* 8(1): 93–98.
Björkman, Ingmar, and Mats Forsgren. 2000. "Nordic International Business Research." *International Studies of Management & Organization* 30(1): 6–25.
Bonaccorsi, Andrea. 1992. "On the Relationship Between Firm Size and Export Intensity." *Journal of International Business Studies* 23(4): 605–635.
Boter, Håkan, and Carin Holmqvist. 1996. "Industry Characteristics and Internationalization Processes in Small Firms." *Journal of Business Venturing* 11(6): 471–487.
Calof, Jonathan L., and Paul W. Beamish. 1995. "Adapting to Foreign Markets: Explaining Internationalization." *International Business Review* 4(2): 115–131.
Cavusgil, S. Tamer, and Yezdi M. Godiwalla. 1982. "Decision-Making for International Marketing: A Comparative Review." *Management Decision* 20(4): 47–54.
Chandler, Gaylen N., Dawn R. DeTienne, Alexander McKelvie, and Troy V. Mumford. 2011. "Causation and Effectuation Processes: A Validation Study." *Journal of Business Venturing* 26(3): 375–390.

Chetty, Sylvie, Arto Ojala, and Tanja Leppäaho. 2015. "Effectuation and Foreign Market Entry of Entrepreneurial Firms." *European Journal of Marketing* 49 (9–10): 1436–1459.

Child, John, and Linda H.Y. Hsieh. 2014. "Decision Mode, Information and Network Attachment in the Internationalization of SMEs: A Configurational and Contingency Analysis." *Journal of World Business* 49(4): 598–610.

Collinson, Simon, and John Houlden. 2005. "Decision-Making and Market Orientation in the Internationalization Process of Small and Medium-Sized Enterprises." *Management International Review* 45(4): 413–436.

Coviello, Nicole. 2006. "The Network Dynamics of International New Ventures." *Journal of International Business Studies* 37(5): 713–731.

Coviello, Nicole, and Hugh J. Munro. 1995. "Growing the Entrepreneurial Firm. Networking for International Market Development." *European Journal of Marketing* 29(7): 49–61.

Crick, Dave, and Martine Spence. 2005. "The Internationalisation of 'High Performing' UK High-Tech SMEs: A Study of Planned and Unplanned Strategies." *International Business Review* 14(2): 167–185.

Eberhard, Manuel, and Justin Craig. 2013. "The Evolving Role of Organisational and Personal Networks in International Market Venturing." *Journal of World Business* 48(3): 385–397.

Engel, Yuval, Mariëtte Kaandorp, and Tom Elfring. 2017. "Toward a Dynamic Process Model of Entrepreneurial Networking Under Uncertainty." *Journal of Business Venturing* 32(1): 35–51.

Evers, Natasha, and Colm O'Gorman. 2011. "Improvised Internationalization in New Ventures: The Role of Prior Knowledge and Networks." *Entrepreneurship & Regional Development* 23(7–8): 549–574.

Finnish Ministry of Economy and Employment. 2012. "Finnish Food Industry." www.temtoimialapalvelu.fi/files/1607/Elintarviketeollisuus2012_web.pdf. Accessed November 2.

Fisher, Greg. 2012. "Effectuation, Causation, and Bricolage: A Behavioral Comparison of Emerging Theories in Entrepreneurship Research." *Entrepreneurship Theory & Practice* 36(5): 1019–1051.

Fletcher, Margaret, and Simon Harris. 2012. "Knowledge Acquisition for the Internationalization of the Smaller Firm: Content and Sources." *International Business Review* 21(4): 631–647.

Gabrielsson, Peter, and Mika Gabrielsson. 2013. "A Dynamic Model of Growth Phases and Survival in International Business-to-Business New Ventures: The Moderating Effect of Decision-Making Logic." *Industrial Marketing Management* 42(8): 1357–1373.

Galkina, Tamara. 2013. "Entrepreneurial Networking: Intended and Unintended Processes." PhD diss., Hanken School of Economics.

Galkina, Tamara, and Sylvie Chetty. 2015. "Effectuation and Networking of Internationalizing SMEs." *Management International Review* 55(5): 647–676.

Granovetter, Mark S. 1973. "The Strength of Weak Ties." *American Journal of Sociology* 78(6): 1360–1380.

Hair Jr., Joseph F., William C. Black, Barry J. Babin, and Rolph E. Anderson. 2010. *Multivariate Data Analysis: Global Perspective.* Upper Saddle River, NJ: Pearson Education.

Harms, Rainer, and Holger Schiele. 2012. "Antecedents and Consequences of Effectuation and Causation in the International New Venture Creation Process." *Journal of International Entrepreneurship* 10(2): 95–116.

Hewerdine Lisa Jane, Maria Rumyantseva, and Catherine Welch. 2014. "Resource Scavenging. Another Dimension of the Internationalisation Pattern of High-Tech SMEs." *International Marketing Review* 31(3): 237–258.

Hurmerinta Leila, Eriikka Paavilainen-Mäntymäki, and Mélanie Hassett. 2016. "TEMPUS FUGIT: A Hermeneutic Approach to the Internationalisation Process." *Management International Review* 56(6): 805–825.

Jack, Sarah, Sarah Drakopoulou Dodd, and Alistair R. Anderson. 2008. "Change and the Development of Entrepreneurial Networks Over Time: A Processual Perspective." *Entrepreneurship & Regional Development* 20(2): 125–159.

Johannisson, Bengt. 1988. "Business Formation—A Network Approach." *Scandinavian Journal of Management* 4(3): 83–99.

Johanson, Jan, and Jan-Erik Vahlne. 1977. "The Internationalisation Process of the Firm—A Model of Knowledge Development and Increasing Foreign Market Commitments." *Journal of International Business Studies* 8(1): 23–32.

Johanson, Jan, and Jan-Erik Vahlne. 2009. "The Uppsala Internationalization Process Model Revisited: From Liability of Foreignness to Liability of Outsidership." *Journal of International Business Studies* 40(9): 1411–1431.

Jones, Marian V., and Nicole Coviello. 2005. "Internationalisation: Conceptualising an Entrepreneurial Process of Behaviour in Time." *Journal of International Business Studies* 36(3): 284–303.

Kalinic, Igor, Saras D. Sarasvathy, and Cipriano Forza. 2014. "Expect the Unexpected: Implications of Effectual Logic on the Internationalization Process." *International Business Review* 23(3): 635–646.

Langley, Ann. 1999. "Strategies for Theorizing from Process Data." *Academy of Management Review* 24(4): 691–710.

Leonidou, Leonidas C., and Constantine S. Katsikeas. 1996. "The Export Development Process: An Integrative Review of Empirical Models." *Journal of International Business Studies* 27(3): 517–551.

Liesch, Peter W., Lawrence S. Welch, and Peter J. Buckley. 2011. "Risk and Uncertainty in Internationalisation and International Entrepreneurship Studies: Review and Conceptual Development." *Management International Review* 51(6): 851–873.

Lloyd-Reason, Lester, and Terry Mughan. 2002. "Strategies for Internationalisation Within SMEs: The Key Role of the Owner-Manager." *Journal of Small Business and Enterprise Development* 9(2): 120–129.

Luostarinen, Reijo. 1979. "Internationalization of the Firm, an Empirical Study of the Internationalization of Firms with Small and Open Domestic Markets with Special Emphasis on Lateral Rigidity as a Behavioral Characteristic in Strategic Decision-Making." PhD diss., Helsinki School of Economics.

Mainela, Tuija, and Vesa Puhakka. 2009. "Organising New Business in a Turbulent Context: Opportunity Discovery and Effectuation for IJV Development in Transition Markets." *Journal of International Entrepreneurship* 7(2): 111–134.

Michailova, Snejina. 2011. "Contextualizing in International Business Research: Why Do We Need More of It and How Can We Be Better at It?" *Scandinavian Journal of Management* 27(1): 129–139.

Minzberg, Henry, and James A. Waters. 1985. "Of Strategies, Deliberate and Emergent." *Strategic Management Journal* 6(3): 257–272.

Musteen, Martina, John Francis, and Deepak K. Datta. 2010. "The Influence of International Networks on Internationalization Speed and Performance: A Study of Czech SMEs." *Journal of World Business* 45(3): 197–205.

Nummela, Niina. 2010. "Change in SME Internationalization: A Network Perspective." In *International Growth of Small and Medium Enterprises*, edited by Niina Nummela, 248–263. New York: Routledge.

Nummela, Niina, Sami Saarenketo, Päivi Jokela, and Sharon Loane. 2014. "Strategic Decision-Making of a Born Global Firm: A Comparative Study from Three Small Open Economies." *Management International Review* 54(4): 527–550.

Ojala, Arto. 2009. "Internationalization of Knowledge-Intensive SMEs: The Role of Network Relationships in the Entry to Physically Distant Market." *International Business Review* 18(1): 50–59.

Ostgaard, Tone A., and Sue Birley. 1996. "New Venture Growth and Personal Networks." *Journal of Business Research* 36(1): 37–50.

Paavilainen-Mäntymäki, Eriikka. 2009. "Unique Paths: The International Growth Process of Selected Finnish SMEs." PhD diss., Turku School of Economics.

Perks, Keith J., and Mathew Hughes. 2008. "Entrepreneurial Decision-Making in Internationalization: Propositions from Mid-Size Firms." *International Business Review* 17(3): 310–330.

Perry, John T., Gaylen N. Chandler, and Gergana Markova. 2012. "Entrepreneurial Effectuation: A Review and Suggestions for Future Research." *Entrepreneurship Theory & Practice* 36(4): 837–861.

Pettigrew, Andrew M. 1987. "Context and Action in the Transformation of a Firm." *Journal of Management Studies* 24(6): 649–670.

Reid, Stan D. 1981. "The Decision-Maker and Export Entry and Expansion." *Journal of International Business Studies* 12: 101–112.

Ruokonen, Mika, Niina Nummela, Kaisu Puumalainen, and Sami Saarenketo. 2006. "Network Management—The Key to Successful Rapid Internationalisation of a Small Software Firm?" *International Journal of Entrepreneurship and Innovation Management* 6: 554–572.

Sarasvathy, Saras D. 2001. "Causation and Effectuation: Toward a Theoretical Shift from Economic Inevitability to Entrepreneurial Contingency." *Academy of Management Review* 26(2): 243–263.

Sarasvathy, Saras D. 2008. *Effectuation: Elements of Entrepreneurial Experience.* Cheltenham, UK: Edward Elgar.

Sarasvathy, Saras D., Nicholas Dew, Stuart Read, and Robert Wiltbank. 2008. "Designing Organizations that Design Environments: Lessons from Entrepreneurial Expertise." *Organization Studies* 29(3): 331–350.

Schweizer, Roger. 2012. "The Internationalization Process of SMEs: A Muddling-Through Process." *Journal of Business Research* 65(6): 745–751.

Schweizer, Roger, Jan-Erik Vahlne, and Jan Johanson. 2010. "Internationalization as an Entrepreneurial Process." *Journal of International Entrepreneurship* 8(4): 343–370.

Slotte-Kock, Susanna, and Nicole Coviello. 2010. "Entrepreneurship Research on Network Processes: A Review and Ways Forward." *Entrepreneurship Theory & Practice* 34(1): 31–57.

Spence, Martine, and Dave Crick. 2006. "A Comparative Investigation into the Internationalisation of Canadian and UK High-Tech SMEs." *International Marketing Review* 23(5): 524–548.

Weick, Karl E. 1979. *The Social Psychology of Organizing*. Reading, MA: Addison-Wesley.

Welch, Catherine, and Eriikka Paavilainen-Mäntymäki. 2014. "Putting Process (Back) in: Research on the Internationalization Process of the Firm." *International Journal of Management Reviews* 16(1): 2–23.

Ylirenko, Helena, Erkko Autio, and Vesa Tontti. 2002. "Social Capital, Knowledge, and the International Growth of Technology-Based New Firms." *International Business Review* 11(3): 279–304.

Part IV
Internationalization

11 Growth Ambitions and Internationalization Among Newly Started Small Swedish Firms

Gert-Olof Boström, Karl Johan Bonnedahl and Lars Silver

1. Introduction

Small firms are essential for any national economy due to their aggregate number of employees, their role in technological change and productivity growth, and essentially in economic development (Boter and Lundström 2005; Glower 1999; Eurostat 2016). Whereas much research takes departure in the broader SME category, an explicit delimitation to the smaller firms means that we will find many self-employed and enterprises where the main intention is to secure a livelihood for the owner/manager rather than to expand business operations. Nevertheless, small firms hold important roles for employment and income generation not least in local and regional settings. The smallest category of firms naturally also contains many new ventures, firms which have not yet proven if they will survive or fail in the long run. As such, they constitute crucial components in development and change on a societal level: New ventures are needed for a dynamic and developing economy. Such processes could relate to the development of new technologies, new forms of organization and marketing, and to various ways to approach sustainable development, not least by the use of new business models (e.g. Bocken *et al.* 2014).

In order to understand the potential success of small firms, and the realization of processes such as the ones mentioned above, we turn to entrepreneurship research. Gnyawali and Fogel (1994) developed a model combining elements such as opportunity, ability to enterprise and propensity to enterprise, in order to explain entrepreneurial development. It is argued that the combination of an entrepreneur's capacity and drive, together with a slight stroke of chance, is what defines the development of an enterprise. The model builds on an extensive overview of the literature of the times, and the article from 1994 bears witness to how entrepreneurship research focused on small business growth as something both achievable and preferable at a society level, mostly in terms of job opportunities and expansion of the economy. Only later on did concepts such as social entrepreneurship and sustainable businesses emerge to further the explanations of entrepreneurial development (Dean and McMullen 2007; Hultman *et al.* 2016; Nicholls 2010).

Taking the perspective from Northern Europe, and more specifically from the *Northern Sparsely Populated Areas* (NSPA; e.g. Gløersen *et al.* 2005, 2009), it is often a necessity that an expanding small business needs to set sights to larger, often international, markets. Consequently, NSPA firms, including Swedish firms, have a long tradition of international business, and this chapter focuses on growth ambitions of small and particularly new ventures in a two-stage process. First the entrepreneur's general ambitions to expand the firm's operations (from here on: to grow) is in focus as this is seen as paramount in relation to activity in any market, including foreign markets. However, as indicated above, there is a need for international growth among the NSPA firms, and foreign markets may present particular challenges, which is why attention is given to what obstacles entrepreneurs perceive for increasing export and how these obstacles should be overcome. These analyses are done in order to understand how small businesses of today act in order to secure a place in the international market.

2. Background

Finding the Opportunity

According to neoclassical economic theory, which holds a predominant role in economic policy and analysis, growth of individual firms would be related to imperfections of markets, situations in which resources could be more efficiently used through entrepreneurial activities. This logic would also explain the lack of uniformity in the size of firms in a market and the differences in resources available to different firms. One impact of this difference regarding resources would be variations in ability to grow (Penrose 1959), and research has reported a number of disadvantages held by small-sized firms compared to larger firms (Ates and Bititci 2011; Beaver and Jennings 2000).

Nevertheless, small firms exist, and within the academic field of entrepreneurship, the roles of the entrepreneurial individual and emerging opportunities have been emphasized (e.g. Cohen and Winn 2007; Schaltegger and Wagner 2011). Consistent with our experiences of real-world markets, where deviations from the perfect markets of neoclassical economics are the rule, opportunities can be understood as emerging from imperfections (e.g. Dutta and Crossan 2005). However, to not get stuck in a deterministic position, we must not only recognize agency, but also understand the entrepreneur's role with more sophistication than when an opportunity seeking "black box" is used. This implies that we also must recognize limitations in the entrepreneurial decision-making of the real world.

This way of arguing leaves us with a combination of a macro description of circumstances relevant for the emergence and growth of SMEs and a micro description, arguably relevant also due to the close relation between the individual entrepreneur and the behavior of the small firm (Boter and

Lundström 2005). It is thus of importance to consider the entrepreneur when analyzing, for example, growth in SMEs. One model that takes both the environment and the entrepreneur into consideration is the one by Gnyawali and Fogel (1994). It was developed to enable an understanding of "the emergence and growth of enterprises in a country" (Gnyawali and Fogel 1994, 43) and takes departure in opportunities. In the model, and consistent with the environment-actor duality, opportunity refers to two issues: the extent to which there are possibilities for new firms in the market and the extent to which the entrepreneur can influence the possibilities for success by their own actions. In order to elaborate on the model of Gnyawali and Fogel, the nuances of the entrepreneur should be taken into consideration. Entrepreneurs are people with different ambitions which affect the business orientation (see, for instance, Lumpkin and Dess 2001; Runyan *et al.* 2008; Wiklund *et al.* 2009). Thus, it is not only market conditions and opportunities that affect the growth of enterprises in a country, but also the entrepreneur's ambitions that are crucial.

Entrepreneurial Orientation and Growth of Small Business

By looking at nascent entrepreneurship, researchers have understood that there are different kinds of entrepreneurs: those who only start a business in order to make a living, and those who start a business explicitly to see how far they can take that idea, in terms of growth. According to this research, most entrepreneurs are of the former type, and have what we can call a "small business orientation," meaning that they are unwilling or uninterested in rapid growth (Stewart and Roth 2001). The alternative "entrepreneurial orientation" has been described as a strategic choice (Miles *et al.* 2000), but small business orientation is also a choice. In some cases, small business owners even chose not to grow when they had ample opportunities to do so (Runyan *et al.* 2008).

Consistent with an entrepreneurial orientation, entrepreneurs engage in entrepreneurial activity. What actually constitutes an entrepreneurial activity has been contested (Davidsson *et al.* 2002), but as Fuller and Moran (2001) have described it, entrepreneurial action typically concerns acting in a complex environment in order to maximize the potential for growth. Entrepreneurial orientation is, however, dependent on the managerial qualities in SMEs (Koeller and Lechler 2006), and management skills have been considered a strong prognosticator for success (Cressy 2006). Here we can see the common denominator with Håkan Boter's idea that entrepreneurs need to have both the willingness and a certain quality (Boter and Lundström 2005).

Internationalizing the Small Business

Based on the notion of opportunity, and recognizing agency as well as limitations, entrepreneurs who have the willingness and a certain capacity may succeed in expanding their firm's operations. However, it turns out that internationalization, which is a relevant strategy not least in the sparsely populated Northern Europe, presents a number of challenges. If the uncertainty in local and regional expansion is already high, foreign markets often challenge the capable entrepreneur with a set of different norms and values together with new regulations and languages (Child *et al*. 2002; Hofstede 2001; Rhee and Cheng 2002; Sousa and Bradley 2006).

Hence, in relation to the model presented by Gnyawali and Fogel (1994), internationalization poses a variety of challenges which call for additional concepts. With ambitions to increase international sales, firms may meet challenges of, in principle, four main types (cf. Bonnedahl 2011; Leonidou 2004; Miesenbock 1988). Their access to foreign markets can be restricted by obstacles relating to "the home and host environment within which the firm operates" (Leonidou 2004, 281), such as tariffs, distance or differences in regulation. While this type of challenge is external to the firm, concerns market conditions, and can be said to reside on the macro level, other challenges and potential obstacles to international expansion correspond to meso or micro levels of analysis.

As the second type challenge, a firm's capabilities and resources with regard to the handling of opportunities and threats in a foreign market can also pose limitations, as they may be more or less sufficient to overcome any market condition that form an obstacle which is external to the firm (Campbell 1996; Fliess and Busquets 2006). This discussion clearly relates to the capacity and skills of the individual firm and the entrepreneur. Third, enabling or constraining characteristics can be related to a firm's region or networks, thus constituting a form intermediate to the "external" and "internal" obstacles mentioned above (Child, Ng and Wong 2002; Johansson and Elg 2002). An outsidership to the business environment's web of relationships was actually found to be the main root of uncertainty in international business operations when Johanson and Vahlne "revisited" the Uppsala internationalization model (Johanson and Vahlne 2009). Nevertheless, and fourth, the subjective perceptions of the various types of objective, or external, obstacles can still be crucial for decision making on internationalization (Crick 2012; Leonidou 2004; Miesenbock 1988).

Consistent with these challenges, one of the most widespread ideas as to how firms cope with internationalization is to adopt a strategy of incremental expansion (Johanson and Vahlne 1977). However, much of the research on internationalization has been made on large, or even very large enterprises (Teece 2014). This situation is unfortunate as the opportunities for small firms to internationalize are greater today than they were two decades ago (Zander *et al*. 2015). While we here limit the discussion to international sales, mainly through exports (but acknowledging equal opportunities in imports and other international activities), the chances of expanding a small firm through a process of internationalization is part of an overall trend. This may even be seen in large firms being younger than before (Reeves *et al.* 2016). It has also resulted in an emerging trend of investigating small firms as being "born global" (Knight and Cavusgil 2004; Moen and Servais 2002); a research interest which includes one of Boter's doctoral students (Abrahamsson 2016). Furthermore, contemporary research on internationalization of small business engages in questions such as management capabilities (Hennart 2014), the importance of legitimization (Makela and Maula 2005), social networks (Sasi and Aurenius 2008) and not least, the ability to adapt and reconfigure (Gabrielsson and Gabrielsson 2013).

We can therefore anticipate that the willingness to internationalize should as great as ever, given the ample opportunities provided. At the same time, many of the potential pitfalls remain, as does competition. Internationalization opens doors that may turn the small business into a large and multinational enterprise, but it can also lead to the eventual demise of the entire operation.

Challenges to Growth Ambitions

As we have seen, the list of potential obstacles to small businesses going international includes micro and meso level factors, which were also addressed by Gnyawali and Fogel (1994). We need to take a look at these, too, in order to get a more fundamental understanding of the enterprise; that is, to identify factors behind the development of a firm to the level of being a candidate for international expansion. First, and on the micro level, Gnyawali and Fogel (1994, 56) present the ability to enterprise referring to "the sum of technical and business capabilities required to start and manage a business." Thus, this ability concerns the entrepreneur's collection of knowledge that makes it possible to run a business, e.g., marketing management, logistics, research and development. This knowledge must also be under development and adapted to upcoming opportunities and challenges. As one example, the rapid change in business today regarding the use of social media as a marketing channel demands concurrent development and education. According to Boter and Lundström (2005) there is a need for resources available for support and stimulation of managers and key personnel. These authors also want to stress the need for external help in the firms in the form of consultancies. Further, they argue that "The main purpose of small business policy is to increase business competence" (Boter and Lundström 2005, 247).

The second factor at this level in Gnyawali and Fogel's (1994, 53) model is "Propensity to enterprise," referring to "the psychological and behavioral characteristics of entrepreneurs." This adheres to the classic study by McClelland and Winter (1969) and their finding of high need of achievement among entrepreneurs, to the capacity to innovate by Schumpeter (1934), and to the internal locus of control (Shapero 1977). All these studies taken together demonstrate that the entrepreneur needs to have specific personal characteristics in order to succeed in the creation or harvesting of opportunities to expand the business. Scoring high regarding "propensity to enterprise" means that the person has a large motivation and a mind-set required to start and or develop a business.

According to Gnyawali and Fogel (1994), together with opportunity, the ability to enterprise and the propensity to enterprise affect the "likelihood to enterprise." In terms of the context of this paper, these three factors can be understood as factors necessary for expansion. While the summarizing factor (likelihood) absorbs what comes out of the prior ones, the first three are directed by underlying factors, such as when new opportunities are given if regulation changes in favor of an industry or the whole business sector. Likewise, the ability to enterprise is affected, as indicated above, by entrepreneurial skills and business skills, an increase in which augments the likelihood of new venture creation and expansion. Finally, the propensity to enterprise is, not least, affected by socio-economic factors. The personal profile of the entrepreneur is vital according to the model, but the model also wants to encompass the overall attitude of the general public in this factor (Gnyawali and Fogel 1994).

3. Design of the Study

The empirical base for this chapter is a survey among small Swedish firms. Data was collected between December 2015 and February 2016 by a professional marketing survey company. The CEO of each firm in the sample (described below) was called by telephone and interviewed on the basis of a structured questionnaire. Interviewing the CEO follows the idea from Boter and Lundström, who argue "that it is absolutely necessary to focus on the entrepreneur in order to understand and analyze market conditions" (245, 2005). In total, 1959 CEOs participated in the survey.

The structured questionnaire contained a mixture of open-ended questions and questions with fixed alternatives. In brief, the questionnaire themes were growth, innovation, financing, sustainability and international business. Included in the questionnaire were also some background variables.

The size of the firm has been found to affect operations and performance, e.g. through a weaker resource base (Boter and Holmquist 1996; Boter and Lundström 2005; Beaver and Jennings 2000). In order to consider the relationship between size and resources, and potentially operations, stratified random sampling was used in the study. Four categories were defined: newly started firms (firms that have operated three months or less), solo firms (firms that only have one employee), firms having two to nine employees, and firms having ten to forty-nine employees.

The sample was Swedish small firms where the strata were also constituted by location, to cater for differences in, for example, local market size and distance to foreign markets. A random sample of 20 companies for each of the four firm categories in each county in Sweden was used. There are 21 counties in Sweden. The ambition to get 20 firms per strata could, however, only be met in 3 out of 21 counties. While the total aim was 1680 interviews (4 × 20 × 21), the reached number of interviews was 1569, a total deviation of 111. The deviations were primarily due to lack of firms in certain categories in most of the counties.

The open-ended questions were carefully analyzed in accordance with the following process: alphabetic lists for all responses to the question were made in order to find describing themes for the responses. The response that the respondents had written first were considered as the top-of-mind alternative—the first thing that came to mind for the respondent when the question was read.

The analysis was done with the following rules: overall descriptions of the questions were done with weighted numbers. Thus, the overall description is a reflection of the actual situation in Sweden. When the analyses were between groups, unweighted numbers were used. Thus, there are two dimensions of analysis for each question: the distribution of growth ambitions for the firms was done with weighted numbers; however, to find out differences in ambitions between newly started firms, solo firms, two-to-nine-employee firms and ten-to-forty-nine-employee firms, unweighted numbers were used.

4. Findings

Newly started firms show a relatively high willingness to grow in the study. Almost a third (29.9 %) of the recently started firms stated their intention to expand rapidly. This is somewhat higher than the average for all respondents, and an expected difference as early stages of development make some expansion necessary, while older firms may have reached stages of maturity in their markets. Hence, many respondents did not declare an overall ambition (propensity) to expand rapidly. Among firms that have accumulated a certain growth (those between 10 and 49 employees), existing growth ambitions are either oriented towards gaining a larger market share (16.2 %), or towards consolidating profits (13.7 %).

In order to achieve growth, the firm needs to be located in a market permitting growth (opportunity) and be able to obtain resources for such growth (ability). One dimension that was assessed, that primarily focused on the opportunity and ability to grow, was the scalability of the business proposition. According to the results, newly started firms have a reasonably scalable business proposition (with a mean of 3.52 on a 1 to 5 scale and a median of 3). This can be related to the relatively small proportion of newly started firms that argue that they are able to grow. Certainly, some firms will have the opportunity and ability, but actually lack the propensity to grow. However, newly started firms may also meet a particular set of obstacles. In the study, the major difficulties in order to achieve growth were assessed to be either a strong competition or a lack of time. For larger firms, regarding the groups of firms in this study, a lack of sufficiently competent labor is indicated as an additional difficulty.

In order to overcome deficiencies, the newly started firms argue that additional market penetration in terms of networking, support and selling would handle the opportunity issue (which includes the level of competition), while the issue of time would be handled by finding ways to increase the amount of time available, which most likely means delegating tasks to others. Regarding the possibility to use external support, the newly started firms were in general lukewarm (a median of 2.54 on a 1 to 5 scale). The results may be in line with the notion that the higher the ambition is to grow, the more support from outside actors is needed in order to achieve that goal. In general, the results show that most firms nevertheless prefer to grow without outside support.

Among available opportunities to grow, internationalization is obviously one way of acquiring additional market share and profitability. To relate to the concept of born globals, only 8.4 % of the newly started businesses in our sample had started with an international market. The share of exporting firms among all respondents was 23.1%. As was the case with expansion in general, the study shows that internationalization is primarily prevented by a lack of access to markets (opportunity) and time (propensity) constraints. Added complexities that could create obstacles to international expansion were legal demands and certificates (ability). In addition, for the rapidly expanding firms, financing (ability) was a scarce resource as well.

Among the newly started firms, it was primarily the issue of acquiring time (19.2 %), and the development of the organization (15.4 %), that were mentioned as critical resources needed in order to further internationalization efforts. It is thereby relatively clear that newly started firms in one way or the other need the internal capabilities to augment internationalization. The same issues were at the core of internationalization for more mature firms as well

5. Discussion and Conclusions

In order to understand more about the dynamics in an economy, whether we have the traditional aim to promote employment or want to find tools that could help move society into a sustainable direction, knowledge about growing enterprises and about factors that enable or impede expansion is important. However, in spite of the many new challenges facing society as well as individual firms, our data from small Swedish firms reveal that central features of the circumstances that determine the success and expansion of small firms remain robust. It appears that while in the short run issues such as connecting to the market are most important in order to get the new firm started, internationalization is more an issue of translating these acquired competencies to new markets. Thus, at the outset opportunity and propensity seem more important as the newly started firm gets going. In the second stage of the internationalization process, the internal ability to adapt to new circumstances seems more important than opportunity.

To begin with, we must acknowledge that expansion is not, and cannot be, the aim of all entrepreneurs and business owners (cf Mochire *et al.* 2006). Further, among those with growth ambitions, many only aim for some growth or no growth at all. The fact that such ambitions—a small business orientation—predominate among the smallest firms, tells us that it is also often a matter of choice related to the life situation of a person or family that should be respected by analysts and policy makers.

As responses in our data show, some of the firms without high growth ambitions could however change plans if opportunities arise, to which potential causes would include various types of support and counseling, but such solutions were generally not favored by firms in our study.

This way of acting can be related to the mainstream and still largely applicable approach by Gnyawali and Fogel (1994), who took departure in markets with low barriers to entry. Somewhat paradoxically but arguably for this reason, the primary force affecting opportunities according to the model is governmental policies and procedures, such as those related to labor and taxation. In the context of our data, with the European common market as the major target for small firm internationalization, the model would not be fully applicable.

This situation implies that the step to go international is often smaller—or at least taken faster—compared to contexts where the near market is large, such as in major urban areas on the European continent. It is reasonable that in smaller markets there is also a more urgent need to plan for expansion into new markets for relatively small firms. In spite of the trend to internationalize more rapidly, the newly started firms displayed a significantly lower degree of internationalization. This might be explained by the need for smaller firms to hone their abilities before internationalizing, hence targeting the other main factor behind "propensity," ability (cf. Gnyawali and Fogel 1994). Nevertheless, our data give no reason to deny the positive sides of small firm abilities, such as flexibility, fast decision-making processes and the ability to respond quickly and adapt to changes due to a simple flat internal structure (Ghobadian and Gallear 1997).

Our conclusion from this inquiry is that firms are typically not born globally, even if that is still important in certain sectors. Born globally firms typically require a market that is clearly already international, and/or competencies that many firms lack. Internationalization is for most firms a process in which there are many obstacles along the way. Firstly, the firms need to acquire certain skills, but also time to focus on internationalization. Thus, it appears reasonable to argue that firms first establish themselves in the marketplace, which provides some of the resources necessary in order to internationalize. Secondly, the firms need to overcome obstacles such as rules and regulations, as well as financial constraints. These obstacles can be dealt with through experience (rules and regulations) as well as obtaining a track record (financing). Thus, again, time is important to provide a solid foundation for internationalization. However, since the firms in this study typically will find their home market to be limited in size, internationalization is still over time an important part of growing the firm. One conclusion from this research is to discuss internationalization in terms of acquiring experiences and competencies over time, in addition to the emerging concept of being born globally.

References

Abrahamsson, Jan. 2016. "Beyond Going Global: Essays on Business Development of International New Ventures Past Early Internationalization." PhD diss., Umeå University.

Ates, Aylin, and Umit Bititci. 2011. "Change Process: A Key Enabler for Building Resilient SMEs." *International Journal of Production Research* 49(18): 5601–18.

Beaver, Graham, and Peter Jennings. 2000. "Editorial Overview: Small Business, Entrepreneurship and Enterprise Development." *Strategic Change* 9(7): 397–403.

Bocken, Nancy M.P., Samuel W. Short, Padmakshi Rana, and Steve Evans. 2014. "A Literature and a Practice Review to Develop Sustainable Business Model Archetypes." *Journal of Cleaner Production* 65: 42–56.

Bonnedahl, Karl Johan. 2011. "Strategic Implications of European Economic Integration: The Relative Importance of Barrier Categories." *European Journal of International Management* 5(3): 235–252.

Boter, Håkan, and Carin Holmquist. 1996. "Industry Characteristics and Internationalization Processes in Small Firms." *Journal of Business Venturing* 11(6): 471–487.

Boter, Håkan, and Anders Lundström. 2005. "SME Perspectives on Business Support Services: The Role of Company Size, Industry and Location." *Journal of Small Business and Enterprise Development* 12(2): 244–258.

Boyd, Cohen, and Monica I. Winn. 2007. "Market Imperfections, Opportunity and Sustainable Entrepreneurship." *Journal of Business Venturing* 22(1): 29–49.

Campbell, Alexandra J. 1996. "The Effects of Internal Firm Barriers on the Export Behavior of Small Firms in a Free Trade Environment." *Journal of Small Business Management* 34(3): 50–58.

Child, Johan, Sek Hong Ng, and Christine Wong. 2002. "Psychic Distance and Internationalization." *International Studies of Management and Organisation* 32(1): 36–56.

Cressy, Robert. 2006. "Why Do Most Firms Die Young?" *Small Business Economics* 26(2): 103–116.

Crick, Dave. 2012. "SMEs' Barriers Towards Internationalisation and Assistance Requirements in the UK: Differences Between Exporters and Firms Employing Multiple Modes of Market Entry." *Journal of Small Business and Entrepreneurship* 20(3): 233–244.

Davidsson, Per, and Delmar, Frédéric, and Wiklund, Johan. 2002. "Entrepreneurship as Growth: Growth as Entrepreneurship." In *Entrepreneurship and the Growth of Firms*, edited by Per Davidsson, Frederic Delmar, and Johan Wiklund, 21–38. Cheltenham, UK: Edvard Elgar.

Dean, Thomas J., and McMullen, Jeffery S. 2007. "Toward a Theory of Sustainable Entrepreneurship: Reducing Environmental Degradation Through Entrepreneurial Action." *Journal of Business Venturing* 22(1): 50–76.

Dutta, Dev K., and Mary M. Crossan. 2005. "The Nature of Entrepreneurial Opportunities: Understanding the Process Using the 4I Organizational Learning Framework." *Entrepreneurship Theory and Practice* 29(4): 425–449.

Eurostat. 2016. "Small and Medium-Sized Enterprises (SMES)." http://ec.europa. eu/eurostat/web/structural-business-statistics/structural-business-statistics/ sme?p_p_id=NavTreeportletprod_WAR_NavTreeportletprod_INSTANCE_ vxlB58HY09rg&p_p_lifecycle=0&p_p_state=normal&p_p_mode=view&p_p_ col_icolumn-2&p_p_col_pos=1&p_p_col_count=4. Accessed September 19.

Fliess, Barbara, and Carlos Busquets. 2006. "The Role of Trade Barriers in SME Internationalization." OECD Trade Policy Working paper No. 45, Paris: OECD Publishing.

Fuller, Ted, and Paul Moran. 2001. "Small Enterprises as Complex Adaptive Systems: A Methodological Question?" *Entrepreneurship and Regional Development* 13(1): 47–63.

Gabrielsson, Peter, and Mika Gabrielsson. 2013. "A Dynamic Model of Growth Phases and Survival in International Business-to-Business New Ventures: The Moderating Effect of Decision-Making Logic." *Industrial Marketing Management* 42(8): 1357–1373.

Ghobadian, Abby and David Gallear. 1997. "TQM and Organization Size" *International Journal of Operation and Production Management*, 17(2): 121–163.

Gløersen, Erik, Alexandre Dubois, Andrew Copus, and Carsten Schurman. 2005. "Northern Peripheral, Sparsely Populated Regions in the European Union." Stockholm, Nordregio Report 2005, 4.

Gløersen, Erik, Alexandre Dubois, Johanna Roto, Rasmus Ole Rasmussen, and Jose Sterling. 2009. "Development perspectives for the NSPA: Opportunities and Challenges." Stockholm, Nordregio Working Paper 2009, 5.

Glover, Jere W. 1999. "Introduction to *Are Small Firms Important?*" In *Their Role and Impact*, edited by Zoltan J. Acs, ix–xi. New York: Springer Science+Business Media.

Gnyawali, Devi R., and Fogel, Daniel S. 1994. "Environment for Entrepreneurship Development: Key Dimensions and Research Implications." *Entrepreneurship: Theory and Practice* 18(4): 43–62.

Hennart, Jean-Francois. 2014. "The Accidental Internationalists: A Theory of Born Globals." *Entrepreneurship Theory and Practice* 38(1): 117–135.

Hofstede, Geert. 2001. *Culture and Consequences: Comparing Values, Behaviors, Institutions, and Organizations Across Nations*. London: Sage.

Hultman, Martin, Karl Johan Bonnedahl, and Kristie O'Neill. 2016. "Unsustainable Societies—Sustainable Businesses? Introduction to Special Issue of Small Enterprise Research on Transitional Ecopreneurs: Transitional Ecopreneurs—New Ecopreneurial Activities in the 21st Century." *Small Enterprise Research* 23(1): 1–9.

Johanson, Jan, and Jan-Erik Vahlne. 1977. "The Internationalization Process of the Firm-a Model of Knowledge Development and Increasing Foreign Market Commitments." *Journal of International Business Studies* 8(1): 23–32.

Johanson, Jan and Jan-Erik Vahlne. 2009. "The Uppsala Internationalization Process Model Revisited: From Liability of Foreignness to Liability of Outsidership." *Journal of International Business Studies* 40(9): 1411–1431.

Johansson, Ulf and Ulf Elg. 2002. "Relationships as Entry Barriers: A Network Perspective." *Scandinavian Journal of Management* 18(3): 393–319.

Knight, Gary A., and S. Tamar Cavusgil. 2004. "Innovation, Organizational Capabilities, and the Born-Global Firm." *Journal of International Business Studies* 35(2): 124–141.

Koeller, C. Timothy, and Thomas G. Lechler. 2006. "Economic and Managerial Perspectives on New Venture Growth: An Integrated Analysis." *Small Business Economics* 26(5): 427–437.

Leonidou, Leonidas C. 2004. "An Analysis of the Barriers Hindering Small Business Export Development." *Journal of Small Business Management* 42(3): 279–302.

Lumpkin, G. Tom, and Gregorey G. Dess. 2001. "Linking Two Dimensions of Entrepreneurial Orientation to Firm Performance: The Moderating Role of Environment and Industry Life Cycle." *Journal of Business Venturing* 16(5): 429–451.

Mäkelä, Markus M., and Markku V.J. Maula. 2005. "Cross-Border Venture Capital and New Venture Internationalization: An Isomorphism Perspective." *Venture Capital* 7(3): 227–257.

McClelland, David C., and David G. Winter. 1969. *Motivating Economic Achievement*. New York: Free Press.

Miesenbock, Kurt J. 1988. "Small Businesses and Exporting: A Literature Review." *International Small Business Journal* 6(2): 42–61.

Miles, Morgan P., Jeffrey G. Covin, and Michael B. Heeley. 2000. "The Relationship Between Environmental Dynamism and Small Firm Structure, Strategy, and Performance." *Journal of Marketing Theory and Practice* 8(2): 63–74.

Mochrie, Robbie, Laura Galloway, and Eleanor Donnelly. 2006. "Attitudes to Growth and Experience of Growth Among Scottish SMEs." *International Journal of Entrepreneurial Behavior & Research* 12(1): 7–20.

Moen, Øystein, and Per Servais. 2002. "Born Global or Gradual Global? Examining the Export Behavior of Small and Medium-Sized Enterprises." *Journal of International Marketing* 10(3): 49–72.

Nicholls, Alex. 2010. "The Legitimacy of Social Entrepreneurship: Reflexive Isomorphism in a Pre-Paradigmatic Field." *Entrepreneurship Theory & Practice* 4: 611–33.

Penrose, Edith T. 1959. *The Theory of the Growth of the Firm*. Oxford: Basil Blackwell.

Reeves, Martin, Simon Levin, and Daichi Ueda. 2016. "The Biology of Corporate Survival." *Harvard Business Review* 94(1): 46–55.

Rhee, Jay Hyuk, and Joseph L.C. Cheng. 2002. "Foreign Market Uncertainty and Incremental International Expansion: The Moderating Effect of Firm, Industry, and Host Country Factors." *Management International Review* 42(4): 419–439.

Runyan, Rodeny, Cornelia Droge, and Jane, Swinney. 2008. "Entrepreneurial Orientation Versus Small Business Orientation: What Are Their Relationships to Firm Performance?" *Journal of Small Business Management* 46(4): 567–588.

Sasi, Viveca, and Pia Arenius. 2008. "International New Ventures and Social Networks: Advantage or Liability?" *European Management Journal* 26(6): 400–411.

Schaltegger, Stefan, and Marcus Wagner. 2011. "Sustainable Entrepreneurship and Sustainability Innovation: Categories and Interactions." *Business Strategy and the Environment* 20(4): 222–237.

Schumpeter, Joseph Alois. 1934. *The Theory of Economic Development*. Cambridge, MA: Harvard University Press.

Shapero, Albert. 1977. *The Role of Entrepreneurship in Economic Development at the Less than National Level*. Washington, DC: US Department of Commerce.

Sousa, Carlos M.P., and Frank Bradley. 2006. "Cultural Distance and Psychic Distance: Two Peas in a Pod?" *Journal of International Marketing* 14(1): 49–70.

Stewart, Wayne H., Jr., and Philip L. Roth. 2001. "Risk Propensity Differences Between Entrepreneurs and Managers: A Meta-Analytic Review." *Journal of Applied Psychology* 86(1): 145–153.

Teece, David J. 2014. "A Dynamic Capabilities-Based Entrepreneurial Theory of the Multinational Enterprise." *Journal of International Business Studies* 45(1): 8–37.

Wiklund, Johan, Holger Patzelt, and Dean A. Shepherd. 2009. "Building an Integrative Model of Small Business Growth." *Small Business Economics* 32(4): 351–374.

Zander, Ivo, Patricia McDougall-Covin, and Elizabeth L Rose. 2015. "Born Globals and International Business: Evolution of a Field of Research." *Journal of International Business Studies* 46(1): 27–35.

12 Internationalization of SMEs

Family- vs. Nonfamily-owned Firms

Hamid Moini and John Kuada

1. Introduction

Interest in the internationalization process of small and medium-sized firms (SMEs) has increased tremendously in academic research over the last three decades (Dyer and Dyer 2009; Segaro 2012) due to the growing awareness that international SMEs are major contributors to job and wealth creation in all countries (Casillas *et al.* 2011). It has been consistently argued in the extant SME literature that a firm's decision to seek and take advantage of international business opportunities depends partly on its ownership configuration and its ability to leverage strategic capabilities and resources (Donckels and Fröhlich 1991; Gallo and García-Pont 1996; Hitt *et al.* 1997; Peng, 2001; Zahra 2003). With regard to ownership, the understanding is that family-owned businesses tend to be more constrained in their access to financial resources than nonfamily firms (Gallo and García-Pont 1996). But the strong relational networks and social capital, which constitute dominant characteristic of family businesses, tend to compensate for their resource disadvantages. For example, employees of family businesses are reputed for their strong sense of duty towards their businesses (Astrachan 2010) and this encourages them to adopt non-traditional growth-enhancing strategies (Abdellatif *et al.* 2010; Kontinen and Ojala 2010; Kotey and Folker 2007; Okoroafo and Koh 2010). Thus, the differences between family and nonfamily-owned businesses are significant enough to require research attention, especially in investigations of the internationalization processes of small firms.

In spite of this awareness, comparison of the internationalization process of family and nonfamily businesses has been found to be widely neglected in the international business literature (Abdellatif *et al.* 2010). Furthermore, although researchers have been engaged in theory and concept development in this strand of research (Cerrato and Piva 2012; Chrisman *et al.* 2003), the ownership variable seems to be neglected in most empirical investigations of factors that influence the internationalization processes of these businesses. Still, with few exceptions, the available empirical investigations have been completed in bigger developed countries such as the USA (Okoroafo and

Koh 2010; Sundaramurthy and Dean 2008), Spain (Claver, *et al.* 2008; Puig and Fernandez-Perez 2009), France, (Ducassy and Prevopt 2010), and Japan (Abdellatif, *et al.* 2010). Smaller countries appear to have been neglected in the current stream of research. However, investigations in Finland (Kontinen and Ojala 2010, 2011) and the Czech Republic (Moini *et al.* 2010) have suggested that the internationalization processes of small businesses in smaller economies deserve special attention.

Three reasons legitimize such a focus. First, due to the limited home market, businesses in small countries tend to undertake rapid internationalization to achieve economies of scale. Second, the operational contexts of these businesses differ from those of the larger economies. Policy makers in the small economies are more likely to show a greater inclination to adopt policies that shape the operational environments of small businesses with good results (Felsenstein and Fleischer 2002; Nischalke and Schöllmann 2005; Pollard 2003). Third, previous studies have shown that new small businesses are likely to start in the home region of their founders (Stam 2007). Once established, they tend to be economically and socially anchored in that environment and depend greatly on the locationally embedded resources to grow (Pellenbarg *et al.* 2002). These location-bound resources help shape their growth trajectory (Audretsch and Dohse 2007; Rugman and Verbeke 1992; Kenny and Patton 2005). It has also been noted that this locational attachment appears to be more pronounced for small family businesses. Thus, it is a lot easier for government institutions to encourage family business formation in regions where their entrepreneurial citizens live than to convince nonfamily businesses to relocate to such regions.

The study presented in this chapter has been motivated by the above considerations. It is an empirical investigation of the internationalization processes of ten randomly selected small businesses in the northern region of Denmark. The study is not intended to offer comprehensive overviews of how smaller Danish businesses internationalize their operations. It simply tells the stories of these businesses with the hope of throwing additional light on how ownership impacts the internationalization processes of small businesses.

We seek to make three contributions to the existing literature. First, we provide additional evidence that enhances our understanding of the internationalization processes of small businesses located in small remote regions under the assumption that business location matters in understanding the comparative and competitive advantages/disadvantages that small businesses enjoy or suffer. In this regard, our aim is to investigate the similarities and differences in their internationalization process, bearing in mind the role of ownership in these processes. Second, based on the premise that ownership influences the decisions that small business managers make, we seek to compare the decision-making behaviors of family- and nonfamily-owned small businesses. Third, by focusing on businesses in one region, we provide evidence on how regional policies tend to impact the growth trajectories of the businesses.

The next section of the chapter provides an overview of the literature on the internationalization processes of family- and nonfamily-owned small firms. We then describe the methods we have adopted to collect our data and present the results of our interviews with ten owner-managed firms in Northern Denmark. This is followed by our reflections and conclusions.

2. Literature Review and Conceptual Framework

As noted above, the SME literature draws useful distinction between family- and nonfamily-owned firms not only in terms of ownership and resource configurations, but also with respect to the decision-making styles of their managers as well as their locational characteristics. In terms of resources, family businesses tend to demonstrate a greater capacity to leverage intangible resources through their long-term orientation and propensity to adopt relational management approaches (Habbershon and Williams 1999). Furthermore, the personal and emotional stake that family members have in their firms makes them more committed to business success. However, economic profit may not always be the overriding objective of such firms.

In terms of decision making, Tesar *et al.* (2010) suggest that owner-managers of small businesses may be easily classified into three broad categories: (1) craftsman managers, (2) promoter managers, and (3) rational managers. Craftsman managers are normally directly involved with the operations of the enterprise and are usually not interested in innovation. Promoter managers tend to have very strong entrepreneurial skills and charismatic leadership qualities that motivate employees to strive for a better future. They are usually growth-oriented, driven by the desire to expand the market operations and improve the competitive position of their businesses. But they tend to be somewhat impulsive, using their operational experiences to improve their management practices. Rational managers usually have good abilities to reorganize and restructure their businesses in a manner that enables them to compete both in domestic and in international markets. They demonstrate agility—they are able to change their management styles in response to the needs of their businesses.

The differences in decision-making styles among the three categories of managers are important for several reasons. First, individual managers need to understand how and when to make appropriate decisions to grow a business and, if they do not have this understanding, they need to know when to step back and let a more qualified manager take over. Second, the manager needs to anticipate the decisions that are needed to reinforce the growth of the business. If the manager is not able to make these decisions, the business will not grow. Third, as the operational environments of the businesses become increasingly competitive the managers must constantly be aware of their position in the global marketplace. However, the decision on how to compete and when to internationalize can be overwhelming for inexperienced managers and, again, they may have to be replaced by more experienced managers.

The available empirical knowledge suggests that family businesses tend to prefer informal decision-making styles and this allows for flexibility, speed, and pragmatism in their relations with key stakeholders (Kotey and Folker 2007; Sharma *et al.* 1997). Some demonstrate the characteristics of promoter managers in certain situations and rational managers in other situations—i.e. adjusting their decision-making styles to fit the exigencies of their operations. Managers of nonfamily family-owned businesses typically exhibit rational decision-making characteristics.

With regard to location, the prevailing understanding is that location-specific policies may combine with owner-managers' social network positions in their communities to provide family businesses with intangible resources that may compensate fully or partly for the advantages that non-family businesses may enjoy. This explains why some family businesses may perform better than their nonfamily counterparts within the same industry and location in spite of their apparent limited financial resources.

Institutional policies may influence the degree to which businesses depend on the domestic market or exhibit internationalization ambitions during the early years of their existence. When policies do not encourage internationalization, firms tend to be latecomers on the international scene. Furthermore, studies have shown that family firms are more likely to initiate their internationalization processes later than their nonfamily counterparts within the same industry and location due to their risk-averse behavior and adaptation inertia. Their internationalization process is therefore likely to conform to the gradual, incremental process suggested in the Uppsala model (Kontinen and Ojala 2010).

Firms also differ in terms of their resource leveraging capabilities. It has been argued that family businesses tend to rely on *patient financial capital* and adopt long-term orientations to their investment decisions (Sirmon and Hitt 2003). Thus, Astrachan (2010) asserts that family businesses are among the longest-lived organizations in the world. The fear of losing control over the business makes owner-managers reluctant to leverage external financial resources and therefore prefer a more gradual approach to growth in general and internationalization in particular (Casillas and Acedo 2005; Gallo and Garcia-Pont 1996; Gallo and Sveen 1991; Graves and Thomas 2008).

Some studies have shown that family businesses exhibit tremendous adaptive capacities, responding successfully to changing operational environments when they enter new markets (Dyer and Whetten 2006). Their adaptive capacities enhance their competitive advantage in providing solutions to business customers with fluctuating demands (Kontinen and Ojala 2010). Such enterprises have opportunities to create new high growth businesses, ushering in creative destruction that challenges larger businesses (Tripsas 1997).

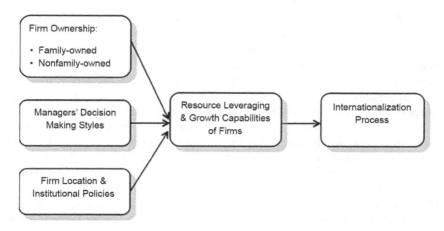

Figure 12.1 Selected Determinants of the Internationalization Process of Small Firms

Other studies have shown that family businesses are likely to face enormous challenges in their internationalization processes. For example, factors such as the level of technological sophistication, operating capacity, and enterprise resources (e.g. financial and human capital) have been listed as sources of constraint in their internationalization process (Leonidou *et al.* 2010). With respect to technology, the argument is that due to financial resource constraints, family businesses may operate with outdated technology and would, therefore, be less able to meet customer requirements with respect to volume and product quality. This would reduce their competiveness in sectors where technologically sophisticated businesses exist (Bonaccorsi 1992). In addition to these factors, family businesses may be less able to obtain adequate information about foreign market opportunities and business practices due again to human and financial resource limitations (Leonidou and Katsikeas 1996; Moini, *et al.* 2010; Morschett *et al.* 2010). Furthermore, in family businesses the division between business and personal objectives often becomes blurred (Fernández and Nieto 2006). As the family investments are not diversified, their owners can be expected to be risk-averse (Donckels and Fröhlich 1991). These theoretical perspectives are schematically summarized in Figure 12.1 (page 209) and constitute the conceptual framework for the study.

3. Research Methodology

As noted earlier, most published studies dealing with internationalization of smaller firms and comparisons of initial decisions to export focus on Europe, and more specifically, on the larger countries. In order to better understand how internationalization of small firms in a small country proceeds we collected data from five small family-owned firms and five similar sized nonfamily-owned firms located in Northern Denmark. We have decided to locate our empirical investigation in Northern Jutland Region of Denmark because it has characteristics that can constrain or promote small business development. The region is characterized by high rates of innovation and new product development within certain industry sectors—especially mobile telephone and related businesses. But incomes in the region are 8 percent lower than the national average and have been increasing at a slower rate than the national average. This means firms in the region may not be domestic market-dependent. Finally, there is a good relationship between higher education institutions, political and administrative institutions, and the business community in the region. These inter-institutional linkages have shaped the environment for private enterprise development. We will investigate how these factors have influenced resource leveraging and internationalization processes of the firms.

Since our interest in this study is to gain insight into how and why the firms engage in international business activities, we consider it appropriate to interview the key decision makers in a selected number of firms—mainly the owners of these firms. We selected 10 firms from a database of 600 firms using the following three criteria: (1) the business is located in the northern region of Denmark, (2) the firm has less than 250 employees, and (3) the firm was already engaged in international activities. Three additional criteria were used to identify the family-owned businesses: (1) the family is either the only or the majority owner, (2) the family must be represented in top management of the business, and (3) the business must perceive itself as a family-owned business.

The data collection was carried out through personal interviews at the premises of the firms. Our choice of interview approach was based on the understanding that managers may assign different meanings to the critical events in the history of their firms. These meanings are best revealed through semi-structured and interactive interviewing. By grouping together collections of such meanings we hope to identify similarities, differences, and patterns in the activities and experiences of the respondents.

During the interviews, questions were asked and the interviewers took notes. Complete write-ups were prepared after each interview, focusing on the specific characteristics of each case situation. Supplementary data were also collected from secondary sources mainly to understand the history and the products of each firm. This approach is consistent with recent studies of the activities of small businesses, which have the objective of investigating the dynamic decision-making processes of entrepreneurs and their internationalization processes (Moini *et al.* 2010). A summary of the participating firms is presented in Table 12.1 (page 211).

Table 12.1 Firms' Profile

Family-owned Firms

ScanBelt	Started in mid-1980s; currently owned by Mr. Morten Vejlstrup, with 30 employees. Produces modular plastic belts. Sees flexibility as its main competitive advantage. Company adopts systematic approach in search of international opportunities and hopes to target Brazil and USA. Owner would want to grow the company without letting go of their core values, their flexibility and security of their investment.
Fjerritslev Tryk	Founded over 100 years ago. Currently owned by Mr. Peter Eigenbroth, his wife and their son. Produces thick books printed on thin paper; this is the company's competitive advantage since few other firms do that today. Main foreign markets are Sweden and Norway, but there are ambitions to expand to other markets.
Frontego	Founded in 1990; currently owned by Mr. Tage Nielsen and his wife. Produces wooden doors and canopies and considers flexibility in producing customized products as its competitive advantage. It currently exports to Sweden and Norway and considers language and cultural barriers as the main constraints to further internationalization.
PSE Group	Founded by two brothers in 2002. Manufactures and sells varieties of sports clothing & equipment and considers its brands to be the best in the market segment. Exports to Sweden, Norway, Finland, and Germany. Considers finance, currency fluctuations and language barriers as constraints to further international expansion.
Gl Bested	Established in 1942 and bought by the current owner in 2008. Produces sheet metal, machine components, and forging in stainless steel. Considers quality its main competitive advantage. Exports to Norway but less to Sweden, Germany, United Kingdom, and Malta. Sees no major problems in further expansion abroad.

Nonfamily-owned Firms

Judex	Founded in 1981 and produces software for the healthcare sector. It sees good knowledge of the medical business as a key competitive advantage. Its key foreign market is the USA, where 30% of its sales come from. It exports mainly through distributors.
Kellpo	Established in 1995 to produce machines and equipment mainly for the manufacturing industry and for hospitals. It sees unique tool making skills as its main competitive advantage. Sells its products in countries including China, Germany and Norway and generates 50% of its sales abroad.
Scanca Isolering	Established to produce isolation materials for storage tanks used for storing liquids and gas. Considers itself an expert in this narrow line of business. Internationalizes by following key customers abroad and derives its sales from these sources.

(Continued)

Table 12.1 (Continued)

Nonfamily-owned Firms	
Logimatic Engineering	Established in 1987 to design electricity installations, automation, and software solutions for the maritime industry. Sees the quality of its technology and flexibility as its main competitive advantage. Enjoys stable exports to Norway, Sweden, Spain and Germany and derives 30% of its turnover from these markets. Sees language barriers as a key challenge in entering new markets such as Russia and China.
Tylstrup Kager	Started in 1965 to produce cakes and candies. Considers the quality of its products as its main competitive advantage. Sells to Sweden, Norway and Finland. Sees language barriers as a main challenge in entering new markets.

4. Results

Family-Owned Firms Perspective

Family-owned businesses in Denmark have a long tradition of contributing not only to the local but also to the national and international economies. Many such firms have grown into major players in the global marketplace. Some large Danish multinational firms began as small family operations, adjusting to numerous domestic and international economic, social, and technological challenges, by changing their business models and finding more effective and efficient ways to compete and become internationally engaged. Some of the family-owned firms in this study have followed a similar path.

The following five cases illustrate some of the challenges and opportunities that owners of Danish family-owned firms are facing today. These firms have functioned over a number of years and mostly are still successfully competing domestically or internationally. They also represent firms that are managed by a group of dynamic owners with broad perspectives of their operations and growth potential.

The oldest family-owned firm in the study was established over 100 years ago. The youngest firm was established in 2002. One firm was started by a previous family member and was passed on to the current owners. Other individuals started three other firms and the current family owners bought the firms later. One of these three firms has already been passed on to the next generation in the family. Finally, two brothers established the last firm. The owners of family-owned firms whom we interviewed can be classified as two craftsman owners,[1] one promoter owner,[2] and two rational owners.[3]

Three of the firms believe that they are primarily job shops. While a craftsman owner manages one of these firms, rational owners manage the other two. The remaining firm focuses on sales and marketing and is managed by a promoter owner.

In order for the family-owned firms to succeed and grow, owners need to make decisions, and one would expect that the three types of owners would approach decisions differently. The owners typically made decisions about new products and markets, including international markets, sometimes with input from other family members or teams of employees appointed by the owner. The exception to this finding was the PSE Group, where decisions were made by the board of directors and implemented by relevant managers according to policies and procedures.

Three family-owned firms began by offering a product perceived by the original owner to be unique. Reflecting on the history of those firms, the current owners pointed out that the founders recognized an opportunity in the market and proceeded to fill it. Through systematic product improvements and innovation, they have managed to maintain their growth and market expansion. One failed in the process due to its inability to quickly recognize the changing market conditions. Even today, the owners continue to believe that they offer a unique product of relatively high quality to their customers, and ascribe their primary competitive advantage to the manufacture of a high-quality product that is based on innovative technology and supported by superior customer service. The owner of one of the firms believes that his competitive advantage derives from the fact that his company has the best brands of products for their target segments combined with their highly effective customer service (e.g. their convenient return policies).

Some of the firms are not well known within their local environments, and this does not bother their owners. For example, the owner of ScanBelt believes that less than 10 percent of people in the town in which it is located know about its existence, even though they are possibly one of the top five largest employers in the town. He justifies this lack of public recognition to the fact that their products are not the typical products that people normally use or see on the street. If people are asked about ScanBelt products, he thinks most will respond, "Oh, I have seen it somewhere or understand what it is," but may not know from what it is made (plastic, rubber, or steel).

Today, all five family-owned firms serve international markets to some degree. Some of them export directly. One firm exports directly but also maintains a sales and distribution center abroad. The initial involvement in international operations differs substantially among the five family-owned firms. Some owners actively pursued entering into foreign markets. Others, such as Fjerritslev Tryk, found their way into foreign markest by accident. In this case, their first foreign customer was a Swedish publisher whose other Danish printer had gone bankrupt. Since Fjerritslev Tryk print machines were very similar to the bankrupt company's, the Swedish company placed their order with Fjerritslev Tryk.

Family-owned firms active in international markets generate somewhere between 10% and 92% of their sales volume from exports. Four of the owners in the five cases presented here believe that profits generated from international sales are more than or equally as profitable as those generated from domestic sales. They believe there are significant obstacles to international operations. Most obstacles are not major; for example, collecting payment and pricing products for export are typically perceived as minor obstacles. Two of the owners consider their inability to speak foreign languages, as well as, their lack of understanding of foreign cultures, as major obstacles to their international operations.

We also asked the five owners how they examined and assessed international operations in relation to their firms. Do they systematically examine their international operations? Four firms reported they systematically explore export opportunities but only one of the firms has hired qualified staff to manage its export operations. One firm, which manages to export only 10% of its products, neither systematically explores export opportunities nor has hired anyone to improve its exports sales. The owner explained the process as follows:

"We did not start with a specific plan but rather based on a 20-year experience we know what it takes, and we know what time frame it takes to start up. We know what to expect, we know which sign to look for, and we know where we need to help people. We know also in case people buy loose parts for further production what to recommend, we know what training they need, we know what promotion to do toward them, and how they go about promoting the strength and weaknesses of the product."

One of the five family-owned firms started exporting almost from the beginning of its operations. The remaining firms used a variety of forms to enter their first foreign market. Three of the five owners interviewed had no policies to evaluate international opportunities. On the other hand, the most successful exporters in the study had policies to search for new geographic markets and new opportunities. Owners of three of the firms that do not have a formal policy to evaluate foreign opportunities have an ongoing process whereby they consider new opportunities as they arise, sometimes without making any real commitment.

Most of the owners expect that the road to progress in the next five years will be bumpy, as they have experienced some difficulties due to global financial crisis. How the growth and the other objectives for these firms will be realized is not clear. Unfortunately, one of the firms (Gl Bested) has already found it impossible to continue its operations and filed for bankruptcy shortly after our interview. Only PSE Group expects to grow, develop new products and markets, and perhaps diversify. It appears they have a very structured day-to-day process plan for the years ahead. But they are all willing to employ qualified people to compensate for their limitations. As the owner of Fjerritslev Tryk informs us, "The most important thing about being an entrepreneur is to hire people that are smarter than you."

Nonfamily-Owned Firms Perspective

Danish nonfamily-owned firms are not necessarily more established than their Danish family-owned counterparts. Many of them also faced the need to internationalize their operations shortly after they were established due to the relatively small domestic markets. But in most instances, owners were not concerned with developing strategic business models. Demand for their products grew in response to unsolicited orders from customers in a few European countries.

Although the European market is not homogeneous, there are sufficient similarities in markets for a variety of products. Industrial markets especially tend to be relatively similar and stable. Only in countries where the political system has changed recently is it possible to detect major changes in market demand. Political changes in China in the early 1990s have created a new environment and opportunities for some Danish nonfamily-owned firms. But owner-managers of these firms have a great deal to consider in their attempts to compete with their more established counterparts in the rest of the world. Nonfamily-owned firms have been well established in Denmark for centuries. Most Danish firms evolved from individual initiatives and were mainly managed by craftsman owners at their founding. Three of the owner-managers in these cases identified themselves as craftsman, emphasizing the fact that their firms are focusing on the technology or production capabilities of their firms. Thus, according to the owner of Fjerritslev Tryk, "while much has changed in the industry, craftsmanship is still the focus of our firm." The other two owner-managers believe that over the years their firms' focus has evolved. Today, their businesses' focus is not only on the technology but also on the business and marketing aspects of the firm. Their products are highly customized in order to meet customers' designs and needs. So, they see themselves as owners who manage their companies in a logical and rational manner despite all the problems in the economy.

The oldest enterprise among the five cases was established after World War II as a cookie and candy maker, and the most recent one was established in 1995, manufacturing machines mostly for the medical industry and a whole series of other major production activities.

From a managerial perspective, these nonfamily-owned firms focus on well-developed lines of products and services. They believe that they offer high quality products suitably priced for domestic and foreign markets. Although they have a tendency to view their operations as job shops, they represent highly advanced and technologically sophisticated manufacturing operations and are relatively well endowed with financial resources. Owner-managers of these firms believe that their competitive advantage is embedded in technology, superior product quality, and service. No one mentioned price as his competitive advantage. But they are experiencing pressures from foreign competitors. The owner of Kelpo reflects on the competitive situation as follows: "We are good toolmakers. In the last 10 years everybody was telling us to move our production to China because you will not survive producing tools in a country like Denmark. We have a rough time right now but have survived."

All of the nonfamily firms look for growth and market expansion; however, they are concerned about technology and the role cutting edge technology plays in growth and market expansion. One owner said that being a small firm in a remote part of Denmark makes it very difficult for them to compete with global giants in the field. Therefore, it is very critical for their firm to grow. Although they are willing to sacrifice short-term profitability for the sake of growth, they need to control the sales and marketing of their products in order to grow. Another owner attributes the survival of his firm in the last 25 years to two principles: (1) they always emphasize profitability, and (2) the preservation of their investment is their primary goal. They will not accept any project that is not profitable. However, they are willing, to a certain degree, to accept lower profit margins (but not a loss) on new projects which have the possibility of bringing other contracts in the future. They are also willing to stretch their efforts and resources to serve as many customers as possible. As the owner of Kelpo puts it, "Our philosophy is to never run away from any order. We always go the whole way."

Some of the Danish nonfamily-owned firms are in a unique position when it comes to the impact of the global economic conditions on their turnover and profitability. In one case the owner-manager reported that most of their customers are governments and public health institutions around the world and their business activities are not affected the same way as many others in the private sector. Others are a lot more dependent on international sales and therefore, changes in the domestic economy are not affecting them as much. However, the global financial crisis of 2008 had a tremendous effect on all of these firms. An owner-manager reported that his firm's turnover declined by more than 50 percent due to the fact that the demand for his products declined in a number of countries as many projects were abandoned.

It is interesting to note that four of the cases expect growth in their business in the near future. There is a great deal of optimism that there will be market opportunities both domestically and internationally. In one case, the owner-manager is highly optimistic about the future of his firm. He believes the demand for his firm's products will increase by at least 20% in five years. Expanding into new markets is another area that he feels comfortable to achieve. He is also as optimistic about the future of his firm's finances. In another case, the owner is not sure when the current economic crisis will end, but hopes that his firm will make it through these rough times and will come out far stronger at the end.

The Danish nonfamily-owned firms tend to evaluate future options systematically using a team approach. For example, in one case the firm has a systematic decision-making process involving the four founders and other shareholders who make all major decisions in the firm. The board of directors is also involved in those decisions. Even if the four founding members make a decision they usually seek the approval of the board and other minor shareholders. However, the founders of the firm normally handle the day-to-day decisions in the firm. Decisions about the international activities of the firm are also made the same way. Logimatic regularly plans for activities such as new products, new markets, increase of their market share, and diversification of their activities, as well as their international business.

The five nonfamily-owned firms started international operations by exporting their products shortly after start-up and mostly into neighboring countries; this is consistent with conclusions from studies presented by earlier researchers. Some of the firms have entered into contractual agreements with partners abroad. They systematically evaluate international business opportunities and select those that contribute to their growth and profitability. They plan for their business activities such as new products and markets by watching the marketplace to see what type of issues provide opportunity for their firms to come up with new solutions for these issues. One firm reported that they remain highly flexible and constantly search for opportunities all over the world. Even if they find opportunities that are beyond the scope of their strategic plans they are willing to take the risk and either move away from their previous plans or modify them so that they can take advantage of the new opportunity. It seems the company has been quite successful in their efforts.

Although many of the nonfamily-owned firms perceive obstacles to international operations, these obstacles vary from firm to firm. For example, one firm faces regulatory requirements for the sale of its medical equipment in the United States. The on-going process of receiving the approval has already taken the firm several years with no end in sight. Other firms perceived obstacles differently; they perceived the inability to speak foreign languages and ethical and cultural differences hampering their business activities overseas. Size and their geographical location are seen by some as competitive disadvantages. As the manager of Judex expresses it, "Finding a business partner overseas due to small size is very difficult. Most hospitals both in the US and Europe prefer to buy from larger domestic companies. We have lesser problems with Scandinavian countries."

Nonfamily-owned firms represented in this study believe that future markets for their product are growing in Europe and internationally. They have a strong international perspective, and they regularly explore the potential of international markets and plan for such potential. In one case, the owner is planning to transform his firm into a European firm instead of a Danish company. Germany, the largest European country and the world's fourth largest economy has the greatest potential for his firm. While his firm is the largest toolmaker for the packaging industry in Denmark, it ranks 40th in Germany. He feels his firm must become larger in order to gain the respect of its potential customers. He also keeps his eyes on the other European markets as well.

5. Cross-Case Comparison and Discussions

Comparison of Danish family-owned and nonfamily-owned firms in this study produced similarities and differences with respect to their internationalization perspectives. Internationalization as a process evolved at the same rate in both the family-owned and nonfamily-owned firms. Since the Danish market is fairly small, both groups of firms have realized that in order to survive, they must start their internationalization process shortly after their establishment. Cases reported above show that both family-owned and nonfamily-owned firms have a long tradition of operating internationally and using several modes of operations.

One similarity is that all of these firms were started by individuals who had an innovative idea, technology, or product that had the potential to have a major impact on an industry, manufacturing process, or consumer life styles. In some cases it was found that the original owners eventually passed on the management of the firms to the next generations but in most cases they are still managing their firms. Due to the small size of the Danish market, both family-owned and nonfamily-owned firms found it difficult to expand their market domestically; therefore, they had to look for markets in neighboring countries. The initial internationalization decisions of most of them were in response to unsolicited orders from abroad from customers who perceived their technologies or products to have unique features. Others decided to internationalize because of the size of their markets and close proximity to neighboring countries.

Previous studies have suggested that small businesses exhibit tremendous adaptive capacities, responding successfully to changing operational environments when they enter new markets (Dyer and Whetten 2006). The capacity to adapt allows them to tailor solutions to unique customer demands, and this enhances their competiveness in international markets (Kontinen and Ojala 2010). Evidence from the present study lends additional support to this perspective. As noted above, both family-owned and nonfamily-owned firms believed that their products have unique attributes and superior quality and that this has made them competitive within the markets that they operate.

For some family-owned firms, internationalizing operations seemed to be a difficult decision that had a major impact on the entire firm and its resources (three firms had less than 22% export ratio), while nonfamily-owned firms found the internationalization process a normal extension of their domestic operations (only one firm had an export ratio of less than 50%). This result is also in line with findings from previous studies that family firms are usually latecomers to the international business scene compared to their nonfamily counterparts within the same location (Graves and Thomas 2008).

Our theoretical discussions have suggested that family businesses tend to prefer informal decision-making styles when compared with nonfamily firms (Kotey and Folker 2007). This is true for their international business decisions as well. The present study confirms this viewpoint. The evidence shows that once the decision to internationalize has been taken, nonfamily-owned firms are more likely to formalize and internalize the decision than family-owned firms. Owners of family-owned firms frequently did not choose to do so. When family-owned firms received orders from abroad they examined them one at a time, assessed the potential risk in filling the order, and then decided if they would fill the order. The nonfamily-owned firms tended to introduce policies and procedures concerning international opportunities earlier and generally relied on a team decision rather than decisions made just by the owners. The informal approach to the internationalization decision that the family firms adopt tends to produce some advantages. As noted earlier this allows for flexibility, speed, and pragmatism in their relations with key stakeholders (Sharma *et al.* 1997). This enabled them to learn from these experiences and improve their products to meet foreign customers' needs. Thus, they felt closer to potential customers abroad (mostly European markets) and have been able to notice similar applications for their products, particularly in evolving industries and/or economic sectors.

Most family-owned and nonfamily-owned firms started their foreign market entry by exporting their products. As they gained more international experience, a couple of the nonfamily-owned firms have used other foreign markets entry methods such as licensing and joint ventures. On the other hand, a couple of the family-owned firms expanded the internationalization of their operations by setting up sales offices, distribution, and even manufacturing abroad very early in their internationalization process. One of the family-owned firms was willing to purchase licenses to distribute foreign products in their markets. In agreement with previous studies we found that the entry mode choices the firms make may be a reflection of their managers' attitude to risk: family-owned firms appear to be more risk averse than the nonfamily-owned firms (Casillas and Acedo 2005; Graves and Thomas 2008). The risk factor is also reflected in their market outreach. Family-owned firms mostly look for established markets such as the United States, Germany, France, and Scandinavian countries. They sell existing products with as little modification as possible. Nonfamily-owned firms, on the other hand, tend to explore markets in the emerging economies such as China, Russia, and Malaysia. They are also more willing to adapt their products to foreign customers' applications and local industry standards in order to enter foreign markets.

Previous studies have suggested that shortages of some specific enterprise resources may constrain the internationalization of small firms (Leonidou *et al.* 2010). In this study we have found that family-owned firms saw their inability to speak foreign languages, shipment procedures, the management of foreign financial transactions, and problems of understanding business practices in foreign countries as serious constraints to growth.

220 Hamid Moini and John Kuada

Nonfamily-owned managers emphasize such other problems as the inability to know the actual needs of potential customers or market requirements and industry standards in specific countries as main constraints. These firms actively seek information to fill in their knowledge gaps as their international operations expand.

Both family-owned and nonfamily-owned firms managed their growth processes in a similar manner. Growth in both groups of firms tend to be driven by introducing new products, technologies, and manufacturing processes that provide bases for start-ups in other industries (see Judex, a nonfamily-owned firm and PSE Group, a family-owned firm). Consequently, some of the firms (Scanca Isolering and Tylstrup Kager, both nonfamily-owned firms, as well as ScanBelt, Frontego, and Gl Bested, all family-owned firms) were purchased or taken over by their current owners. Many of them changed ownership and managerial structures early in the growth stage and were internationalized by their new owners. The fundamental difference between the family-owned and nonfamily-owned firms tends to be their longer-term management orientation. But it seems family-owned firms tend to be more stable. Owners of nonfamily-owned firms are more likely to change ownership while owners of family-owned firms retain ownership and grow their firms. This evidence is in line with findings from previous studies indicating family-owners' desire to growth incrementally in order not to lose control over their investments (see Gallo and Sveen 1991; Gallo and Garcia-Pont 1996).

Finally, it appears from the results that age can be a key factor in understanding the management and decision-making styles of the owners. Owners of both PSE Group and ScanBelt were much younger and at the same time extremely aggressive. These owners have grown their firms rapidly and evaluate their market options more systematically. When the internationalization decision needs to be made, it is made appropriately and consistently with expectations of growth. The exceptions to this approach are Gl Bedsted, and to some extent, Fjerritslev Tryk, which tend to be more conservative and not quick enough to respond to market conditions for their products. As a result, the first one has already filed for bankruptcy and the second one is shedding some assets in order to preserve itself.

6. Conclusions

We have noted in the introduction to this chapter that previous empirical studies of the internationalization process of small firms have been done in relatively big countries and have not included ownership as a potential explanatory variable. The present study contributes to filling this knowledge gap with its focus on family- and nonfamily-owned small firms in Denmark—a relatively small Nordic country. Its overall conclusion is that ownership, management decision-making styles and location of firms are among the key variables in understanding the ability of both family- and nonfamily-owned firms to leverage resources and shape their international-ization processes. Evidently, the small size of the Danish market appears to be a strong motive for internationalization; it encouraged owners to respond quickly to foreign offers and inquiries. In most of the firms, international operations frequently take precedence over domestic operations.

We have also noted some similarities between the two groups of firms with respect to their growth strategies. Firms with relatively more aggressive strategies tend to expand their markets and successfully internationalized their operations. In other words, irrespective of ownership, small Danish firms need to examine their competitive posture, assess their market posi-tion, and evaluate their technological competence in the international con-text in order to survive. Doing this systematically and adopting proactive strategies appear to pay off.

Our research design, however, leaves a number of questions unanswered and therefore invites further studies. The first is the limited generalizability of the study, having been based on only ten cases. For example, future research should help uncover how different the family- and nonfamily-owned firms operating in the northern region of Denmark are from those operating in other parts of Denmark or other smaller countries in Europe. Furthermore, the present study has not collected data from institutional actors. We are therefore not in a position to determine what policy initiatives have been taken in the past and the relative impacts of these initiatives on the two groups of firms. Bearing in mind that local, regional, and national govern-ments are concerned about employment, taxes, and economic stability and want to help these firms to grow, we need additional research to under-stand how contextual factors, including policy instruments from various public entities, can motivate small family and nonfamily-owned firms to internationalize.

Notes

1 *Craftsman managers are normally directly involved with the operations of the enterprise and are usually not interested in innovation. They owe their survival to their ability to supply products that are totally uneconomical for larger enter-prises to produce. They may change with experience, adjusting their managerial styles to the needs of the changing business environment and internal growth processes.*

2 *Promoter managers actively promote their enterprises and products. They tend to have very strong entrepreneurial skills and charismatic leadership qualities that motivate employees to strive for a better future. They are somewhat impulsive, using their operational experiences to improve their management practices. They are also usually growth-oriented, driven by the desire to expand the market opera-tions of their businesses and improve its competitive position. But as rapid growth and expanding organizational complexity brings uncertainty, these managers are likely to adopt conservative business and leadership practices.*

3 *Rational managers are basically promoter managers who manage to grow their businesses and change their management styles in response to the needs of their enterprises. They usually have a good ability to reorganize and restructure*

their businesses in a manner that enables them to compete both in domestic and in international markets. They plan systematically for technical development and automatically introduce innovation. Their employees are highly skilled and perform homogenous functions within set standards that are determined by the overall philosophy and core competence of the enterprise.

References

Abdellatif, Mahamat, Bruno Amann, and Jacques Jaussaud. 2010. "Family Versus Nonfamily Business: A Comparison of International Strategies." *Journal of Family Business Strategy* 1(2): 108–116.

Astrachan, Joseph H. 2010. "Strategy in Family Business: Toward a Multidimensional Research Agenda." *Journal of Family Business Strategy* 1(1): 6–14.

Audretsch, David B., and Dirk Dohse. 2007. "Location: A Neglected Determinant of Firm Growth." *Review of World Economics* 143(1): 79–107.

Bonaccorsi, Andrea. 1992. "On the Relationship Between Firm Size and Export Intensity." *Journal of International Business* 23(4): 605–635.

Casillas, Jose C., and Francisco J. Acedo. 2005. "Internationalization of Spanish Family SMEs—Analysis of Family Involvement." *International Journal of Globalization and Small Business* 1(2): 134–151.

Casillas, Jose C., Ana M. Moreno, and Jose L. Barbero. 2011. "Entrepereneurial Orientation of Family Firms: Family and Environmental Dimensions." *Journal of Family Business Strategy* 2(2): 90–100.

Cerrato, Daniels, and Mariacristina Piva. 2012. "The Internationalization of Small and Medium-sized Enterprises: The Effect of Family Management, Human Capital and Foreign Ownership." *Journal of Management & Governance* 16(4): 617–644.

Chrisman, James J., Jess H.Chua, and Parmodita Sharma. 2003. "Current Trends and Future Directions in Family Business Management Studies: Toward a Theory of the Family Firm." *Coleman Foundation White Paper Series*, 1–62.

Claver, Enrique, Laura Rienda, and Diego Quer. 2008. "Family Businesses' Risk Perception: Empirical Evidence on the Internationalization Process." *Journal of Small Business and Enterprise Development* 15(3): 457–471.

Donckels, Rik, and Erwin Fröhlich. 1991. "Are Family Businesses Really Different? European Experiences from STRATOS." *Family Business Review* 4(2): 149–160.

Ducassy, Isabelle, and Frédéric Prevopt. 2010. "The Effects of Family Dynamics on Diversification Strategy: Empirical Evidence from French Companies." *Journal of Family Business Strategy* 1(4): 224–235.

Dyer, W. Gibb, and W. Justin Dyer. 2009. "Putting the Family into Family Business Research." *Family Business Review* 22(3): 216–219.

Dyer, W. Gibb, and David A. Whetten. 2006. "Family Firms and Social Responsibility: Preliminary Evidence from the S&P 500." *Entrepreneurship Theory and Practice* 30(6): 785–802.

Felsenstein, Daniel, and Aliza Fleischer. 2002. "Small-Scale Entrepreneurship and Access to Capital in Peripheral Locations: An Empirical Analysis." *Growth and Change* 33(2): 196–215.

Fernandez, Zulima, and Maria J. Nieto. 2006. "Impact of Ownership on the International Involvement of SMEs." *Journal of International Business Studies* 37(3): 340–351.

Gallo, Miguel A., and Carlos Garcia-Pont. 1996. "Important Factors in Family Business Internationalization." *Family Business Review* 9(1): 45–59.

Gallo, Miguel A., and Jannicke Sveen. 1991. "Internationalizing the Family Business: Facilitating and Restraining Factors." *Family Business Review* 4(2): 181–190.

Graves, Chris, and Jill Thomas. 2008. "Determinants of the Internationalization Pathways of Family Firms." *Family Business Review* 21(2): 151–167.

Habbershon, Timothy G. and Mary L. Williams. 1999. "A Resource-Based Framework for Assessing the Strategic Advantages of Family Firms." *Family Business Review* 12(1): 1–25. doi:10.1111/j.1741-6248.1999.00001.x.

Hitt, Michael A., Robert E. Hoskisson, and Hicheon Kim. 1997. "International Diversification: Effects on Innovation and Firm Performance in Product Diversified Firms." *Academy of Management Journal* 40(4): 767–798.

Kenney, Martin, and Donald Patton. 2005. "Entrepreneurial Geographies: Support Networks in Three High-Tech Industries." *Economic Geography* 81(2): 201–228.

Kontinen, Tanja, and Arto Ojala. 2010. "Internationalization Pathways of Family SMEs: Psychic Distance as a Focal Point." *Journal of Small Business and Enterprise Development* 17(3): 437–454.

Kontinen, Tanja, and Arto Ojala. 2011. "Social Capital in Relation to the Foreign Market Entry and Post-Entry Operations of Family SMEs." *Journal of International Entrepreneurship* 9(2): 133–151.

Kotey, Bernice, and Cathleen Folker. 2007. "Employee Training in SMEs: Effect of Size and Business Type-Family and Nonfamily." *Journal of Small Business Management* 45(2): 214–238.

Leonidou, Leonidas C., and Constantine S. Katsikeas. 1996. "The Export Development Process: An Integrative Review of Empirical Models." *Journal of International Business Studies* 27(3): 517–551.

Leonidou, Leonidas C., Constantine S. Katsikeas, and D.N. Coudounaris. 2010. "Five Decades of Business Research into Exporting: A Bibliographic Analysis." *Journal of International Management* 16(1): 78–91.

Moini, Hamid, Frantisek Kalouda, and George Tesar. 2010. "Internationalization of Family-Owned Businesses in the Czech Republic." *International Journal of Entrepreneurial Venturing* 2(3/4): 400–418.

Morschett, Dirk, Hanna Schramm-Klein, and Bernhard Swoboda. 2010. "Decades of Research on Market Entry Modes: What Do We Really Know About External Antecedents of Entry Mode Choice?" *Journal of International Management* 16(1): 60–77.

Nischalke, Tobias, and Andrea Schöllmann. 2005. "Regional Development and Regional Innovation Policy in New Zealand: Issues and Tensions in a Small Remote Country." *European Planning Studies* 13(4): 559–579.

Okoroafo, Sam C., and Anthony C. Koh. 2010. "Family Businesses' Views on Internationalization: Do They Differ by Generation?" *International Business Research* 3: 22–28.

Pellenbarg, Piet H., Leo J.G Van Wissen, and Jouke Van Dijk. 2002. "Firm Migration." In *Industrial Location Economics*, edited by Phillip McCann, 110–150. Cheltenham, UK: Edward Elgar.

Peng, Mike W. 2001. "The Resource-Based View and International Business." *Journal of Managment* 27(6): 803–829.

Pollard, Carol. 2003. "E-service Adoption and Use in Small Farms in Australia: Lessons Learned from Government Sponsored Programme." *Journal of Global Information Technology Management* 6(2): 45–63.

Puig, Nuria, and Paloma Fernández-Pérez. 2009. "A Silent Revolution: The Internationalization of Large Spanish Family Firms." *Business History* 51(3): 462–483.

Rugman, Alan M., and Alain Verbeke. 1992. "A Note on the Transnational Solution and the Transaction Cost Theory of Multinational Strategic Management." *Journal of International Business Studies* 23(4): 761–771.

Segaro, Ethiopia. 2012. "Internationalization of Family SMEs; The Impact of Ownership, Governance, and Top Management Team." *Journal of Management & Governance* 16(1): 147–169.

Sharma, Pramodita, James J. Chrisman, and Jess H. Chua. 1997. "Strategic Management of the Family Business: Past Research and Future Challenges." *Family Business Review* 10(1): 1–37.

Sirmon, David G., and Michael A. Hitt. 2003. "Managing Resources: Linking Unique Resources, Management and Wealth Creation in Family Firms." *Entrepreneurship: Theory and Practice* 27(4): 339–358.

Stam, Christiaan D. 2007. "Making Sense of Knowledge Productivity: Beta Testing the KP Enhancer." *Journal of Intellectual Capital* 8(4): 628–640.

Sundaramurthy, Chamu., and Michelle A. Dean. 2008. "Family Businesses' Openness to External Influence and International Sales: An Empirical Examination." *Multinational Business Review* 16(2): 89–106.

Tesar, George, Hamid A. Moini, John Kuada, and Olav J. Sørensen. 2010. *Smaller Manufacturing Enterprises in an International Context: A Longitudinal Exploration*. London: Imperial College Press.

Tripsas, Mary. 1997. "Unraveling the Process of Creative Destruction: Complementary Assets and Incumbent Survival in the Typesetter Industry." *Strategic Management Journal* 18(S1): 119–142.

Zahra, Shaker A. 2003. "International Expansion of US Manufacturing Family Businesses: The Effect of Ownership and Involvement." *Journal of Business Venturing* 18(4): 495–512.

13 Marketing Mix Decisions of Traditionally Internationalized Firms vs. Born Internationals

Jorma Larimo and Minnie Kontkanen

1. Introduction

The marketing mix elements of product, price, distribution and promotion offer important tools for a firm to internationalize. Depending on the level of adaptation made for each element in foreign markets, the customer acceptance of product and/or service may differ. Thus, the adaptation levels of marketing mix elements have implications on the ease of expansion into the first foreign markets and into additional markets, which may also be reflected in the export performance. In addition, the need to cooperate with local or international firms may be more important when great adaptations are required for international markets. Thus, for an export or marketing manager, decisions related to the marketing mix are important.

During the last 20 years, one of the key research focus areas in the analysis of exports and internationalization of SMEs has been the features and behavior of rapidly internationalizing companies referred to as "born internationals," "born globals" and "international new ventures." As a result, our knowledge has increased concerning these companies and their differences compared to traditionally internationalizing companies. However, we still have limited understanding of the potential similarities and differences in the adaptation-standardization level of marketing mix strategies of Traditionally Internationalized companies (TRs) compared to Born Internationals (BI), and the implications of these similarities and differences on export performance.

In the context of TRs, the marketing strategy adaptation-standardization level and the influence of various environmental and internal factors on performance have been the main areas of interest in international marketing strategies research (Leonidou and Katsikeas 2010). Nevertheless, although recently other marketing elements have also received increasing attention, the number of studies exploring the degree of standardization of all four main marketing strategy elements (product, price, distribution, and communication) is still limited (Shoham 2003; Sousa and Lengler 2009; Stoian *et al.* 2009). Even less attention is given to the analysis of the link with export performance. In addition, the results have been quite contradictory. This could be explained, at least partly, by the fact that for the most part, the direct relationship between marketing mix strategies and performance has been studied without taking the context into account—in other words the fit between situational factors and chosen strategy has not been taken into account (Theodosiou and Leonidou 2003; Schmid and Kotulla 2009; Schmid and Kotulla 2011). Thus, there is a need to explore in more detail whether TRs and BIs use different types of marketing strategies in terms of the level of adaptation and whether this has an effect on performance. In addition, an interesting aspect to study is whether the potential moderating effects are similar between these two types of companies.

Thus, the goal of the study is to explore the similarities and differences between TRs and BIs in terms of the adaptation level of marketing mix elements and their effect on the export performance. Also of interest to this study is the role of moderating effects on the relationship between adaptation level of marketing strategies and export performance. In more detail, the goal is to analyze the relationship between the degree of adaptation of the four key marketing mix elements—product, price, distribution, and communication—and export performance, using both objective and subjective measures of export performance. The resource-based view (RBV) is used as a basis to analyze the studied relationships.

The study contributes to the discussion of the similarities and differences of TRs and BIs, in terms of their international marketing strategies and their performance implications and thus gives guidance to the successful internationalization of SMEs. Another important area of contribution is the contingency approach and situation-strategy fit discussion.

The structure of the chapter is as follows: We will first give a general overview of the standardization/adaptation of the marketing mix—performance literature, and develop hypotheses on the level of adaptation of product, price, promotion and distribution elements and performance for TRs and BIs. Secondly we will discuss the role of moderating factors in the level of adaptation of the marketing mix strategies—performance relationship. Thirdly, we will present key methodological and sample related issues. This is followed by the presentation of the empirical results and finally we will end with discussion of the role of the level of adaptation of marketing strategies on performance for TRs and BIs.

2. Marketing Mix Adaptation Levels and Export Performance

Based on previous studies some of the key differences between TRs and BIs are that BIs expand more rapidly into several foreign markets, often use more networking and strategic alliances in their operations and operate more often in high-tech sectors and in niche markets than TRs (Cavusgil and Knight 2015; Rialp *et al.* 2005). Such differences in the internationalization strategies would also indicate differences in terms of the most common approach to the adaptation/standardization level of international marketing strategies. However, as was discussed earlier, this has been explored to only a limited extent in prior studies. A study by Gabrielsson *et al.* (2012) is one of the rare studies which explicitly explored these differences. They found that, in their sample of Swedish and Finnish ICT companies, both globalizing internationals and born globals used a more standardized marketing strategy than did TRs.

Therefore, we suggest that,

H1: TR firms utilize more adapted marketing mix strategies than BIs.

In general, prior literature identifies three perspectives which guide the design of international marketing strategy so that it can compete effectively and efficiently in international markets (Lages *et al.* 2013; Theodosiou and Leonidou 2003). These are standardization, adaptation and contingency perspectives. Based on the standardization approach, marketing mix strategies should be standardized, because markets are considered to become more similar in several respects and thus standardization allows achievement of economies-of-scale and the maintenance of a consistent, high-quality image worldwide (Shoham 2003). Proponents of adaptation, on the other hand, argue that in spite of the globalization tendencies, variations between markets are still great and require adaptations in marketing mix strategies. The contingency perspective, on the other hand, offers an approach to overcome the two extreme perspectives. According to contingency perspective, standardization and adaptation are two ends of the same continuum where the degree of standardization/adaptation can vary depending on the contingency factors relating to a specific situation (Hultman *et al.* 2009).

The results of the direct effect of a standardization/adaptation level of marketing mix strategies on performance are inconsistent. Some studies have reported a positive relationship (Lee and Griffith 2004) and some a negative relationship (Sousa and Bradley 2008). However, most of the results imply an insignificant relationship (O'Cass and Craig 2003; Stoian *et al.* 2009). The results may also vary depending on which element of the marketing mix strategy has been studied and how the performance has been measured. Thus, the before-mentioned issues may partly explain the inconsistent results. Prior literature, however, has argued that export performance is not directly related to the adoption of marketing strategy standardization or adaptation, but rather to the extent that the adopted strategy matches the unique context that the firm is confronted by within a particular overseas market (Schmid and Kotulla 2011). In addition, recent findings reject the direct effect of marketing strategy standardization level on performance (Gabrielsson *et al.* 2012; Hultman *et al.* 2009). Therefore, confusing results can also be explained by the fact that in most cases, the direct relationship between marketing mix strategies and performance has been studied without taking into account the context. Thus, we suggest that

H2: The adaptation level of marketing mix strategies does not have a direct relationship with performance either for TRs or BIs.

3. Contingency Factors and Their Moderating Effects on Export Performance

In line with the contingency approach (Theodosiou and Leonidou 2003) and strategic fit (Schmid and Kotulla 2011), we assume that contingency factors will have a moderating effect on the relationship between the adaptation level of marketing mix strategies and export performance.

In the following, the focus will be on seven contingency factors and their moderating effect on the relationship between the adaptation level of marketing mix strategies and performance for both TRs and BIs. The contingency factors are firm size, number of target countries, customer type, product uniqueness and quality, managers' prior international experience and the commitment of management in international operations.

When taking the context into account in explaining the relationship between the level of adaptation of the marketing mix elements and export performance, it is believed that there are no differences between TRs and BIs. Thus, the following hypotheses are the same for both TRs and BIs.

Firm size: Stoian *et al.* (2009) specifically studied whether firm size moderated the relationship between overall adapted marketing mix strategy and performance. They found that for larger firms, higher adaptation leads to lower objective performance, but in the case of smaller firms there was no effect. However, when performance was measured by a subjective measure (satisfaction with export performance) there was an even clearer moderating effect. The relationship between adaptation and satisfaction was negative for larger firms, but positive for smaller firms. In addition, Tan and Sousa (2013) investigated the meta-analysis and found a positive relationship between firm size and the level of product, promotion and distribution strategy. Sousa and Bradley (2008), on the other hand, found that larger firm size supported the use of a more adapted pricing strategy. However, it is believed that larger firms can benefit from standardization more than smaller firms, as they are able to make considerable investments in production capacity and thus make use of the economies of scale. Based on this assumption, we suggest that:

> H3: The negative relationship between adapted marketing mix strategies and performance increases with firm size.

Number of target countries: No studies could be identified exploring the potential role of the number of target countries in moderating the relationship between marketing strategy mix and performance. However, a couple of studies have examined the effect of the number of target countries on the degree of adaptation of marketing mix strategies. Cavusgil *et al.* (1993) found that adaptation of positioning and the use of a promotional approach were greater when a product was exported simultaneously to multiple markets, but the opposite result was noted for product elements, where adaptation was higher when the product was exported to a single market. In addition, no significant differences in terms of adaptation were found for the packaging and labeling elements. Tan and Sousa (2013) found that the number of target markets had a negative relationship with the standardization of promotion and distribution strategy and a positive relationship with the standardization of price strategy. Sousa and Bradley (2008) found a negative relationship with the adaptation level of a pricing strategy and performance. Prior results thus do not provide a clear indication of the relationship between the number of target countries and the degree of adaptation of all the marketing mix strategies. However, we can assume that the more concentrated the sales effort of the company is on a few markets, the less market power the firm has, and thus the conditions under which competitive advantage is transferable would not be met.

> H4: The negative relationship between adapted marketing mix strategies and performance increases with the number of target countries.

Business customers: It is commonly viewed and empirically verified that industrial products sold to business customers seem to be more standardized than consumer products sold to final customers, because, for example, various cultural elements demand more adaptation in the latter than in the former situations (Leonidou 1996; Menguc 1997). In addition, it may be assumed that this does not concern only the product element of the marketing mix, but also the other elements like distribution and communication. In some studies, however, no support for the relationship was found (Michell *et al.* 1998; Schilke *et al.* 2009). Thus, we suggest that:

> H5: The negative relationship between adapted marketing mix strategies and performance increases when customers are mainly business customers.

MNCs as customers: No studies were found exploring the moderating role of MNCs as a customer type. However, the foreign companies may have followed their customers in the domestic and other markets into other foreign markets. In these cases, one could expect that the level of adaptations in various marketing mix elements is clearly lower than in cases where the buyers are totally or mainly target-country-based customers. Thus, it is suggested that,

> H6: The negative relationship between adapted marketing mix strategies and performance increases when customers are mainly multinationals.

The roles of **product uniqueness** and **product quality** in export marketing mix strategies have been studied only to a limited extent. In some studies, the effect of the product uniqueness on adaptation level has been explored. Based on the results, in some cases a positive relationship and in other cases no relationship between the variables has been found (O'Cass and Craig 2003). In the review by Theodisou and Leonidou (2003) no prior studies exploring the relationship between product quality and the level of adaptation in marketing strategies was found.

However, both uniqueness and quality of the product can be a source of competitive advantage that may lead to perceived customer benefits and act as an entry barrier to competition, and so would have the characteristics of a core competence as proposed by Viswanathan and Dickson (2007, 53). This would mean that conditions, under which competitive advantage is transferable, are met and the use of a standardized marketing mix strategy would lead to higher performance. Thus, it is suggested that,

> H7: The negative relationship between adapted marketing mix strategies and performance increases with the level of product uniqueness.
>
> H8: The negative relationship between adapted marketing mix strategies and performance increases with the quality of the product.

Managers' international experience and *management commitment to international operations* are important resources in creating successful international business operations. Some studies exploring the role of firm level international experience have found support for the positive relationship; others have found a negative relationship, and some have found no significant relationship with adaptation level (Leonidou 1996; Sousa and Bradley 2008; Tan and Sousa 2013). Tan and Sousa (2013) found a negative relationship between the level of management commitment and both the level of standardization of product and price strategy; they also found a positive relationship with promotion standardization. It seems that none of the previous studies has explored the moderating effect of before-mentioned factors. However, it may be believed that when the management of the SME has more international experience they know better and they are able to analyze the market situation, customer needs, alternative distribution channels etc. in a better way, and they therefore are able to plan the potential or needed adaptations to various marketing mix elements more efficiently. In firms where the management does not have this kind of experience, the possibilities to evaluate the potential adaptation of various marketing mix elements is more limited. In addition, if management is not committed to international operations they will limit their effects in the required market analysis and most probably will not show interest in changing existing marketing strategies. Lack of proper analysis as a result of low management commitment may lead to weak performance.

Thus, we suggest that:

> H9: The positive relationship between adapted marketing mix strategies and performance increases with the level of managerial international experience.

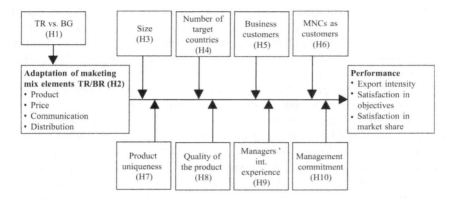

Figure 13.1 Summary of the Framework

> H10: The positive relationship between adapted marketing mix strategies and performance increases with the level of managerial commitment to international operations.

A summary of the framework of the study is presented in Figure 13.1 on page 231.

4. Methodology, Data Collection and Sample

The empirical part of the study is based on a two-step mail survey complemented with a telephone survey, the process being completed between June and November 2006 among Finnish SMEs. The selection of target companies was based on four criteria, in that the firm: 1) had 10–249 employees, 2) had an annual turnover of less than 50 million euros 3) operated in the manufacturing or ICT sectors, and 4) had been established between 1960 and 2000. These criteria produced the target group of 1481 firms that were sent a four-page-long questionnaire. In firms having less than 50 employees, the survey was sent to the managing director of the firm, and in bigger companies to the person in charge of international operations. Fifty-two of the questionnaires were returned due to the company ceasing to exist or being otherwise untraceable, reducing the number of target firms to 1429. A total of 269 firms responded to the questionnaire, indicating an effective response rate of 18.8 percent. For this study, two additional criteria were set: the share of export had to have been 10 percent or more in 2005, and the company should have had two or more export target countries in 2005. These additional conditions reduced the sample size to 221 companies. From these, the number of TRs (started exporting after three years of establishment or share of exports was <25% within three years of establishment) was 147 and BIs 68 (started exporting within three years of establishment and share of exports was by then at least 25%). However, six cases could not be classified because of missing information. In addition, not all information was available for all the cases and thus depending on the model, the sample sizes in different regression models may be lower than the sample sizes mentioned above.

Measures used in prior studies were adopted in the study. *Degree of adaptation* was measured by asking the respondents to rate the total degree of standardization of the product, price, communication and distribution strategy (1 = fully standardized . . . 5 = fully adapted), which is similar to that identified by Theodosiou and Leonidou (2003). *Firm size* has often been measured by the number of employees and turnover (Kustin 2010). In this study, we adopt the first measure. *Number of target countries* was measured by a single item—respondents were asked to state how many countries the firm exported to in 2005, representing a similar type of measurement, for example, to that of Hultman *et al.* (2009).

Two variables were used to explore the type of customer. We distinguish between *business customers* (coded as 1) and final customers (coded as 0) and between *MNC as main customers* (coded 1) and others (coded 0) including mainly local companies. *Product uniqueness* was measured by asking the respondents to rate how well the statement, "Our product satisfies a unique need which is not easy to be substituted by our competitors' products" and *Product quality* by rating how well the statement, "Customers regard our product as of a higher quality than our competitors' product" described the company (1 = very poorly . . . 5 = very well). Subjective measurement was used to measure the level of *International manager experience* and *International management commitment* (1 = very low—5 = very high).

Export performance was measured using both an objective measure and two subjective measures in order to avoid the criticized unidimensional measurement (Leonidou and Katsikeas 2010). One of the most common export performance measures has been export intensity (Sousa and Lengler 2009; Stoian *et al.* 2009). Thus, in order to increase the comparability of results, an objective performance measure of export intensity was utilized. In order to take into account the multidimensional nature of export performance, the degree of satisfaction in fulfilling the objectives set for the exports and market share in main markets were applied in the measurement (Alashban *et al.* 2002; Stoian *et al.* 2009). In testing the moderation effects, variables were mean-centered in order to minimize problems with multicollinearity.

5. Results

Descriptive statistics and correlations among the variables in the study are presented in Table 13.1, in Appendix 13.1 (page 237). Tables 13.2 and 13.3 in Appendices 13.2 and 13.3 (pages 238 and 240) show the regression results for hypothesis testing. In *H1* we suggested that the level of standardization/

adaptation would not have a direct effect on export performance. As can be seen in Table 13.2, Appendix 13.2, we found support for the suggestion in the cases of price, communication and distribution strategies both in the samples of TRs and BIs. However, product strategy had a direct positive effect on satisfaction with market share in core markets for TRs and fulfilling the objectives set for exports in the case of BIs.

In H2 we assumed that TRs would utilize more adapted marketing mix strategies than BIs. However, based on the t-tests, there was no significant difference in the level of adaptation of marketing mix strategies between TRs and BIs.

In the following, the potential moderating effects are examined for TRs and for BIs (see Table 13.3, Appendix 13.3 on page 240). We hypothesized that the greater the *size of the firm,* the more adapted marketing mix strategies would have a more negative relationship with performance (*H3*). Only limited support was found for this hypothesis. The results for the subsamples of TRs and BIs differed clearly. In the case of TRs, no interaction effect was found, but in the case of BIs, a significant negative interaction effect was found with pricing and with distribution strategy. The results indicate that the greater the size of BIs, the more an adapted *pricing strategy* would decrease the satisfaction with fulfilling the objectives set for exports and an adapted *distribution strategy* would decrease the satisfaction with the market share in core markets, thus supporting our suggestion.

Through hypothesis *H4* we suggested that the *number of target countries* would moderate the relationship between marketing mix strategies and performance. Again, only in the case of BIs were some interaction effects found when the performance was measured by the satisfaction with fulfilling the objectives set for exports. The more adapted the *product and communication strategies* were, the higher was performance when there was an increase in the number of target countries. The results indicate that when the number of target countries is high, more adapted product and communication strategies should be used in order to increase the satisfaction with fulfilling the objectives set for exports, thus contrary to our expectations.

In *H5* we assumed that when the *customers were mainly business firms,* more adapted marketing mix strategies would decrease performance. We found no support for the interaction effect among TRs and BIs. In the case of BIs, some minor support was found for *H6* in which we assumed that when *customers were mainly MNCs,* a more adapted marketing mix strategy would decrease performance. The empirical results confirmed that for BIs, a more adapted *distribution strategy* would decrease *export intensity* when customers were mainly MNCs.

For the moderating role of *product type,* we suggested that the use of more adapted marketing mix strategies when the product uniqueness (*H7*) and quality (H8) are high would lower performance. We found *no support* for the hypothesis. On the other hand, some *minor positive interaction* effects were found between uniqueness and distribution strategy for BIs and between quality and distribution strategy for TRs and quality and product strategy for BIs.

The assumption related to the moderating role of *managers' international experience (H9)* was that the use of more adapted strategies when there is a higher level of experience would increase the performance. The results show that in the case of BIs more adapted *product strategy* would increase the satisfaction with fulfilling the objectives. Again, clear differences were found for the moderating role of *management international commitment (H10)*. No interaction effect was found for the TRs. However, for BIs there was a significant negative interaction effect with all marketing mix strategies on satisfaction with fulfilling the objectives. The results indicate that the higher the level of management international commitment, a more adapted product, pricing, communication and distribution strategy would decrease the satisfaction with fulfilling the objectives set for exporting, thus supporting the use of more standardized marketing mix strategies.

6. Discussion and Conclusions

The goal of the study was to explore the similarities and differences between TRs and BIs in terms of the adaptation level of marketing strategies and their effect on the export performance, taking into account the effect of potential moderators. Moderating factors included in the study were firm size, number of target countries, customer and product types, managers' international experience and management commitment to international operations. The ten developed hypotheses were tested in the empirical part of the study, which was based on survey results from 221 Finnish SMEs (10–249 employees) with exports constituting at least 10 percent of total sales and at least two export target countries in 2005.

Similarities between TRs and BIs were found in the direct performance implications of the marketing mix elements. We found that price, communication and distribution strategy did not directly influence any of the performance types for either of the firm types. The results are in line with previous literature and support the criticism that situation-strategic fit needs to be taken into account when trying to understand the performance implications (Shoham 2003; Stoian *et al.* 2009; Schmid and Kotulla 2011). However, product strategy had a direct positive effect on one of the performance types for both TRs and BIs, supporting the findings by for example, Sousa and Lengler (2009). In addition, the results indicate that there were no significant differences in the adaptation level of marketing strategies between TRs and BIs. The result is surprising, taking into account the differences in the key characteristics of TRs and BIs.

However, especially interesting are the differences found in the subsamples of TRs and BIs regarding the impact of moderating factors. For TRs, only one out of the eight suggested moderating factors had a significant interaction effect with some of the marketing strategies on performance.

On the other hand, for BIs seven of the moderating factors had a significant effect. Firm size, number of export countries, MNCs as a customer type, product uniqueness and management commitment are the moderators for which significant interaction effects were found for BIs but not for TRs. Only product quality and managers' international experience were found to have moderating effects for both TRs and BIs.

What could explain these differences in the two subsamples? The original assumption was that even though TRs and BIs differ in many respects, the potential performance implications of the decisions on the level of marketing strategies could be explained by the situation-strategic fit and therefore there would be no differences in the role of moderating effects on performance between TRs and BIs. However, the role of situation-specific factors may be even more complicated than suggested in the paper. It may not be enough to explore the role of one moderating factor on the relationship between adaptation level and performance, but rather it may be necessary to take into account the combined effect of several potential moderators. We could assume that in the case of TRs, more variation could be found in the different moderating factors, compared to BIs. Thus, also the potential combinations of situational factors could be larger compared to BIs and therefore limited interaction effects were found in the subsample of TRs.

When analyzing the results based on the subsample of BIs, we can see a clear variance in the impact of moderating factors. The role of moderating factors varied depending on the marketing mix strategy and performance type, offering support for the argumentation of high context specificity of the marketing strategy-performance relationship. However, it seems that when comparing the effects of different moderating factors, management commitment on international operations had a significant interaction effect on all the four marketing strategies, indicating a more important role compared to the other moderating factors. What is also interesting is the negative interaction impact on performance, indicating that the higher the level of management international commitment, the more adapted marketing mix strategies would decrease satisfaction on fulfilling the objectives set. In addition, in terms of performance measures, the results indicate that the interaction effect was most often found on fulfilling the objectives set for the exports.

The results are interesting specifically for export and marketing managers in BIs planning marketing mix adaptation levels to support their expansion in international markets. In order to increase the internationalization, it is recommended that they should adapt product strategy, especially when the quality of the product is high. An appropriate adaptation of product characteristics according to the local customer requirement may put emphasis on cooperation with local companies. However, the need to cooperate may be reduced when firms already have high manager level international experience, which can be utilized in the design of appropriate product adaptation. The results also indicate that when there is high commitment to international activities, a higher level of standardization would make it easier to achieve the goals set for internationalization. In addition, when BIs are cooperating strongly with MNCs, the standardized distribution strategy seems to support the possibility of increasing internationalization intensity, giving further evidence that standardization strategy may help the co-operation with other firms in export efforts.

The findings also give guidelines regarding the partner selection for potential export cooperation. Selection of partners with similar product quality, approaches on distribution strategy and type of customers could be beneficial for successful cooperation activities.

The main contribution of the paper is considered to be specifically in exploring the similarities and differences between TRs and the BIs in terms of the adaptation level of marketing strategies and their effect on export performance. It gives support for the basic idea presented in the contingency perspective and situation-strategy fit that the appropriate level of standardization/adaptation of different marketing mix strategies depends on the situational factors and therefore it is not the direct effect of the level of adaptation of marketing mix strategy that determines the performance implications (Schmid and Kotulla 2011; Theodosiu and Leonidou 2003). Specifically, the study contributes in showing the clear differences between TRs and BIs in terms of the effects of moderating factors. The results indicate the need for further studies in which the context is explored in more detail, taking into account the combined effect of relevant moderating factors.

Secondly, the study contributes by exploring the role of the four marketing mix strategies at the same time, and thirdly by investigating their influence on three performance types. The results clearly indicate that some context factors may have important moderating effects, but depending on the specific context factor, different marketing mix strategies and performance types are influenced. Therefore, the study provides new insights into the marketing mix strategy-performance relationship.

It is important to take into account that the results of this study are valid only in the main export countries exploited by the firms polled. It is noteworthy that the number of target countries was quite high for most of the firms. Thus, the results should be interpreted with caution. In the future, it would be important to assess the marketing mix adaptation and performance for each target country separately. In addition, as the results indicate, the effect of the situational factors depends on the marketing strategy element under review: it is not enough to have general-level hypotheses assuming the same moderating effects for all marketing strategies, but rather the attempt should be made to explore in more detail the linkages between individual market strategies and situational factors and thus utilize the situation-strategy fit concept more specifically.

Appendix 13.1

Table 13.1 Descriptives and Correlations

Variable	Mean	S.D.		1.	2.	3.	4.	5.	6.	7.	8.	9.	10.	11.	12.	13.
1. Product and services strategy	3,01	1,173	Pearson correlation	1												
			Sig. (2-tailed)													
2. Pricing strategy	3,34	1,183	Pearson correlation	0,393	1											
			Sig. (2-tailed)	0,000												
3. Communication strategy	3,01	1,176	Pearson correlation	0,366	0,416	1										
			Sig. (2-tailed)	0,000	0,000											
4. Place strategy	3,09	1,182	Pearson correlation	0,367	0,483	0,542	1									
			Sig. (2-tailed)	0,000	0,000	0,000										
5. Firm size	54,29	48,627	Pearson correlation	0,067	0,057	0,075	0,116	1								
			Sig. (2-tailed)	0,335	0,415	0,289	0,101									
6. Number of export countries	14,98	12,870	Pearson correlation	−0,001	0,143	0,044	−0,071	0,359	1							
			Sig. (2-tailed)	0,993	0,039	0,532	0,314	0,000								
7. Product uniqueness	3,14	1,168	Pearson correlation	0,125	0,090	−0,010	−0,037	−0,044	0,124	1						
			Sig. (2-tailed)	0,082	0,215	0,894	0,612	0,534	0,078							
8. Product quality	3,94	0,752	Pearson correlation	0,062	−0,019	−0,002	−0,031	−0,002	0,144	0,280	1					
			Sig. (2-tailed)	0,384	0,788	0,976	0,674	0,981	0,039	0,000						
9. Management's int. exp.	3,79	1,010	Pearson correlation	0,050	0,009	0,143	0,079	0,050	0,242	0,174	0,227	1				
			Sig. (2-tailed)	0,505	0,900	0,061	0,302	0,494	0,001	0,018	0,002					
10. Management's commitment	4,22	0,792	Pearson correlation	0,015	0,061	0,021	−0,038	0,018	0,307	0,108	0,216	0,518	1			
			Sig. (2-tailed)	0,846	0,422	0,785	0,621	0,805	0,000	0,144	0,003	0,000				
11. P1: Export intensity	0,53	0,283	Pearson correlation	0,126	0,064	0,007	−0,029	0,119	0,511	0,164	0,227	0,256	0,252	1		
			Sig. (2-tailed)	0,067	0,354	0,917	0,677	0,077	0,000	0,019	0,001	0,000	0,000			
12. P2: Compared to goals	3,32	0,921	Pearson correlation	0,191	0,010	−0,034	−0,037	−0,005	0,108	0,139	0,270	0,126	0,202	0,130	1	
			Sig. (2-tailed)	0,009	0,891	0,650	0,621	0,948	0,133	0,054	0,000	0,091	0,006	0,071		
13. P3: Market share	3,34	0,797	Pearson correlation	0,179	0,060	0,086	0,016	−0,057	−0,052	0,140	0,173	0,163	0,206	0,055	0,479	1
			Sig. (2-tailed)	0,018	0,435	0,268	0,839	0,443	0,489	0,063	0,021	0,030	0,006	0,463	0,000	

Appendix 13.2

Table 13.2 Direct Impacts

TRADITIONALLY INTERNATIONALIZED FIRMS

Variable	Model 1 Performance 1 Export Intensity	Model 2 Performance 2 Compared to Goals	Model 3 Performance 3 Market Share
Product and services strategy	0,038	0,073	0,165[b]
Pricing strategy	–0,027	–0,023	0,091
Communication strategy	–0,010	–0,149	–0,026
Distribution strategy	0,003	0,077	–0,036
Firm size	0,000	–0,001	0,000
Number of export countries	0,012[d]	0,016[a]	–0,008
Customer type 1. Business firm	0,122[b]	–0,078	–0,044
Customer type 2. MNCs	0,051	0,319	–0,003
Product uniqueness	0,002	0,104	0,090
Product quality	0,045	0,268[b]	–0,049
Management's int. exp.	0,043	0,033	0,083
Management's commitment	–0,032	0,134	0,189[a]
Constant	–0,008	1,295[a]	1,739[c]
Adjusted R Square	0,282	0,097	0,063
F (ANOVA)	4,475[d]	1,946[b]	1,584
N	98	95	98

BORN INTERNATIONALS

Variable	Model 1 Performance 1 Export Intensity	Model 2 Performance 2 Compared to Goals	Model 3 Performance 3 Market Share
Product & services strategy	0,010	0,504[d]	0,098
Pricing strategy	0,037	0,040	–0,062
Communication strategy	0,005	–0,139	0,047
Distribution strategy	–0,019	–0,168	–0,056

(Continued)

Table 13.2 (Continued)

BORN INTERNATIONALS

Variable	Model 1 Performance 1 Export Intensity	Model 2 Performance 2 Compared to Goals	Model 3 Performance 3 Market Share
Firm size	−0,001	−0,004	−0,003
Number of export countries	**0,005**[a]	0,000	−0,001
Customer type 1. Business firm	−0,069	−0,187	**−0,619**[b]
Customer type 2. MNCs	−0,008	−0,325	−0,170
Product uniqueness	0,026	−0,121	−0,051
Product quality	0,050	**0,362**[b]	**0,360**[b]
Management's int. exp.	−0,018	0,053	−0,012
Management's commitment	0,063	0,033	0,135
Constant	0,101	1,442	**2,060**[b]
Adjusted R Square	0,058	0,319	0,075
F (ANOVA)	1,294	3,230[c]	1,371
N	53	52	51

Statistical significance levels: a <= 0,1; b <= 0,05; c <= 0,01; d <= 0,001

Appendix 13.3

Table 13.3 Significant Interaction Effects with Product, Price, Communication and Distribution Strategy, TRs & BIs

TRADITIONALLY INTERNATIONALIZED FIRMS

Variable	Model 4 Performance 1 Export Intensity	Model 5 Performance 2 Compared to Goals	Model 6 Performance 3 Market Share	Model 7 Performance 1 Export Intensity	Model 8 Performance 2 Compared to Goals	Model 9 Performance 3 Market Share
Number of export countries	0,012[d]	0,018	-0,012	0,012[d]	0,016	-0,009
Customer type 1. Business firm	0,115	-0,050	-0,066	0,142[b]	-0,083	-0,089
Product quality	0,041	0,278[b]	-0,045	0,044	0,247	-0,080
Constant	0,348[d]	3,367[d]	3,423[d]	0,332[d]	3,390[d]	3,464[d]
Adjusted R Square	0,267	0,037	0,067	0,265	0,106	0,059
F (ANOVA)	2,878[d]	1,198	1,370	2,909[d]	1,627	1,327
N	98	95	96	98	95	96

	Model 10	Model 11	Model 12	Model 13	Model 14	Model 15
Number of export countries	0,010[d]	0,018	-0,006	0,013[d]	0,015	-0,010
Customer type 1. Business firm	0,181[b]	-0,019	0,065	0,123[a]	-0,101	-0,015
Product uniqueness	0,002	0,37	0,063	-0,002	0,165[a]	0,177[b]
Product quality	0,041	0,301[b]	-0,010	0,047	0,303[b]	-0,045
DistrStr_x_Quality				0,020	0,157	0,366[d]
Constant	0,325[d]	3,344[d]	3,382[d]	0,358[d]	3,387[d]	3,385[d]
Adjusted R Square	0,283	0,065	-0,017	0,277	0,085	0,149
F (ANOVA)	2,916[d]	1,329	0,923	2,971[d]	1,477	1,902[b]
N	98	95	96	98	95	96

BORN INTERNATIONALS

Variable	Model 4	Model 5	Model 6	Model 7	Model 8	Model 9
Product and services strategy	0,072	0,883[c]	0,168	0,006	0,508[d]	0,051
Communication strategy	0,034	-0,340[b]	0,074	-0,017	-0,141	0,167
Product quality	0,051	0,076	0,354	0,044	0,262	0,366[b]
Management's int. exp.	-0,120[b]	0,403[b]	-0,031	0,015	0,172	0,019
Management's commitment	0,181[b]	-0,246	0,209	0,075	-0,028	0,304
ProductStr_x_TargetCou	-0,005[b]	0,026[c]	0,002			
ProductStr_x_Quality	0,159[c]	-0,100	-0,023			
ProductStr_x_Int.Exp.	0,010	0,293[b]	-0,039			
ProductStr_x_Commitment	-0,031	-0,762[c]	-0,053			
PriceStr_x_Firmsize				-0,001	-0,006[b]	-0,004
PriceStr_x_Uniqueness				-0,011	-0,043	-0,221[c]
PriceStr_x_Commitment				-0,043	-0,346[b]	-0,048
Constant	0,670[d]	3,300[d]	3,668[d]	0,811[d]	3,346[d]	3,680[d]
Adjusted R Square	0,209	0,446	-0,078	0,121	0,373	0,146
F (ANOVA)	1,715[a]	3,174[c]	0,805	1,372	2,604[c]	1,462
N	53	52	51	53	52	51

	Model 10	Model 11	Model 12	Model 13	Model 14	Model 15
Product & services strategy	0,008	0,497[d]	0,115	0,009	0,464[d]	0,039
Product quality	0,035	0,258	0,360[b]	0,028	0,214	0,211
CommunStr_x_TargetCou	-0,003	0,014[b]	0,009			
CommunStr_x_Commitment	-0,063	-0,527[b]	-0,222			
DistrStr_x_Firmsize				0,000	-0,004	-0,007[b]
DistrStr_x_MNCs				-0,195[c]	0,007	0,364

(Continued)

Table 13.3 (Continued)

	Model 10	Model 11	Model 12	Model 13	Model 14	Model 15
DistrStr_x_Uniqueness				0,051[b]	−0,063	−0,095
DistrStr_x_Commitment				−0,091	−0,493[b]	−0,360
Constant	0,770[d]	3,325[d]	3,696[d]	0,726[d]	3,273[d]	3,731[d]
Adjusted R Square	0,078	0,379	0,034	0,180	0,319	0,177
F (ANOVA)	1,234	2,678[c]	1,097	1,602	2,289[b]	1,589
N	53	52	51	53	52	51

Statistical significance levels: b ≤ 0,05; c ≤ 0,01; d ≤ 0,001

References

Alashban, Aref A., Linda A. Hayes, George M. Zinkhan, and Aanne L. Balazs. 2002. "International Brand-Name Standardization/Adaptation: antecedents and Consequences." *Journal of International Marketing* 10(3): 22–48.

Cavusgil, S. Tamir, and Gary Knight. 2015. "The Born Global Firm: An Entrepreneurial and Capabilities Perspective on Early and Rapid Internationalization." *Journal of International Business Studies* 46(1): 3–16.

Cavusgil, S. Tamer, Shaoming Zou, and G.M. Naidu. 1993. "Product and Promotion Adaptation in Export Ventures: An Empirical Investigation." *Journal of International Business Studies* 24(3): 479–506.

Gabrielsson, Peter, Mika Gabrielsson, and Tomi Seppälä. 2012. "Consequences of Strategic Fit and Performance." *Journal of International Marketing* 20(2): 25–48.

Hultman, Magnus, Matthew J. Robson, and Constanine S. Katsikeas. 2009. "Export Product Strategy Fit and Performance." *Journal of International Marketing* 17(4): 1–23.

Kustin, Richard. 2010. "The Earth Is Flat, Almost: Measuring Marketing Standardization and Profit Performance of Japanese and U.S. firms." *Journal of Global Marketing* 23(2): 100–108.

Lages, Luis Filipe, Jose Mata, and David A. Griffith. 2013. "Change in International Market Strategy as a Reaction to Performance Decline." *Journal of Business Research* 66(12): 2600–2611.

Lee, Chol., and David A. Griffith. 2004. "The Marketing Strategy-Performance Relationship in an Export-Driven Developing Economy." *International Marketing Review* 21(3): 321–334.

Leonidou, Leonidas C. 1996. "Product Standardization or Adaptation: The Japanese Approach." *Journal of Marketing Practice: Applied Marketing Science* 2(4): 53–71.

Leonidou, Leonidas C., and Constantine S. Katsikeas. 2010. "Integrative Assessment of Exporting Research Articles in Business Journals During the Period 1960–2007." *Journal of Business Research* 63(8): 879–887.

Mengüç, Bülent. 1997. "Product Adaptation Practices in the Context of Export Activity: An Empirical Study of Turkish Manufacturing Firms." *Journal of Euromarketing* 6(2): 25–66.

Michell, Paul, James Lynch, and Obaid Alabdali. 1998. "New Perspectives on Marketing Mix Program Standardization." *International Business Review* 7(6): 617–634.

O'Cass, Aron, and Julian Craig. 2003. "Examining Firm and Environmental Influences on Export Marketing Mix Strategy and Export Performance of Australian Exporters." *European Journal of Marketing* 37(3): 366–384.

Rialp, Alex, Josep Rialp, and Gary A. Knight. 2005. "The Phenomenon of Early Internationalizing Firms: What Do We Know After a Decade (1993–2003) of Scientific Inquiry?" *International Business Review* 14(2): 147–166.

Schilke Oliver, Martin Reiman and Jacquelyn S. Thomas. 2009. "When Does International Marketing Standardization Matter to Firm Performance?" *Journal of International Marketing* 17(4): 24–46.

Schmid, Stefan, and Thomas Kotulla. 2009. "Standardization and Adaptation in International Marketing and Management—From a Critical Literature Analysis to a Theoretical Framework." In *Strategies and Management of Internationalization*

244 Jorma Larimo and Minnie Kontkanen

and Foreign Operations, edited by Jorma Larimo, 309–348. Vaasa: University of Vaasa.

Schmid, Stefan, and Thomas Kotulla. 2011. "50 years of Research on International Standardization and Adaptation- From a Systematic Literature Analysis to a Theoretical Framework." *International Business Review* 20(5): 491–507.

Shoham, Aviv. 2003. "Standardization of International Strategy and Export Performance: A Meta-Analysis." *Journal of Global Marketing* 16(1–2): 97–120.

Sousa, Carlos M.P., and Frank Bradley. 2008. "Antecedents of International Pricing Adaptation and Export Performance." *Journal of World Business* 43(3): 307–320.

Sousa, Carlos M.P., and Jorge Lengler. 2009. "Psychic Distance, Marketing Strategy and Performance in Export Ventures of Brazilian Firms." *Journal of Marketing Management* 25(5–6): 591–610.

Stoian, Maria-Cristina, Alex Rialp, and Josep Rialp. 2009. "International Marketing Strategy and Export Performance: Standardization, Adaptation or a Middle Road?" Paper presented at the 36th AIB UK and Ireland Chapter Conference, Glasgow, Scotland, April 2–4.

Tan, Qun, and Carlos M.S. Sousa. 2013. "International Marketing Standardization: A Meta-Analytic Estimation of Its Antecedents and Consequences." *Management International Review* 53(5): 711–739.

Theodosiou, Marios, and Leonidas C. Leonidou. 2003. "Standardization Versus Adaptation of International Marketing Strategy: An Integrative Assessment of the Empirical Research." *International Business Review* 12(2): 141–171.

Viswanathan, Nanda K., and Peter R. Dickson. 2007. "The Fundamentals of Standardizing Global Marketing Strategy." *International Marketing Review* 24(1): 46–63.

14 Sourcing by Born Global Firms

Per Servais and Erik S. Rasmussen

1. Introduction

Tesar *et al.* (2003) researched the internationalization of small European firms, and they found that recently small and medium-sized enterprises (SMEs) have started systematically to examine alternatives open to them in the rapidly changing market. Some SMEs have embarked on the development of market-oriented strategies only in their domestic market while other SMEs have explored export markets. Those SMEs that are attempting to defend their domestic markets face strong competition from abroad (Kahiya 2013; Love and Roper 2015; Moini 1995). SMEs that have decided to explore export markets are finding it difficult to export their products on their own and are looking for external partners (Tesar *et al.* 2003).

An increasing number of smaller firms behave in a manner that is contradictory to existing frameworks of explaining internationalization behavior, namely the stages model. These firms have been termed "international new ventures" (INVs) (McDougall *et al.* 1994), "born globals" (Knight and Cavusgil 1996; Knight 1997; Madsen and Servais 1997), "instant internationals" (Preece *et al.* 1999), or "global startups" (Oviatt and McDougall 1994). Knight and Cavusgil (1996, 17) state that "the Born Global phenomenon presents an important new challenge to traditional internationalization theory." One shortcoming in the stream of literature on international new ventures, however, has been the overwhelming focus on the sales side, whereas insights into local and international sourcing by INVs are absent. This chapter deals with the dilemma raised by Tesar *et al.* (2003) about small firms' network participation—that sourcing is equally a part of the operations of INVs. International sourcing is vital for European SMEs, and connecting simultaneously to both sourcing and international marketing networks challenges newly established firms. That international sourcing is an important part of the entrepreneurial internationalization process in many SMEs has been documented in research on SMEs by, for example, (Horgos 2013; Jia *et al.* 2014; Overby and Servais 2005; Servais *et al.* 2007.). For many SMEs, sourcing is the first step of the internationalization process, and there is a lack of studies with a focus on international sourcing—both from theoretical and empirical points of view.

As demonstrated, for example, by (Hessels and Parker 2013), SMEs must be seen as key players in the internationalization of firms from small and industrialized countries, especially in Europe. The focus of the research on SME internationalization has traditionally been on exporting, but purchasing and sourcing can be a way for an SME to gain access to resources abroad and develop its competitive advantage. Learning from international suppliers could lead to both informal and formal relations with new partners abroad (Luostarinen and Gabrielsson 2006; Welch and Luostarinen 1993).

Following the research gap discussed above, the purpose of the chapter is, therefore, to explore sourcing in new international ventures and the motives for international purchasing and to present a case study of a Danish born global firm and some suggestions for further research.

2. Overview of Research On INVs

Several articles set out to give an overview in the form of a literature review of some parts of the research on International New Ventures, International Entrepreneurship, Born Globals and similar expressions for firms that internationalize from their founding (see, for example, Jones *et al.* 2011; Knight and Liesch 2016). Thorough reviews of empirical findings can be found, for example, in several studies (Aspelund *et al.* 2007; Cesinger *et al.* 2012; Keupp and Gassmann 2009; Rialp *et al.* 2005). It must be emphasized that comparisons across studies are extremely difficult because definitions of the phenomenon of early and rapidly internationalizing firms are very different. There may be a relatively high degree of consensus among scholars when conceptualizing the phenomenon, and often the conceptual definition suggested by Oviatt and McDougall (1994) is used, but there is much higher fragmentation when it comes to operational definitions used in empirical work. It is an important research gap in the empirical literature that no such commonly accepted operational definition of the phenomenon had been developed.

One of the most comprehensive and updated overview articles on INVs is Jones *et al.* (2011). This article explores the domain of international entrepreneurship (IE) research by thematically mapping and assessing the area. Given that IE is positioned at the nexus of internationalization and entrepreneurship where entrepreneurial behavior involves a cross-border business activity or is compared across countries, they identify 323 relevant journal articles published in the period from 1989 to 2009. They examine the subject matter of IE research and inductively synthesize and categorize it into major themes and sub-themes. The review is substantial and comprehensive, pointing to the fact that only a very few researchers have looked into the sourcing activities of the international new ventures.

In a recent review article, Peiris *et al.* (2012) analyze 291 scholarly articles on INVs published in the period 1993–2012. The most prevalent sector for IE studies was found to be manufacturing (142 articles), and the focus of IE research appears to have narrowed down to high-technology firms, new ventures (95 articles), and SMEs with <500 employees (161 articles). First, it suggests an integrative framework based on international business, entrepreneurship, strategic management, social network, and marketing theories. The suggested model highlights the significant role played by the entrepreneur/team, firm and network resources that act as antecedents to international opportunity development and value innovation. Second, it suggests four typologies of firms (born global, enduring global, early exporter, and mature exporter) that can be studied under the IE theme. It is interesting to observe that they do not identify contributions concerning the international sourcing aspects of the new venture. To develop a typology of born global firms or INVs that include international sourcing as a key activity of the entrepreneurial firm, it is necessary to draw upon the first research on INVs and look at the typologies used.

3. Typologies of International New Ventures

Looking closer at the definition of the seminal work by Oviatt and McDougall (1994, 49), we find that the authors refer to an INV as "a business organization that, from inception, seeks to derive significant competitive advantage from the use of resources and the sale of outputs in multiple countries." They don't really define resources, quantify the scale of foreign sales, or specify the scope (number of countries), within or across different continents. However, more importantly, Oviatt and McDougall (1994) do specify that the most distinguishing factor for an INV is its commitment to creating value across countries, handling either a few or multiple value-chain activities. Oviatt and McDougall (1994) tried to be more specific concerning the concepts used in the definition, not by using supplementary definitions but through a typology of firms created from the number of value chain activities combined with the number of countries by identifying four types of international new ventures. The different types vary according to the number of countries involved in the companies' operations and according to the number of value chain activities these companies coordinate across countries. Figure 14.1 on page 248 illustrates the categorization.

The new international market makers covers quadrants 1 and 2 in Figure 14.1. These companies are traditional importers and exporters that profit by moving goods to nations where they are demanded. The new international market makers most likely internalize the systems and knowledge of inbound and outbound logistics. These companies can be either export/import start-ups or multinational traders. Export/import start-ups focus on serving a few nations that are familiar to the entrepreneur. Multinational traders serve an array of countries and are constantly scanning for trading

	Number of Countries involved	
	Few	*Many*
Few value chain activities coordinated across countries Many value chain activities coordinated across countries	1. Export/import start-up 3. Geographically focused start-up	2. Multinational trader 4. Global start-up

Figure 14.1 Types of International New Ventures (Oviatt and McDougall 1994)

opportunities in areas where they have established networks or can quickly set up new ones. The geographically focused start-ups (quadrant 3) derive an advantage from serving well the specialized needs of a region of the world by using foreign resources. They are more geographically restricted to the location of the specialized need than the multinational traders. The fourth category of companies (quadrant 4), global start-ups, derive significant competitive advantage from extensive coordination among multiple organizational activities that take place in geographically unlimited locations.

Another core of Oviatt and McDougall's early conceptualization of an INV is that it has a "proactive international strategy" which they contrast to the posture of organizations that "evolve gradually from domestic firms to MNEs" in a more reactive way (Oviatt and McDougall 1994, 49). The different types vary according to the number of countries involved in the companies' operation and according to the number of value chain activities these companies coordinate across countries. Hallbäck and Larimo (2006) also questions earlier research on international new ventures and the tendency towards a rather homogenous view on international new ventures as they set out to identify the possible variety of international new ventures. Astonishingly, only a few researchers have looked into these typologies. Hallbäck and Larimo (2006) departs from the work by Oviatt and McDougall (1994) but applies a long-term perspective on firms' development and the inclusion of several factors as possible agents of the difference as their study aimed at exploring several questions: Are INVs different from one another regarding their international development? Moreover, if they are, how and why are the differences manifested in these firms? Based on the analysis of eight INVs, the results highlight the importance of the founding conditions, the internationalization motives, and the international experience of the founding managers on the INV's development in the early phase. Both initial and subsequent development of the INVs varied concerning the geographical reach and type of operations abroad. Hallbäck and Larimo (2006) observed that a growing number of INV studies concentrated on other-than-traditional manufacturing industries or had no industry limitations at all (Larimo and Pulkinen 2002). The results implied the increase of INVs both in manufacturing and service industries as well as in industries of both high and low knowledge intensity.

Going further on situational conditions, in the context of start-up growth, the results suggest that the high-growth firms differ from the low-growth firms in their motivations for start-up. Hence Hallbäck and Larimo (2006) underlines that internationalization can be seen as a strategy for firm growth and the firms pursuing rapid international growth may be expected to differ from local new ventures in their motivations regarding start-up establishment as well as internationalization. In conclusion, Hallbäck and Larimo (2006) calls for an inclusion of the INVs' differences in the international level of value chain activities and not limiting the studies to primary activities such as outward operations and logistics. Activities such as procurement, R&D, financing and other support activities, and the geographical dispersion of these activities, ought to be included, too. Furthermore, a wider time horizon to incorporate and differentiate between the pre-founding, early, and subsequent internationalization phases of the different INVs is needed.

4. SMES' International Sourcing Expansion

According to Melin (1992), a firm's internationalization can be perceived as a part of an ongoing strategy process of the firm. The main difference between internationalization and other types of growth strategy processes can be found in two dimensions. Firstly, the firm transfers products, services, and resources across borders. This difference implies that the company must select in which country or countries the transaction should be performed. Secondly, the firm must choose how to enter foreign markets (Andersen 1997). A firm's international expansion is, however, not confined to export activities alone. In a review of the academic literature, Liang and Parkhe (1997) reveal a striking imbalance: one side of the coin—the exporter side—has been extensively studied, while the other side the importer side and the associated motives have largely been neglected. This finding is further stressed by the findings of Lye and Hamilton (2000). In a similar vein, Cavusgil (1998) highlights perspectives on some fundamental questions in the field of international marketing and some promising research avenues. Among the mentioned avenues is the analysis of firm expansion in international markets with inward and outward internationalization, for example.

Since the late 1980s, a growing concern for manufacturing firms' international sourcing (inward) activities has emerged, stressing the importance of this phenomenon on firms' success (Scully and Fawcett 1994). The connection between import and export activities within a firm and how it affects the internationalization process of the firm has received only scattered interest in the literature (Korhonen *et al.* 1996). The dovetail has been identified primarily through studies on specific business operations such as licensing, subcontracting, and counter trade. In a study of several Finnish industrial firms, Korhonen *et al.* (1996) found that the vast majority of Finnish firms began international activities on the inward side rather than with export, thus pointing to the potential importance of inward activities as a jumping-off point for outward activities. Typical inward operations were imports of physical products such as raw materials, machinery, and components, but also imported services, such as installation, testing, servicing, and maintenance, although at a low level compared to physical products. Korhonen *et al.* (1996) stress that import-export connections could be found at different stages of the internationalization process. These observations link to the research by Oviatt and McDougall (1994) whose original idea was that the sourcing of input as well as the selling of output should be important dimensions in the categorization of international new ventures.

Entrepreneurial Buying

A literature review of entrepreneurs' buying behavior (Ellegaard 2006) shows remarkably little research in this field. Besides the more descriptive studies such as that conducted by Overby and Servais (2005), only a few papers deal with purchasing in newly started firms. As we have seen in the born global literature, sales and export have received much attention; purchasing and the import phenomena, however, have received only very little attention (Quayle 2002). Quayle's survey of 400 SMEs to establish the purchasing priorities and practices of small companies represents one contribution. He found that 65% of the responding companies perceived purchasing to be unimportant but argued that this could be due to a lack of understanding of the value potential of the purchasing task. He argued that effective purchasing needs resources, something which the entrepreneur has in short supply. In another contribution, Low and Macmillan (1988) pinpointed a few other specific entrepreneurial characteristics that condition the purchasing task. For instance, most entrepreneurs lacked a healthy record of accomplishment, which means that suppliers are often reluctant to extend credit.

In addition to the contributions that focus directly on purchasing, some writers have treated related phenomena that, seen from a purchasing perspective, are highly relevant. Various contributions have focused broadly on the network or alliance management issues that confront entrepreneurs (Birley 1985; Larson 1991; Lorenzoni and Ornati 1988). The entrepreneur is described as an orchestrator of inter-firm linkages, combining a wide set of diverse competencies (Lipparini and Sobrero 1994). A critical task for the entrepreneur is to create, manage, and recombine relationships with external parties. Various authors mention the specific entrepreneurial need for relational capability (Larson 1992; Lorenzoni and Ornati 1988). This need comes about as a result of specific conditions, under which most entrepreneurs work. For example, Lipparini and Sobrero (1994) note that entrepreneurs control only a very small part of the supply network and therefore rely much more on external parties than other company types. Entrepreneurs face significant challenges because typically they have not built relationships as well as business and market knowledge and so forth (newness), and because they possess limited resources (smallness).

The above overview indicates that the certain circumstances entrepreneurs work under represent not only a general management challenge but also a specific purchasing challenge compared to larger firms. Lacking resources for internal growth which are typical of the larger company, these dense relationships serve as vehicles for growth through external resources (Lechner and Dowling 2003; Lorenzoni and Ornati 1988). Small companies also utilize supplier relationships to improve innovation by connecting external and internal expertise and capabilities (Lipparini and Sobrero 1994). Moreover, dense ties also serve to reduce risk and uncertainty (Larson 1992). A few studies suggested that close supplier relationships come in various forms. A few contributions looked at the specific networking capabilities of the entrepreneur, which are instrumental in establishing network ties and securing resource access (BarNir and Smith 2002), and Walter *et al.* (2006) demonstrated the importance of entrepreneurial network capability to business performance. Network capability is defined as the entrepreneur's "ability to initiate, maintain, and utilize relationships with various external partners." High network capability includes coordination, relational and internal communication skills, as well as partner knowledge. In a similar study Baron and Markman (2003) investigated social competence, containing the four components social perception, impression management, social adaptability, and expressiveness. The components were not all positively related to financial success, which supported the authors' argument that not all behavioral characteristics of entrepreneurs are equally important. One study found that these companies were more likely to develop progressive relationships with suppliers when positioned in an expanding industry compared to a declining industry (Jones and Kustin 1995). The other demonstrated that export-oriented small companies (clustered) were inclined to have closer relationships than those concentrating on the domestic market (Jones and Kustin 1995).

Motives for International Sourcing

While there has been growing research interest in the last decade on international business opportunities for small and medium-sized firms, this interest aims predominantly at firms' outward activities, whereas firms' international sourcing activities have received only limited attention (Mainela *et al.* 2014). This limited attention (Welch and Luostarinen 1993) to the international sourcing opportunities seems surprising for two main reasons: first, the ultimate success of exporters depends on the behavior of foreign purchases and the quality of the purchasing process. In fact, Biemans and Brand (1995) assert that buyer-seller relationships have changed considerably in recent years from seller initiation to an increasingly active search by the buyer (i.e., reverse marketing). Although not referring specifically to import behavior, Biemans and Brand (1995) point to four international trends that contribute to the increased strategic relevance of purchasing: reduction in the number of suppliers, up-scaling of demands on suppliers, increasing cooperation with suppliers, and decreasing time to market.

The importance of international sourcing activities for firm performance and future competitiveness is supported in the literature from two viewpoints (Overby and Servais 2005). First, international purchasing fosters competition among suppliers in the domestic market through imports of products and services (products and services that may have been available in the domestic market, but on less favorable terms). Second, international purchasing has a direct impact on the performance of the firm in general through improved quality, lower prices, and the array of available products (Overby and Servais 2005). Behind the decision to internationalize purchasing activities are two rationales: that the product/service is not available on the domestic market and/or that the foreign supplier has competitive advantages derived from the production conditions of these firms. The missing availability on the domestic market may result in the buyer redefining the need to suit the offers from domestic suppliers. However, empirical research reveals that industrial buyers in established firms overall are well informed of offerings by foreign suppliers (Birou and Fawcett 1993; Scully and Fawcett 1994). The different production conditions by foreign suppliers are the second explanation, but research has shown that not all international exchange takes place between countries with very different production factors (Servais and Jensen 2001).

Birou and Fawcett (1993) examined a random sample of 1,000 persons in charge of purchases in American manufacturing firms. The aim was to establish a benchmark for the evaluation of competitive advantages and potentials by international purchasing. Among the reasons why they began to purchase abroad were quality, presence, and price. The motives for a firm to engage in international purchasing are, of course, of pivotal interest when studying the field of international sourcing. Traditionally, lower prices or cost advantage has been the main motive for international purchasing. Scully and Fawcett (1994) investigated international purchases in 72 small and medium-sized American manufacturing firms. These 72 firms were divided into two groups: small firms with fewer than 500 employees (44% of the respondents) and large firms with more than 500 employees (the rest). The aim of the survey was, among other things, to demonstrate the connection between the experienced competitive situation and the tendency to make international purchases. Small firms are less internationally oriented compared to large firms. Small firms have less experience with international purchases than large firms, and large firms planned their activities more. The firms were asked to choose among nine different reasons for their international purchases. An important answer in both categories was lower prices, where small firms often emphasized service and large firms often emphasize counter trade. The conclusion was that small firms often are more reactive. Seen numerically, the large firms represent the largest percentage of international purchasers, but as a whole, the purchasing amount of the small firms makes up the largest share of all purchasing. The size of the firm does not influence from which regions the firms choose their suppliers.

However, several studies indicate (Monczka and Trent 1992) that importing firms expect foreign purchases to drive improvement in four critical areas: cost reduction, quality improvement, increased exposure to worldwide technology, and delivery and reliability improvements. Other important reasons for international sourcing include increasing the number of available sources, reacting to foreign sourcing practices of competitors, the introduction of competition to the domestic supply base, and establishing a presence in a foreign market.

Overby and Servais (2005) made a survey of the foreign purchase behavior of small and medium-sized industrial firms in Denmark. The article focused on three issues:

1. To what extent were SMEs involved in international sourcing?
2. How did SMEs initially make contact with foreign suppliers, and what were their motives for choosing a supplier?
3. How did SMEs perceive relationships with foreign suppliers regarding perceived problems and cooperation?

The survey showed that small and medium-sized industrial firms are highly involved in international purchasing both within the European Union and abroad. Surprisingly, this involvement did not appear to be significantly driven by lack of domestic availability. Instead, the primary drivers for choosing a foreign supplier were price and quality. Finally, product adaptation appeared to be a significant element of relationship formation between importers and their suppliers. The motives mentioned above have laid down a base for several empirical studies of manufacturing firms' international purchases in both Europe and the United States; for a comprehensive review, please refer to Overby and Servais (2005). More importantly, these studies support the motives as vital for the importing firms. Other important reasons for international sourcing include increasing the number of available sources, reacting to foreign sourcing practices of competitors, the introduction of competition to the domestic supply base, and establishing a presence in a foreign market. However, all the mentioned studies are concerned with established firms; overall, it is worthwhile to underline that the inward international sourcing activities in newly established ventures are under-researched.

Motivating Factors

One of the influencing forces in the original model is the motivating force of competition. It could also be a necessity for a firm that competes in an internationalized industry sector. When the focal firms are sourcing firms, the competition on the sales side is of less importance. What is particularly important is the existence of potential suppliers in the domestic market and, if they exist, how the new venture perceives the competition among domestic suppliers is also important.

The enabling force has been in focus within international entrepreneurship since its early start as an empirical phenomenon. This refers to a new reality of today with decreasing barriers, both institutional and cultural, which was not the case around 40 years ago when Johanson and Vahlne (1977) presented their first theoretical model of internationalization. Oviatt and McDougall (2005) specifically refer to technology as an enabling force for an accelerated internationalization process. Several researchers have stressed that born global start-ups lack resources required to reach world markets. Further, the extant internationalization theories may not be adequate to indicate viable channel alternatives for born global firms (Gabrielsson and Kirpalani 2004).

Mediating Factors

Internationalization activities typically require resources and time to carry out the activities. Since small firms typically are assumed to have fewer resources to search for suppliers and build relationships with them, the size of the firm may help analyze the differences in the extent of internationalization. Scully and Fawcett (1994) examined international purchases in 72 small and medium-sized American manufacturing firms. They found that small firms were less internationally oriented compared to large firms. Hence, the size of the firm may influence international sourcing activities since we know that smaller firms have fewer resources to search for suppliers and build relationships with them. The experience of the firm and the purchaser are further important variables representing different dimensions of experience. Experience may facilitate speed and extent of internationalization (Johanson and Vahlne 1977), even though inexperienced firms may also engage in international purchasing. Oviatt and McDougall (2005) also stress the importance of who the person or group is that discovers or enacts an international opportunity. They emphasize the personal characteristics (e.g., years of international business experience) and psychological traits (e.g., risk-taking propensity).

Entrepreneurs observe and interpret the potential of the opportunity, the potential of communication, transportation, and computer technology to enable internationalization. Oviatt and McDougall (2005) underline that these influences on perceptions clarify or disturb the entrepreneur's decision making. Therefore, objective measure of technology and competition cannot explain accelerated or delayed international entrepreneurial behavior. Rather, explaining that behavior relies on understanding how the entrepreneurial actor interprets or mediates the opportunity—the enabling and motivating forces. In this vein, several studies have indicated that the experience of the firm and the purchaser influences the speed and expansion of the firm in internationalization activities and the establishment of relationships (Johanson and Vahlne 2009). Arnold (1989) found similar results for global purchasing activities. Scully and Fawcett (1994) found that small firms are less experienced (measured in years of experience) with international purchases than large firms, and large firms planned their activities more.

Moderating Factors

Harris and Wheeler (2005) examined important relationships of three successful entrepreneurs; the authors tried to answer three main questions.

1. What are the functions of relationships in the internationalization process?
2. From where do important relationships come?
3. What strategies concerning relationship development do entrepreneurs pursue?

The study generated two interesting phenomena. First, an entrepreneur's international relationships do not just simply carry out a marketing function, or give access to the network, or provide information, but they direct strategy and can transform the firm, and sometimes be considered one of the firm's most important assets. Second, these important relationships do not necessarily come from the firm's customers, suppliers, or distributors; they also may come from personal contacts in either a social or job-related setting. Hence, a broad set of interconnected relationships forms the network of the firm. Relationships and networks have been important in the field of international entrepreneurship, especially with regard to smaller firms, to help them overcome both their lack of funds and resources (Mort and Weerawardena 2006). Working on six case studies from low-tech and high-tech industry sectors, they examined the mechanisms and processes of the firms' networking capabilities. Very often, networks contribute to the success of born globals by helping them to identify new market opportunities and build market knowledge. The entrepreneur/manager develops networking capabilities to address their vision of reaching global markets; this will allow the firm to exploit opportunities for internationalization. However, entrepreneurs /managers need time to develop these dynamic networking capabilities, which evolve over time, and the process is path dependent (Mort and Weerawardena 2006). The authors distinguish two types of networks: fundamental and secondary. The former are those held by the founder/owner/entrepreneur—and are "acquired" by the firm on the day of its inception—and are used to exploit initial market opportunities. The secondary networks are those built by the owner-manager during the firm's growth process to exploit other market opportunities and fight competition. Findings suggest that it is the job of the owner-manager to identify and put to good use primary and secondary networks. Firms must be proactive, innovative, and not averse to risk taking, reflecting the behavioral characteristics of international entrepreneurship (Oviatt and McDougall 2005).

Weerawardena *et al.* (2007) argue that entrepreneurs/managers build the necessary capabilities with a global/geocentric mindset, some prior international experiences, and a learning attitude. As seen previously, contacts and international education direct them to pursue opportunities in foreign markets (Oviatt and McDougall 1994); these characteristics, plus motivation and ambition, distinguish the born global manager from other managers (Madsen and Servais 1997). The entrepreneurs/managers build the distinctive capabilities of external/market-focused learning, internally focused learning, and the necessary networking capabilities, which enable small and innovative born globals to develop knowledge-intensive products; they also initiate the necessary marketing capabilities that enable the firm to position itself in prestigious market niches. Finally, the combination of the capabilities mentioned above creates accelerated internationalization and, perhaps, superior performances (Weerawardena *et al.* 2007).

Network capability is important in helping new-born firms wishing to internationalize overcome their resource scarcity (Mort and Weerawardena 2006). Networks are, in fact, critical in helping these firms lower the risks and uncertainties when facing foreign markets, and they, therefore, play a fundamental role in this analysis, too. These three capabilities allow the firm to develop knowledge-intensive products, namely those characterized by high-knowledge content, shaped through innovation and personal creativity, with cutting-edge design, or with high technological know-how or deep understanding of the market needs. As suggested by Madsen and Servais (1997), to survive, born global firms must be at the leading edge of the development of their product markets or niches, and, by satisfying them, they will avoid head-to-head competition with large multinational enterprises (Knight and Cavusgil 1996). Zhou *et al.* (2007) add that home-based social networks are mediators in the relationship between inward and outward internationalization and firm performance. Social networks bring three main information benefits:

1. They increase the awareness of foreign market opportunities.
2. They bring advice and experiential learning.
3. They bring referral trust and solidarity.

The authors believe that these benefits, by providing internationally oriented firms with credibility and facilitating the development of new capabilities for rapid internationalization at a lower risk, may help them overcome the lack of resources and the liability of foreignness that often constrain their expansion. Personal ties and interconnections also influence internationally oriented firms to initiate an export, identify foreign partners, provide tacit knowledge on international business practices, and open managerial minds and vision.

4. A Case Study

Survey research from Denmark (Rasmussen *et al.* 2012; Servais *et al.* 2008) has clearly demonstrated that the born global/INV type of firm can be found in any industry and that the percentage of such firms has been increasing over the last 20 years. The firms often rely on low-commitment entry modes for their export, meaning that international sourcing becomes an important starting point of the internationalization process of the firms. As part of this ongoing research, some in-depth qualitative studies have been done. We intend to present a case study from data collected in a qualitative research project. (The Born Global project under The Science and Enterprise Network is an initiative aimed at promoting networks between scientists and small and medium-sized enterprises.) Fifteen Danish manufacturing companies participated in the project. They are all characterized as born global firms (see introduction for definition) or firms that could become born global firms. Each company is approached through the following three stages of inquiry:

1. Pilot interview.
2. Full-scale, open-ended interview.
3. Final elaborating and clarifying interview.

In the following, we will display the results of one of the firms, Densen Audio Technologies.

Densen Audio Technologies

Densen is a small Danish firm with 12 employees. It designs, manufactures and sells hi-fi equipment to a high-end market segment. The firm has three product lines: receivers, amplifiers and preamplifiers, and CD players. The firm's approach to sound is very different from its competitors, focusing on replicating the recording as close to the original as possible. When products are designed, the focus is on company values and the functions the founder wants the product to have. The founder has, for example, chosen not to enable the use of plug-in earphones because he does not like them and they do not fit the design. Other firms try to accommodate consumer taste; Densen tries to show consumers how sound should be and how equipment should look; the design is the same for all the products.

Thomas Sillesen is the founder and CEO of Densen, situated in Esbjerg. Sillesen has an M.Sc. degree in Quality Management from Aarhus School of Business and has been interested in hi-fi since he was 14. He continued to pursue his hobby during his undergraduate studies. There, he met another freshman who told him "how I could import record players from the U.S. and earn 1,000 Euro each. The problem was [that] they were not sold with the heart, which made it difficult to sell enough to do a decent business."

After a start-up period solely as an import company at the beginning of the 1990s, Sillesen decided in 1992 to begin production of receivers, amplifiers, pre-amplifiers, and CD players to ensure timing and quality. In 1993, he produced the first 200 amplifiers.

"The problem for us was that it was exciting to develop the concepts, but it was boring to bring the product to completion. Five years could pass from idea to final product," said Sillesen. The solution to the problem was that Sillesen taught himself to design and test the layouts on a computer. In 1992, Sillesen took part in a hi-fi exhibition in the UK for the first time. There, he made several contacts with potential customers and gained insights about competitors and suppliers. In 1999, three of Sillesen's most important customers could not pay, and the firm was bankrupt. With nearly 150,000 euro of debt, Sillesen managed to reorganize the firm as a private limited-liability company with himself still as CEO. "What I learned from that experience was never to mix close relationships with business. That is, I do have close relations with customers, but all pay cash on delivery, and I had to outsource some of the production, but not the assembly."

Densen has sub-suppliers in Korea, but Danish sub-suppliers make the essential parts, and the final assembly is made on the premises in Esbjerg. This also goes for prototypes: Densen designs the hi-fi equipment on a computer.

In Denmark, Densen cooperates closely with Printline and B&B Electronics in Horsens and Aluline in Tølløse. "We have local suppliers of cabinets and SMD-assembled PCBs, and we have Korean and Taiwanese suppliers of transformers, CD drives, et cetera because these are inexpensive and set the standards in the industry—everybody uses them—and then we have about 20 other suppliers that more easily can be changed. Changing the supplier of cabinets would be very expensive; over the years we have invested more than 100,000 euro in tools for the supplier to be competitive."

Densen sells to distributors in 35 countries who again sell to outlets. The UK is a very important market for hi-fi equipment, and in this market, Densen has employed one sales person. Densen has a homepage with extensive information for end users, but it has no sales via the net. Densen offers lifelong warranties on its products to their original owners. Since Densen does not have an R&D department, all the products are built from modules; therefore, the products can be shipped to Densen for upgrades. The price of Densen hi-fi items starts at 7,000 euro. Some 85% of its products are exported.

5. Findings

As we see from the case mentioned above, Densen is, in a sense, a typical INV as it shares many of the features presented by Oviatt and McDougall

(2005). They wrote, "We define an international new venture as a business organization that, from inception, seeks to derive significant competitive advantage from the use of resources and the sale of outputs in multiple countries. The distinguishing feature of these start-ups is that their origins are international, as demonstrated by observable and significant commitments of resources (e.g., material, people, financing, time) in more than one nation" (p. 49). Densen certainly seeks a competitive advantage by using foreign suppliers. As mentioned in the section on motives for international sourcing, they do so not for short-term advantages, but by seeking advanced suppliers, specialists in their field. Densen is also a niche-oriented firm seeking market shares in the high-end market segment worldwide. This could not have been achieved without the founder's international outlook, his experience and above all his ability to create relationships with both suppliers and dealers.

As we have stressed in this article, more research is needed, especially on two issues. The first is customers' buying behavior. What are the motives and decision-making process that lead to the choice of a new start-up supplier (global firm) from a foreign country? Secondly, what are the decision-making process and motives that drive the purchasing process in entrepreneurial firms?

Supplier relations are indeed different with regard to value potential, network strategy, and supplier actor rationality. Suppliers constitute different value-creation potentials. Hence, negotiating with suppliers just to save money from a short-term perspective can mean these unique value creation possibilities are missed. Some supplier relations are ideal for strategic utilization, whereas the company needs to safeguard others. Finally, supplier rationalities differ across differing relationships. Some suppliers may be opportunistic, but this rationality cannot be taken for granted from any supplier. Assuming specific rationalities can be detrimental to any buying company, hence relations to suppliers both domestic and foreign must be investigated more thoroughly.

6. Conclusion

Sourcing from abroad can be a way of motivating SMEs to cooperate more internationally and to develop their internationalization further (Hessels and Parker 2013). The inward activities of the SME ought to be at least as important as the outward, and instead of governments' focus on the stimulation of exports from SMEs, there ought to be a focus on purchasing as this typically leads to new relations and to exports.

Oviatt and McDougall (2005) highlight that after an entrepreneurial actor discovers or enacts an opportunity and interprets the enabling and the motivating forces, then the knowledge intensity of the opportunity combined with the know-how already available to the entrepreneurial actor and the characteristics of the entrepreneur's international network largely determine internationalization speed. Furthermore, Oviatt and McDougall (2005) propose that differences in the novelty, complexity, and sophistication of knowledge used in a firm explain the speed of internationalization. This assumption is in agreement with industrial buying behavior as described by McQuiston (1989). Hence, the decision process regarding the choice of the supplier will be described by factors such as product type, perceived risk, and anticipated consequences of the choice. In general, the findings indicate that products purchased from foreign suppliers are more difficult to specify/describe than products sourced from local suppliers. This finding might fit very well with the previously mentioned fact that the products were not available in the domestic market, and at the same time, the products sourced from abroad were more technologically complex as they demanded further tests before usage and were harder to adapt to production compared to products purchased domestically. In general, Servais and Jensen (2001) found that the purchases are evaluated as being of a relatively high order of importance to the company. It is worthwhile noticing that international purchases are perceived as having a large influence on the competitiveness of the firm, closely followed by the perceived influence on the quality of the end-product. The companies' motives for choosing a foreign supplier support this, and it is important to stress that the interviewed firms perceived international purchasing as having a relatively large influence on the competitiveness of the firm. When a firm competes with either a novel or a complex knowledge for developing new products, the assumption in the model from Oviatt and McDougall (2005, 543) is that "this type of firm is likely to have the most accelerated internationalization because it has a unique sustainable advantage that may be in demand in a number of countries." In the case of born global sourcers, this is reversed. One cannot claim that the more a firm does sourcing directly from foreign producers, the more international the firm is. Instead one must assume in the case of born global sourcers that the firm has developed relations with foreign suppliers carefully and this has caused offerings that have enabled the firm to create competitive advantages in the domestic market. However, it is of research interest to look into the possible differences in international sourcing by born global sourcers and those carried out by born global firms. The relations to domestic suppliers comprise another aspect that is important to incorporate in the model. Hence, born global sourcers can, as (sub) suppliers to firms in their vicinity, serve as an important element in these firms' internationalization. Regional development and internationalization (or globalization) are thus often seen as two opposite poles, but as Michael Porter states in his article from 2000 about globalization and regional networks, "The local networks play an important role in the development of the internationalization of especially newly established firms" (Porter 2000).

With the words of Oviatt and McDougall (2005), we hope that more scholars will focus on explaining the observed differences in the speed with which entrepreneurial opportunities are taken internationally. We believe that this revised model of born global sourcers will aid in finding those explanations, not only focused on this particular type of INVs. A comparison to other types of INVs such as born global marketers (Gabrielsson and Manek Kirpalani 2004) could further expand our insights into the various strategies implied by INVs. We sincerely hope that this could be a stepping stone in the excavation of outward-inward connection in other types of international new ventures.

References

Andersen, Otto. 1997. "Internationalization and Market Entry Mode: A Review of Theories and Conceptual Frameworks." *MIR: Management International Review* 37(2): 27–42.

Arnold, Ulli. 1989. "Global Sourcing-an Indispensable Element in Worldwide Competition." *Management International Review* 29(4): 14–28.

Aspelund, Arild, Tage Koed Madsen, and Øystein Moen. 2007. "A Review of the Foundation, International Marketing Strategies, and Performance of International New Ventures." *European Journal of Marketing* 41(11/12): 1423–1448. doi:10.1108/03090560710821242.

BarNir, Anat, and Ken A. Smith. 2002. "Interfirm Alliances in the Small Business: The Role of Social Networks." *Journal of Small Business Management* 40(3): 219–232. doi:10.1111/1540–627X.00052.

Baron, Robert A., and Gideon D. Markman. 2003. "Beyond Social Capital: The Role of Entrepreneurs' Social Competence in Their Financial Success." *Journal of Business Venturing* 18(1): 41–60. doi:10.1016/S0883–9026(00)00069–0.

Biemans, Wim G., and Maryse J. Brand. 1995. "Reverse Marketing: A Synergy of Purchasing and Relationship Marketing." *International Journal of Purchasing and Materials Management* 31(2): 28–37. doi:10.1111/j.1745–493X.1995. tb00206.x.

Birley, Sue. 1985. "The Role of Networks in the Entrepreneurial Process." *Journal of Business Venturing* 1(1): 107–117.

Birou, Laura M., and Stanley E. Fawcett. 1993. "International Purchasing: Benefits, Requirements and Challenges." *International Journal of Purchasing and Materials Management* Spring: 28–37.

Cavusgil, S. Tamer. 1998. "Perspectives: Knowledge Development in International Marketing." *Journal of International Marketing* 6(2): 103–112.

Cesinger, Beate, Adriana Danko, and Ricarda Bouncken. 2012. "Born Globals: (almost) 20 Years of Research and Still Not 'Grown Up'?" *International Journal of Entrepreneurship and Small Business* 15(2): 171–190. doi:10.1504/ijesb.2012.045203.

Ellegaard, Chris. 2006. "Small Company Purchasing: A Research Agenda." *Journal of Purchasing and Supply Management* 12(5): 272–283. doi:http://dx.doi.org/10.1016/j.pursup.2006.08.004.

Gabrielsson, Mika, and V.H. Manek Kirpalani. 2004. "Born Globals: How to Reach New Business Space Rapidly." *International Business Review* 13(5): 555–571.

Hallbäck, Johanna, and Jorma Larimo. 2006. "Variety in International New Ventures—Typological Analysis and Beyond." *Journal of Euromarketing* 16(1/2): 37–57. doi:10.1300/J037v16n01_04.

Harris, Simon, and Colin Wheeler. 2005. "Entrepreneurs' Relationships for Internationalization: Functions, Origins and Strategies." *International Business Review* 14(2): 187–207. doi:10.1016/j.ibusrev.2004.04.008.

Hessels, Jolanda, and Simon C. Parker. 2013. "Constraints, Internationalization and Growth: A Cross-Country Analysis of European SMEs." *Journal of World Business* 48(1): 137–148. doi:http://dx.doi.org/10.1016/j.jwb.2012.06.014.

Horgos, Daniel. 2013. "Global Sourcing: A Family-Firm's Perspective." *Journal of Small Business & Entrepreneurship* 26(3): 221–240. doi:10.1080/08276331.201 3.808028.

Jia, Fu, Richard Lamming, Marco Sartor, Guido Orzes, and Guido Nassimbeni. 2014. "Global Purchasing Strategy and International Purchasing Offices: Evidence from Case Studies." *International Journal of Production Economics* 154: 284–298. doi:http://dx.doi.org/10.1016/j.ijpe.2013.09.007.

Johanson, Jan, and Jan-Erik Vahlne. 1977. "The Internationalization Process of the Firm: A Model of Knowledge Development and Increasing Foreign Market Commitments." *Journal of International Business Studies* 8: 23–32.

Johanson, Jan, and Jan Erik Vahlne. 2009. "The Uppsala Internationalization Process Model Revisited: From Liability of Foreignness to Liability of Outsidership." *Journal of International Business Studies* 40(9): 1411–1431. doi:10.1057/Jibs.2009.24.

Jones, Marian V., Nicole Coviello, and Yee Kwan Tang. 2011. "International Entrepreneurship Research (1989–2009): A Domain Ontology and Thematic Analysis." *Journal of Business Venturing* 26(6): 632–659. doi:10.1016/j. jbusvent.2011.04.001.

Jones, Robert, and Richard Kustin. 1995. "Supplier Relations and Export Activity in a Small-Firm Grouping." *International Journal of Management* 12: 112–122.

Kahiya, Eldrede. 2013. "Export Barriers and Path to Internationalization: A Comparison of Conventional Enterprises and International New Ventures." *Journal of International Entrepreneurship* 11(1): 3–29. doi:10.1007/s10843-013-0102-4.

Keupp, Marcus Matthias, and Oliver Gassmann. 2009. "The Past and the Future of International Entrepreneurship: A Review and Suggestions for Developing the Field." *Journal of Management* 35(3): 600–633.

Knight, Gary A. 1997. *Emerging Paradigm for International Marketing: The Born Global Firm*. East Lansing, MI: Michigan State University, Dept. of Marketing and Supply Chain Management.

Knight, Gary A., and Peter W. Liesch. 2016. "Internationalization: From Incremental to Born Global." *Journal of World Business* 51(1): 93–102. doi:10.1016/j. jwb.2015.08.011.

Knight, Gary A., and S. Tamer Cavusgil. 1996. "The Born Global Firm: A Challenge to Traditional Internationalization Theory." *Advances in International Marketing* 8: 11–26.

Korhonen, Heli, Reijo Luostarinen, and Lawrence Welch. 1996. "Internationalization of SMEs: Inward-Outward Patterns and Government Policy." *Management International Review* 36: 315–329.

Larimo, Jorma, and Johanna Pulkinen. 2002. "Global Orientation, Competitive Advantages and Export Strategies of Different Types of SMEs: Empirical Evidence from Finland." 28th EIBA Conference, December.

Larson, Andrea. 1991. "Partner Networks: Leveraging External Ties to Improve Entrepreneurial Performance." *Journal of Business Venturing* 6(3): 173–188.

Larson, Andrea. 1992. "Network Dyads in Entrepreneurial Settings: A Study of the Governance of Exchange Relationships." *Administrative Science Quarterly* 37(1): 76–104. doi:10.2307/2393534.

Lechner, Christian, and Michael Dowling. 2003. "Firm Networks: External Relationships as Sources for the Growth and Competitiveness of Entrepreneurial Firms." *Entrepreneurship & Regional Development* 15(1): 1–26. doi:10.1080/08985620210159220.

Liang, Neng, and Arvind Parkhe. 1997. "Importer Behavior: The Neglected Counterpart of International Exchange." *Journal of International Business Studies* 28(3): 495–530. doi:10.1057/palgrave.jibs.8490109.

Lipparini, Andrea, and Maurizio Sobrero. 1994. "The Glue and the Pieces: Entrepreneurship and Innovation in Small-Firm Networks." *Journal of Business Venturing* 9(2): 125–140. doi:10.1016/0883-9026(94)90005-1.

Lorenzoni, Gianni, and Oscar A. Ornati. 1988. "Constellations of Firms and New Ventures." *Journal of Business Venturing* 3(1): 41–57. doi:http://dx.doi.org/10.1016/0883-9026(88)90029-8.

Love, James H., and Stephen Roper. 2015. "SME Innovation, Exporting and Growth: A Review of Existing Evidence." *International Small Business Journal* 33(1): 28–48. doi:10.1177/0266242614550190.

Low, Murray B., and Ian C. Macmillan. 1988. "Entrepreneurship—Past Research and Future Challenges." *Journal of Management* 14(2): 139–161. doi:10.1177/014920638801400202.

Luostarinen, Reijo, and Mika Gabrielsson. 2006. "Globalization and Marketing Strategies of Born Globals in SMOPECs." *Thunderbird International Business Review* 48(6): 773–801.

Lye, Ashley, and Robert T. Hamilton. 2000. "Search and Performance in International Exchange." *European Journal of Marketing* 34(1/2): 176–189.

Madsen, Tage Koed, and Per Servais. 1997. "The Internationalization of Born Globals: An Evolutionary Process?" *International Business Review* 6(6): 561–583.

Mainela, Tuija, Vesa Puhakka, and Per Servais. 2014. "The Concept of International Opportunity in International Entrepreneurship: A Review and a Research Agenda." *International Journal of Management Reviews* 16(1): 105–129. doi:10.1111/ijmr.12011.

McDougall, Patricia Phillips, Scott Shane, and Benjamin M. Oviatt. 1994. "Explaining the Formation of International New Ventures: The Limits of Theories from International Business Research." *Journal of Business Venturing* 9(6): 469–487.

McQuiston, Daniel H. 1989. "Novelty, Complexity, and Importance as Causal Determinants of Industrial Buyer Behavior." *Journal of Marketing* 53(2): 66–79. doi:10.2307/1251414.

Melin, Leif. 1992. "Internationalisation as a Strategy Process." *Strategic Management Journal* 13: 99–118. doi:10.1002/smj.4250130908.

Moini, A. Hamid. 1995. "An Inquiry into Successful Exporting: An Empirical Investigation Using a Three-Stage Model." *Journal of Small Business Management* 33(3): 9–25.

Monczka, Robert M., and Robert J. Trent. 1992. "Worldwide Sourcing: Assessment and Execution." *International Journal of Purchasing and Materials Management* Fall: 9–21.

Mort, Gillian Sullivan, and Jay Weerawardena. 2006. "Networking Capability and International Entrepreneurship: How Networks Function in Australian Born Global Firms." *International Marketing Review* 23(5): 549–572. doi:10.1108/0265133061703445.

Overby, Jeffrey W., and Per Servais. 2005. "Small and Medium-Sized Firms' Import Behavior: The Case of Danish Industrial Purchasers." *Industrial Marketing Management* 34(1): 71–83. doi: 10.1016/j.indmarman.2004.08.001.

Oviatt, Benjamin M., and Patricia P. McDougall. 1994. "Toward a Theory of International New Ventures." *Journal of International Business Studies* 25(1): 45–64. doi:10.1057/palgrave.jibs.8490193.

Oviatt, Benjamin M., and Patricia P. McDougall. 2005. "Defining International Entrepreneurship and Modeling the Speed of Internationalization." *Entrepreneurship Theory and Practice* 29(5): 537–554. doi: 10.1111/j.1540–6520.2005.00097.x.

Peiris, Indujeeva K., Michèle E. M. Akoorie, and Paresha Sinha. 2012. "International Entrepreneurship: A Critical Analysis of Studies in the Past Two Decades and Future Directions for Research." *Journal of International Entrepreneurship* 10(4): 279–324. doi:10.1007/s10843-012-0096-3.

Porter, Michael E. 2000. "Location, Competition, and Economic Development: Local Clusters in a Global Economy." *Economic Development Quarterly* 14(1): 15–34. doi:10.1177/089124240001400105.

Preece, Stephen B., Grant Miles, and Mark C. Baetz. 1999. "Explaining the International Intensity and Global Diversity of Early-Stage Technology-Based Firms." *Journal of Business Venturing* 14(3): 259–281. doi:10.1016/S0883–9026(97)00105–5.

Quayle, Michael. 2002. "Purchasing in Small Firms." *European Journal of Purchasing & Supply Management* 8(3): 151–159. doi:http://dx.doi.org/10.1016/S0969-7012(02)00005-9.

Rasmussen, Erik S., Tage Koed Madsen, and Per Servais. 2012. "On the Foundation and Early Development of Domestic and International New Ventures." *Journal of Management & Governance* 16(4): 543–556. doi:10.1007/s10997-010-9162-1.

Rialp, Alex, Josep Rialp, and Gary A. Knight. 2005. "The Phenomenon of Early Internationalizing Firms: What Do We Know After a Decade (1993–2003) of Scientific Inquiry?" *International Business Review* 14(2): 147–166. doi:10.1016/j.ibusrev.2004.04.006.

Scully, Joseph I., and Stanley E. Fawcett. 1994. "International Procurement Strategies—Challenges and Opportunities for the Small Firm." *Production and Inventory Management Journal* 35(2): 39–46.

Servais, Per, and Jan Møller Jensen. 2001. "The Internationalisation of Industrial Purchasing: The Example of Small Danish Manufactures." In *Advances in International Marketing, vol 11*, edited by Catherine N. Axinn and Paul Matthyssens, 227–254. Bingley, UK: JAI Press.

Servais, Per, Erik S. Rasmussen, Bo Bernhard Nielsen, and Tage Koed Madsen. 2008. "Internationalisation of Danish SMEs." In *Handbook of Research on European Business and Entrepreneurship: Towards a Theory of Internationalization*, edited by Léo-Paul Dana, Isabell Welpe, Mary Han, and Vanessa Ratten, 171–184. Cheltenham, UK: Edward Elgar.

Servais, Per, Antonella Zucchella, and Giada Palamara. 2007. "International Entrepreneurship and Sourcing: International Value Chain of Small Firms." *Journal of Euromarketing* 16(1/2): 105–117. doi:10.1300/J037v16n0108.

Tesar, George, Håkan Boter, Håkan Bohman, and Hamid Moini. 2003. "Network Participation and Internationalisation of Smaller Manufacturing Enterprises in Central Europe: A Case for Research." Proceedings of the 19th Annual IMP Conference, Lugano.

Walter, Achim, Michael Auer, and Thomas Ritter. 2006. "The Impact of Network Capabilities and Entrepreneurial Orientation on University Spin-off Performance." *Journal of Business Venturing* 21(4): 541–567. doi:10.1016/j.jbusvent.2005.02.005.

Weerawardena, Jay, Gillian Sullivan Mort, Peter W. Liesch, and Gary A. Knight. 2007. "Conceptualizing Accelerated Internationalization in the Born Global Firm: A Dynamic Capabilities Perspective." *Journal of World Business* 42(3): 294–306. doi:10.1016/j.jwb.2007.04.004.

Welch, Lawrence, and Reijo Luostarinen. 1993. "Inward-Outward Connections in Internationalization." *Journal of International Marketing* 1(1): 44–56.

Zhou, Lianxi, Wei ping Wu, and Xueming Luo. 2007. "Internationalization and the Performance of Born-Global SMEs: The Mediating Role of Social Networks." *Journal of International Business Studies* 38(4): 673–690. doi:10.1057/palgrave.jibs.8400282.

Index